Helms and Hunt

Helms and Hunt

The North Carolina Senate Race, 1984

by William D. Snider

The University of North Carolina Press

Chapel Hill and London

FOR FLO

Manufactured in the United States of America

Library of Congress Cataloging in Publication Data

Snider, William D.
Helms and Hunt.

1. North Carolina—Politics and government—1951–
2. Hunt, James B., 1937– . 3. Helms, Jesse.
4. Elections—North Carolina—History—20th century.
5. United States. Congress. Senate—Elections, 1984.
I. Title.
F260.S54 1985 324.9756'043 84-25735
ISBN 0-8078-4132-3

Contents

Helms and Hunt

Prologue

Some thought the ferocious race for senator from North Carolina between Senator Jesse A. Helms and Governor James B. Hunt, Jr., was the second most important election in the nation. They saw it as a sort of showdown for the soul between the conservative Old South and the progressive forces of the New. Others viewed it as yet another stage in the erosion of the old one-party Democratic South. Still others saw it as simply a southern-fried back-alley brawl, featuring the latest electronic advertising techniques underwritten by the most costly funding in senatorial election history.

As the long and rowdy campaign unfolded in the shadow of the Reagan avalanche of 1984, it was a bit of all these. It was also a flamboyant, often nasty race between two skillful politicians sprung from much the same rural soil but espousing different political and social views.

Many of the senator's admirers considered him a courtly, grandfatherly figure, the "nicest man you ever saw." Others viewed him as an unbending right-wing warrior battling the "tax and spend" liberals or even as an avenging angel come to rescue sinners from their wicked ways. Still others identified him with Ronald Reagan's "Morning in America" crusade for free enterprise, patriotism, and the "Opportunity Society." Not all Helms's supporters liked everything he favored—for example, stern anti-abortion laws or organized prayer in public schools—but they admired his gutsiness, even in pursuit of lost causes. He knew how to "send 'em a message," and they always knew where Jesse stood.

Then there were those who supported Helms because they liked Hunt less. They saw the governor as an overly political, wishy-washy opportunist mostly identified with tax increases and Yankee liberals on the Democratic ticket. They feared his links with "the other Jesse" (the Reverend Jesse Jackson) who made "we want it all" demands at home and anti-administration tirades abroad. They disliked Hunt's tight-knit political organization, which had become entrenched and a bit careless after eight years in power.

The governor's admirers, a substantial majority of the populace as the race began, remembered his dedication to educational and economic uplift over a whole decade of Tar Heel history. They liked his crisp, pragmatic gubernatorial leadership, his conservatism on economic issues, his moderation on social issues, and his conviction that government is a partner not an enemy. They considered him a superb ambassador beyond North Carolina's borders, radiating the optimism of a born leader. It was evident to them that Hunt's Bible Belt upbringing had imbued him more with the New Testament teachings of the Sermon on the Mount than with the thunderings of Old Testament prophets about false gods. While the governor's supporters differed among themselves about his stands on some issues—the nuclear freeze, capital punishment—and whether he was "too political" or "too pious," in sum they thought he championed the vision of a forward-looking North Carolina.

There were also those who supported Hunt because they liked Helms less. They viewed the senator as self-righteously hypocritical, using religion for political purposes. They remembered his role in Willis Smith's defeat of Dr. Frank Graham in the 1950 senatorial race and blamed him for igniting racial feelings, both then and now. They deplored his vision of America as a society besieged by conspiratorial forces both inside and outside the gate and charged him with stirring up hatred about a pluralistic society and caring only for those of his own kind. They feared his ideological intensity and his affinity for right-wing figures abroad and fundamentalist preachers at home. They disliked the way, as one of them put it, he "contaminated serious argument with debating points from the gutter" and practiced tactics of divide and conquer.

These became the contending forces in North Carolina's 1984 senatorial contest. They represented widely varying constituencies, ranging from the branch-head mountain coves of the west to the highly sophisticated academic and high-tech industrial centers of the Piedmont. Many had cast their votes for both the senator and the governor in different elections of the past. When the votes were cast on November 6, Senator Helms prevailed—but only by a narrow margin.

Mr. Clean and the Fire Chief's Son

1. Patriarch and Upstart

In the spring of 1972 Jesse Alexander Helms, a North Carolina television editorialist and newly announced Republican candidate for the United States Senate, walked into a small hardware store in the Piedmont village of Rockwell to shake hands and campaign. There he bumped into B. Everett Jordan, the incumbent senator and textile tycoon whose seat he sought.

Both men broke into laughter, and Jordan said: "I've got this side of the street. Why don't you take the side with the antique store?"

"You'd better watch out," Helms replied. "The bank's on that side."

Jordan was far from nonplussed. "That's all right," he replied. "I've already got my share."

This encounter reveals a lot about North Carolina politics. Humor is never far beneath the surface. Informality prevails. Nobody wants to appear too biggety, and there can be aggressiveness even in declarations of modesty.

Senator Jordan, a genial, popular senator, lost in the Democratic primary that spring before he could confront Helms. Whether he realized it or not, he was making his last hurrah. Jordan represented what political scientist V. O. Key called "a financial and business elite" whose influence had prevailed in North Carolina's political and economic life since the turn of the century. The state's "elite" was hardly patrician by some standards. A rough-hewn, down-home demeanor prevailed, both among the textile and banker-tobacco industrialists who exerted considerable influence from their Piedmont executive suites and among the Coastal Plain tobacco barons who made politics a twenty-four-hour-a-day occupation. Their easygoing informality masked an iron will and a genuine devotion to the Democratic Party, southern conservative style.

It was the lawyers, though, who usually won the top political offices, notably the governorship. There had been occasional breaks in the corporate-lawyer continuity since Senator Furnifold Simmons and Governor Charles B. Aycock overturned the Republican-Populist coalition of the 1890s. The Kitchins early in the century and the Scotts at mid-century upset this "aggressive aristocracy of manufacturing and banking" which regularly placed its representatives in the governor's chair and in Washington. But from the time Simmons put his machine together in 1898 on the issue of white supremacy and removal of "scalawag" government through the 1930s-40s reign of O. Max Gardner's "Shelby Dynasty," North Carolina's political majority had been shaped by an economic oligarchy.

This oligarchy endured despite the occasionally successful challenges of progressive insurgents like Governors W. W. Kitchin (1909–12), Kerr Scott (1949–52), and Terry Sanford (1961–64) because it was basically respectful of broad community needs. Within the confines of one-party government, it never tolerated outright bigots of the stripe found in other Deep South states. North Carolina's independent farmers, small-town merchants, and workers did not elect demagogues of the genre William Alexander Percy of Mississippi described when he called "The Man" Theodore Bilbo "a pert little monster, glib and shameless with that sort of cunning common to criminals which passes for intelligence."

North Carolina's government was also remarkably uncorrupt. Its top officials remained protective of conservative interests and gave their greatest sympathy to problems of corporate capital and large employers, but they were largely decent and responsible. In race relations the state fared better than most of its neighbors, with few episodes of violence or repression. One reason for this, as Key explained, was the influence of the state university at Chapel Hill, which had "pioneered in regional self-examination" and become "famed for academic freedom and for tolerance." North Carolina's progressive plutocrats were generally respectful of Chapel Hill. Some feared its liberalism, but they sent their children there all the same and admired its athletic teams and its international academic reputation.

Senator Jordan, son of a Methodist circuit-rider preacher, was in many ways the perfect example of the state's patriarchal dynasty. A successful textile manufacturer and also a member of Duke University's board of trustees for many years, he dabbled in Democratic politics on the side. That accounted for his unexpected appointment to the Senate by Governor Luther Hodges, a former textile official, in April 1958.

Jordan was no intellectual heavyweight, but through his friendliness and integrity he became an influential member of the Senate establishment. He went on to serve two decades in Washington. Then, with advancing age and failing health, he was defeated by an insurgent young Democratic congressman of Greek ancestry, Nick Galifianakis ("Start with a gal; end with a kiss"). Campaigning with energy and charm, Galifianakis edged out the aging patriarch in the May 1972 Democratic primary, in part because it was widely known that Jordan had cancer.

The results were different that November, however, when Jesse Helms, the ambitious television-radio journalist, embarked on his first statewide political venture. Helms defeated Galifianakis with relative ease, taking 54 percent of the vote. Some believed he never would have decided to run if

Jordan had been well. On the other hand, some Old Guard Democrats had been piqued by Galifianakis's unceremonious dumping of Jordan. Many flocked to the Helms colors, though Galifianakis was far from "radical," even by North Carolina standards. Helms said afterward that intensive organization and well-planned media exposure accounted for his success. That, in part, was true. But another factor helped too: In 1972 Richard Nixon reached the apex of his stormy career—his triumph over George McGovern. McGovern's lack of popularity in North Carolina and Nixon's coattails helped Helms and also edged into office the state's first Republican governor in seventy years.

This shattering of Democratic hegemony in two of its top offices sent tremors through party ranks. The gubernatorial turnover had been almost uniformly unexpected, even though Helms's victory was widely predicted three or four weeks before the election. Suddenly, after flirting with the Republicans since the days of Herbert Hoover, it appeared North Carolina had become a genuine two-party state. Jim Holshouser, the surprised young Republican governor-elect, belonged to the moderate-progressive wing of his party. His faction had been indigenous to the Tar Heel uplands for generations. A lawyer, he had served several terms in the state legislature and also as state Republican Party Chairman.

Jesse Helms, though, son of a Piedmont village police and fire chief, had little in common with the legal-corporate power brokers of either party. Helms had switched party registration only two years before. Besides, he had been a radio-television reporter and commentator, a background unheard of in North Carolina politics.

The attitude of some Tar Heel establishment figures toward Helms was summed up pretty well by Senator Jordan's hardware store comment in 1972: "Why don't you take the side [of the street] with the antique store?" To them, Helms was a fundamentalist upstart, a kind of rustic buffoon and radical right-winger. They saw him as North Carolina's version of the bumpkin demagogues familiar in other southern states. But Jesse Helms was not exactly a Bilbo or even a Lester Maddox. Some prominent Democrats agreed with Governor Jim Hunt's cousin, former House Speaker Joe Hunt, who strongly supported Helms across party lines and called him "one of the nicest and most honest people I know." Even those who considered Helms mean spirited and dogmatic in public found him gracious and kindly in person. He was a complex mixture of bonhomie and tenacity, of grassroots shrewdness and puritanical stubbornness. Even those conservatives who did not swallow all his right-wing ideology nevertheless liked enough of his free-enterprising spirit to set aside their doubts and go along.

Thus Jesse Helms made his entry on the national political scene. Later he confessed that he had been reluctant about running for the Senate because he "didn't want to go through the meat-grinder. I couldn't see myself as having any great appeal for the voters." But the majority thought otherwise.

Helms departed for Washington just in time to champion the rise of the New Conservatism. The liberal establishment's achievements had dwindled in the backwash of Lyndon Johnson's collapsing Great Society. The political "middle" had begun to shift rightward. That shift laid the groundwork for Ronald Reagan's ascendancy in 1980.

Doubtless the bluff, big-hearted Everett Jordan had already "gotten his share" by 1972. So had his Democratic corporate-legal associates who ran North Carolina for seventy years. In 1972 Jesse Helms and Jim Holshouser, an unlikely and uncongenial combination, introduced a new persona and style in Tar Heel politics. Holshouser's tenure proved brief and frustrating, but Helms survived and left his mark as the nation's new high priest of the ideological Right.

2. Salt of the Earth People

During the same year that Jesse Helms announced for his first statewide office, a thirty-five-year-old lawyer from North Carolina's Coastal Plain made a similar decision.

"Jim Hunt is a star. Keep your eye on him," a veteran legislator had said two years earlier after Hunt had been president of the state Young Democrats. James Baxter Hunt, Jr., had a passion for politics. Later they would tell stories about his practicing political oratory while plowing the fields of his father's Wilson County farm. At eleven, he helped his family campaign for W. Kerr Scott, the "Good Roads Governor." Scott's $200 million rural road bond issue of 1949 got the road by the Hunt farm paved and first alerted young Jim to the importance of politics.

Hunt was the classic barefoot boy, a sort of rural Horatio Alger. His father was a soil conservationist; his mother, a teacher and librarian. They lived on a farm that had been in Elsie Hunt's family for three generations. The senior Hunts were substantial, conscientious people. The lives of their two boys, Jim and Bob, were steeped in the Protestant ethic of the Marsh Swamp Free Will Baptist Church and the political ethic of Franklin Roosevelt. Their home, a modest gray frame structure, stood less than a mile from the small community of Rock Ridge on the sandy loam of the Carolina Coastal Plain.

Hunt grew up attending meetings of the state Grange. Intellectual influence came from his mother, who encouraged her sons to read history and literature. Hunt's younger brother, Bob, now a social worker at the Veterans Hospital in Durham, said recently: "Our parents stressed public service as the only honorable way to pursue life. We grew up thinking somehow that just making money was not honorable." As a federal employee, Jim Hunt, Sr., was barred from active politics, but during the Great Depression he had strong views about the saving grace of the New Deal. For the Hunts the Democratic Party ranked just below the Baptist church in their hierarchy of respected institutions.

The Hunt boys reached maturity in the post–World War II South, where folkways were changing in the mushrooming small cities of the Piedmont. Out in the countryside, however, the pace was slower. The Hunts stemmed from rural stock which could identify with Nathaniel Macon, the nineteenth-century Tar Heel statesman, who said: "Don't live near enough to your neighbor to hear his dog bark." Hunt told a reporter last year that more than anything else as a lad he enjoyed riding a shaggy-haired pony named Birdie over the unpaved paths and roads among the pines and oaks near his home. He dreamed then of becoming a rancher out West.

Jim Hunt liked to do his homework late at night after farm chores and football or basketball practice. He was a model student, a Mr. Clean teenager of the Eisenhower fifties—confident, idealistic, and intense. A chubby boy at four, he grew up to become leanly handsome, of moderate build and height and decidedly outgoing demeanor. He was neat almost to a fault, quick to learn, and ambitious. Beneath his comely Scotch-Irish facade lay a strong drive to succeed.

The family of J. B. Hunt, Sr., exemplified a certain rural prototype in North Carolina. A classmate who lived on "Hunt Road" in Guilford County's Pleasant Garden, where the Hunts settled early, described them as "devout Christian people." They lived well but modestly. They believed in education. They were wedded to FDR's New Deal because it brought aid to the countryside in time of distress.

Jim Hunt's great-grandfather, Moses Jackson Thomas James Hunt, had been a Methodist circuit rider, and one of his uncles, a Methodist minister. His grandfather Hunt was a building contractor. "They were fine people," said their neighbor Joseph W. Shore. "Jim Sr. didn't have much to say and there was not much humor about him. But he was highly respected." The Hunts and the Rosses, the governor's grandmother's family, were pious and upright. Their house servant, a large black woman, attended the Pleasant Garden Methodist Church with them. "She would sit on the back seat," Shore recalled.

Jim Hunt's father met his mother when she became an English teacher in Pleasant Garden. Elsie Brame had graduated from the Woman's College in Greensboro, part of the University of North Carolina system. For a while the Hunts lived in Greensboro, where Jim Hunt was born, then in Raleigh, and ultimately outside of Rock Ridge in Wilson County, site of the farm owned by Jim Hunt's great-grandfather Renfrow. When the Wilson County community celebrated Jim Hunt Day in 1975, the future governor said: "We're too small to be a crossroads; we just have a T-junction."

The Hunts plunged wholeheartedly into the rural life of eastern Carolina. They specialized in dairying and tobacco, and raised hogs and peanuts. Elsie Hunt, a warmly effusive yet forceful and outgoing woman, continued her teaching at Rock Ridge High School. The family became members of the same Free Will Baptist church attended by some of the Renfrows and Brames. Jim Hunt later described the Free Will Baptists as having two branches—one was foot-washing and fundamentalist; the other, education minded and evangelical. Marsh Swamp fell into the latter category. J. B. Hunt, Sr., full of flinty rectitude, also took pains to differentiate between the two branches of Free Will Baptists. "We're not ultra-conservative like that Jerry Falwell crowd," he told a reporter in 1984. "They're just a bunch of extremists." But the church had a deeply conservative flavor: When Jim Hunt was growing up, men sat on one side of the aisle and women on the other.

The church left its influence on the Hunt boys. The wife of a former pastor remembers that when Jim was ten years old, he answered the call to be "saved," came down the aisle, and "gave his life to Jesus." Hunt's religion runs deep. His favorite New Testament verse is John 3:16: "For God so loved the world that he gave his only begotten son . . ." Of this verse Hunt says: "He gave everything He had, the best that He had."

Hunt recently described his religious beliefs as a blend of Baptist theology and parental teachings. "I believe that God expects obedience and that there is punishment, but I also believe very strongly—and this may have come more from my parents—that the essence of God is love."

The Hunts set high standards and expected diligent performance. They set up a jar for a "no smoking" fund for their boys. By refraining from smoking Jim and Bob could win the equivalent of the price of a pack and a half of cigarettes every day to be used for vacation and travel. "It worked," Elsie Hunt said later. Jim was also promised a one-thousand-dollar life insurance policy at age fourteen if he did not smoke. He won that too.

The Hunt attitude toward liquor was no different. "We've always had fairly strong beliefs about liquor," his mother said. "It's just a dangerous thing." Her son agrees. "I made a decision that if I never started drinking, I'd never become an alcoholic," Hunt said. He also told a reporter: "The only time I ever drank was as a high school senior in 1955 on a trip to a college basketball tournament. Some friends were drinking beer. I had one taste. It just tasted bad. I never had any problem with it after that."

Hunt remembers two early episodes that inspired his interest in public life. One was his father's involvement in Governor Kerr Scott's road bond issue in 1949. The other was his mother's dedication to teaching. "During the summer months the hard-headed boys who failed English at school would come to our house at night and she'd tutor them," Hunt recalls. Hunt learned early that schooling is important. That led to the $15 million campaign for elementary reading programs he later championed as governor.

Another vivid memory of Hunt's early years—he was thirteen at the time—harked back to the bitter senatorial race between Dr. Frank P. Graham, former president of the University of North Carolina, and corporate lawyer Willis Smith. The Hunts had motored one hundred miles to Pleasant Garden for a family wedding on the weekend of the primary runoff between Smith and Graham in June 1950. "My father and mother interrupted the wedding festivities there and went back to Spring Hill township in Wilson County to vote for Dr. Frank Graham that Saturday morning. Later after the wedding reception I remember seeing my mother crying. She told me Dr. Graham had lost. I felt that deeply."

Hunt had little inclination for devilment. The only damage he ever did to anyone's property, his brother recalls, was when he forgot to remove the drive-in theater speaker from the car window before driving away. But Jim Hunt was inquisitive and bold. A childhood friend says he sometimes dared his friends to follow him into the farm pond on icy winter mornings. Hunt's friends recall he was always energetic; he never sat still for long. Both the Hunt boys had rigorous chores seven days a week. Hunt nicknamed his cows for his girlfriends and later for his political heroes (Hubert Humphrey and Kerr Scott).

People who grew up around Hunt were struck by his sense of fairness. His high school coach and history teacher, Onnie Cockrell, remembers one example: "It was during an important basketball game. Our team manager had Hunt with three fouls, but the official score had him with only two. Jimmy came to me and said he knew he had three fouls and he didn't want to play if he got another because it wouldn't be fair." He had his own ideas about justice and race. Sometimes they differed from those of the strongly conservative eastern Carolina culture. In 1955, his senior year at Rock Ridge High School, he surprised his English teacher and classmates when, a year after the Supreme Court's *Brown* decision, he chose as a theme topic school integration. According to his teacher, he endorsed the concept that, whether it was popular or not, it was only fair that people of all races should be given an equal chance to learn.

Hunt's teacher, Mrs. G. C. Wainwright, said Hunt was very studious; but "he was always talking and discussing things between classes and had trouble getting to the next class on time. I told him once he ought to just stop that until he became governor when he could talk all he wanted to." Jim Hunt captured most of the leadership honors at Rock Ridge High School. He was senior class president, football quarterback, captain of the basketball team, yearbook editor, and class valedictorian. The statement beside his yearbook photograph read: "The more a man knows, the more he is worth."

During the summer following high school graduation, Hunt's duties as president of the state Junior Grange took him to a convention of the National Junior Grange in Hamilton, Ohio. There he met a member of its executive committee, Carolyn Leonard, of Mingo, Iowa. He came home telling his mother that he had "met the sweetest, cutest and prettiest girl." "Jim always had a couple of girls on the string," Elsie Hunt said, "but he came back from that Grange meeting and said he didn't know if he could get that girl he had met, but that if he could, he surely would."

The letters began flowing between Rock Ridge and Mingo. Hunt made hitchhiking trips to Iowa. "I had it down to a fine science," he said of those sixteen-hour journeys. "I would sleep in the car once I was satisfied the driver was safe. . . . I got out a time or two." For protection he carried a switchblade knife. Carolyn Leonard and Jim Hunt were married two years later while Jim was a college sophomore. Carolyn Hunt said of her husband: "He seemed to know a lot about life, where he was going, what he wanted to do."

What Hunt had done that fall after meeting Carolyn was to follow his father's example and enroll at North Carolina State University, the region's top agricultural land-grant institution. Hunt's father had graduated from State in 1933 in wildlife management. As a disciple of the pioneering Anson County agronomist Hugh Bennett, he became a soil conservationist. "He spent his life trying to help the farmer save the soil," his son said of him.

The Hunts lived in student housing, and their first daughter, Rebecca, was born while they were there. Hunt did his student teaching at nearby

Cary. His wife worked too. But Hunt's passion for politics hurt his studies. He had a hard time maintaining a B average. "I had to just about kill myself to do it," he said later. Hunt could not resist extracurricular activities. He was absorbed in politics. His classmate lawyer Phil Carlton says he read about politics and government and kept a file of stories about state and national affairs. Even while majoring in agricultural education he had his eye on broader horizons. He visited the General Assembly in Raleigh and listened to legislative debates. He became an active political leader and had trouble deciding whether to accept the student body presidency or a national office in the Future Farmers of America. On the advice of his agriculture teacher he chose the former. That way, they reasoned, more students would come to know him.

After winning the student body vice presidency as a sophomore, Hunt was elevated to the presidency when the president-elect left school. He served two years. It was then that Hunt developed a circle of friends later to play a role in his gubernatorial career. Among them were Eddie Knox, later mayor of Charlotte and candidate for governor; Tom Gilmore, a state legislator from Guilford and candidate for governor too; and Phil Carlton, whom Hunt would appoint to the North Carolina Supreme Court. These friends noted Hunt's serious interest in public affairs. He liked to read books rather than socialize on Saturday nights. "He'd talk about North Carolina being too poor, that changes needed to be made," said Knox.

After Hunt graduated cum laude and won the Outstanding Senior Award in 1959, he remained at State another year to earn his master's degree in agricultural economics. His thesis, "Acreage Controls and Poundage Controls: Their Effects on Most Profitable Production Practices for Flue Cured Tobacco," was later used by the Department of Agriculture to develop its acreage-poundage program.

Politics continued to intrigue Jim Hunt. In 1959 he served as vice president of the North Carolina Young Democrats. Then in 1960 he became state chairman of the College Young Voters for an ambitious young attorney named Terry Sanford in his successful campaign for governor.

That fall, as Hunt entered law school at the University of North Carolina at Chapel Hill, he was swept up in the excitement of the Kennedy-Nixon presidential election. That led him, during his second year of law school, to become national college director for the Democratic National Committee. The Hunts moved to Washington during 1962 and 1963, where Jim continued his studies at George Washington University law school. The Hunts' son, Baxter, was born there in April 1963, shortly before they returned to Chapel Hill for Hunt's final year in law school.

One professor at State, Abe Holtzman, said: "After the first day in class

I came home that night and said to my wife, 'I've got a young man in my class who one day will be governor of North Carolina.' " Hunt's teachers at Chapel Hill had the same impression as those at Rock Ridge and North Carolina State. Throughout his academic career classroom studies came second to politics. As a result Hunt got through law school as a "fair" student, and then failed the state bar examination.

Hunt was shocked. He had never failed anything before. He had spent much time that spring working in Judge L. Richardson Preyer's unsuccessful primary campaign for governor. "I'm sure I didn't study as much as I should have," he said later. "I had made really good grades in law school when I studied. They'd dropped down my last semester because I was so involved in that campaign."

By that time, though, the Hunts were prepared for a new adventure. Jim had wanted to join the Peace Corps, but the organization wouldn't accept married couples with children. Instead, with the help of one of his North Carolina State professors, he got a Ford Foundation grant, to become an economic adviser to the government of Nepal. In 1964 the Hunts left for Katmandu, where they remained for two years. "Carolyn and I had a strong feeling that we wanted to serve," Hunt said. "We believed in foreign missions and in helping our fellow man. I read a book called *The Fabulous Flemings of Katmandu.* It was about the first American medical missionaries in Nepal. They needed people who knew something about agriculture."

In Nepal the Hunts had dinner one evening with Professor Warren Ashby, a philosophy professor on leave from the University of North Carolina at Greensboro. "Jim Hunt told me then," Ashby later recalled, "that his ambition was to become governor of North Carolina." While they were in Nepal, the Hunts had a second daughter, Rachel, who was born in a missionary hospital at Katmandu. Hunt also boned up on the law. On returning home he took the bar examination again and passed.

Jim Hunt's experiences in the Sanford and Preyer campaigns had introduced him to one of the state's shrewdest political kingmakers, the wealthy Winston-Salem oil jobber Bert Bennett. Bennett, who had been Sanford's roommate at Chapel Hill and later became his chief gubernatorial adviser, tagged Hunt as a winner. Bennett and Sanford had built a progressive organization across North Carolina, tying in with Kerr Scott's branch-head boys. Sanford had managed Scott's successful senatorial campaign in the 1950s. Bennett, who was known as a superb nuts-and-bolts organizer, moved in to manage Sanford's 1960 gubernatorial race. After Judge Preyer failed to succeed Sanford as governor in 1964, Bennett sought another protégé and found him in Jim Hunt. At first Bennett had been impressed with Hunt's college friend, Phil Carlton, who had worked in Preyer's headquarters in the 1964 campaign, but Carlton, then a chief district judge in Edgecombe County, had no interest in moving into statewide politics in the early 1970s. "I just got out of [Hunt's] way," he said later.

In the meantime Hunt, having passed the bar examination, returned to his North Carolina roots. He joined the Wilson law firm of Kirby and Webb. The firm's senior partner, J. Russell Kirby, was later state Democratic Party chairman. Hunt plunged into community affairs. He championed a move to consolidate the Wilson and the Wilson County public schools. The Wilson establishment opposed this change because many feared racial integration and higher taxes. After Dr. Martin Luther King's assassination in 1968, Hunt was one of the few whites who, as a member of the local Good Neighbor Council, marched in a candlelight parade to the Wilson County Courthouse for a memorial service. Of this episode Hunt later said: "There were some things said, but you do what needs to be done for your community."

Hunt was then thirty. He had already been elected president of the Wilson County Young Democrats in 1967. Gradually he began to expand his Bennett-Sanford-Preyer contacts into the nucleus of his own organization. He decided to seek the presidency of the North Carolina Young Democrats. He cultivated political friends in every part of the state, many of whom later became his famous "keys." Hunt had no trouble winning the office he sought, which had served as a stepping-stone for many ambitious young politicians. It became one for Hunt, who already had his eye on more important goals.

Another opportunity came in 1970. Governor Bob Scott, Kerr's son, and Jimmy Johnson, state Democratic Party chairman, chose Hunt to head a commission to rewrite the state party rules. This gave him a chance to move about the state, holding hearings and touching bases with friends.

Bert Bennett was much impressed with his young protégé. He told Ken Eudy of the *Charlotte Observer* in 1984 that the best politicians must have the greatest desire to win. "When you have that one desire—no second—plus talent, and you love what you're doing, that's a hell of a combination. And that's what makes Jim Hunt tick."

Hunt had similar words of praise for Bennett. "Bert is a rare individual," he said. "There's nobody like him in politics. He doesn't seek power for himself. He wants good people elected and then he leaves them alone." Judge Preyer also lauded Bennett's talents. "Without his organizing ability I don't believe there would be a Terry Sanford or a Jim Hunt regime. . . .

He inspired great loyalty from his key people all over the state. They would absolutely follow Bert into the flames. He has that kind of personal loyalty."

By the early seventies Jim Hunt had, with the help of Bennett, set his cap for the lieutenant governorship. Governor Bob Scott had used that office as a staging area for the Governor's Mansion. In the same year Jesse Helms announced for the Senate, Jim Hunt announced for lieutenant governor.

3. "A Shy Young Fellow"

On the verge of his resignation from the presidency in the summer of 1974, Richard Nixon, by then besieged and lonely, called four members of Congress to seek consolation. One was the freshman senator from North Carolina, Jesse Helms. Helms said later that the President had called in response to a note Helms wrote him earlier. "My wife and I had been to church and the sermon was about loneliness," he said. "I got to thinking that this guy's got to be lonely, so I just dropped him a note."

Helms supported Nixon almost to the end of Watergate. But then he gagged on the White House tapes, especially Nixon's vulgar language. As a young aide to Senator Willis Smith in the early fifties, Helms had gotten to know Senator Nixon, but he had never noticed such outbursts then. "Why I'd never heard him say 'damn'. . . . I was repulsed by the language [in the tapes]. Perhaps he was just trying to match Kennedy and Johnson in the use of profanity."

From that moment Senator Helms gradually abandoned the Nixon ship. But he had never supported the President completely. He vigorously opposed Henry Kissinger's appointment as secretary of state and his friendship with Nelson Rockefeller. (Helms was later to say of Rockefeller, "He's a wife stealer.")

A foreign policy that favored negotiating with the Kremlin made Helms nervous. "My loyalty is to the principles of conservatism," he told a group of young conservatives in 1973, "not to any particular regime. . . . It pains me to say this, but the current administration [Nixon's] cannot escape a large measure of blame for the current easy acceptance of Leviathan-like government expansion. This expansion has, if anything, become even faster under the current administration."

Helms's attitude toward Nixon pointed up the inviolability of his rock-ribbed conservatism. Reared, like Hunt, in the rural South, Helms remembers his upbringing in a glow of nostalgia. All good people then, he recalls, were churchgoing and spiritually motivated. America has lost its way. What this country needs, he insists, is a spiritual revival.

Helms's view of himself emerged rather clearly during one of his encounters with Congressman Nick Galifianakis during his initial senatorial campaign in 1972. In a speech to the North Carolina Associated Press Broadcasters Association in Raleigh, Helms charged that his opponent had described him as a "racist" and a "hate monger." Furthermore, Helms added, Galifianakis had spread a rumor that Helms had changed his church affiliation "when blacks joined." Helms's voice trembled as he told the broadcasters that, first, Raleigh's First Baptist Church had no black members and, second, the real reason he moved his church membership was that his new church was only a short distance from his home—near enough for his crippled son to walk to Boy Scout meetings.

Helms did have a crippled son. In 1968 he and his wife adopted Charles, a nine-year-old orphan afflicted with cerebral palsy. They reared him along with their daughters, Jane and Nancy. Charles graduated from North Carolina State University in 1980 in forestry and now works for R. J. Reynolds in Winston-Salem. "He's a blessing," his foster father says of him.

Reporters covering Helms's first campaign for the Senate almost uniformly concluded that, far from being a fire-eating, glad-handing extrovert, Jesse Helms sometimes appeared rather shy and introverted. He was a middle-aged man, they noted, of nondescript appearance but rather owl-like in his dark horn-rimmed glasses, tall (six feet, two inches) and angular, lean but not thin. Some of Helms's childhood friends called him "grasshopper" because of his bulging eyes and long legs. His sister's name for him was "telephone pole" because he was thin and tall. "Mother had a hard time getting him to eat," she said. "He was always in a hurry."

To many outside the South Helms presented a mock-courtly southern facade. In personal demeanor he was almost always courteous and effusive, especially with women and older people. He exuded a complex mixture of cheerfulness and aggressiveness laced with piety and shrewdness. "He looks like a Casper Milquetoast, but he isn't," one reporter said.

Helms grew up in the southern Piedmont village of Monroe (population three thousand), once the center of a cotton-growing economy. His father, Jesse A. Helms, Sr. (known as "Mr. Jesse"), started his career as a reserve fireman. Later he became fire chief, deputy sheriff, and police chief, holding some of those positions simultaneously. The Helmses lived three doors down the street from the fire department. Jesse's family, of Scotch-Irish extraction, had been in the neighborhood since the mid-eighteenth century. A George Helms received a land grant from King George III in 1758. Two Helms brothers, George and Tillman, farmed a plot in Union County, site of Monroe, in the mid-1700s.

Helms's father and a distant cousin, Ethel Mae Helms, were married on Christmas Eve, 1912. (The senator once described the union as a "Helms squared.") Researching the family genealogy, Helms's wife, Dorothy, found that it was likely that Jesse, Sr., was descended from George and Ethel Mae from Tillman. "In Union County the Helmses from Monroe pronounced their name 'Helms' and those from the county 'Hell-ums'," said a contemporary of the senator.

Jesse's brother, Wriston, was six years his senior and today is a retired Woolworth's store manager in Pascagoula, Mississippi. His younger sister, Mary Elizabeth McNeely, lives in Monroe with her retired husband, Ruskin.

Jesse himself was born on October 18, 1921. The Helmses lived modestly in the rural North Carolina of those days. Jesse, Sr., had only a fifth-grade education, but his son considers him "the wisest man I've ever known." Others shared a high regard for the tall, cigar-smoking "Mr. Jesse." His son-in-law, Ruskin McNeely, sometimes accompanied him on law-enforcement missions and complimented his knack for handling lawbreakers. "One time the sheriff had a criminal prospect cornered in a house trying to get him to surrender," McNeely recalled. "The man yelled out the window, 'If you'll call Mr. Jesse, I'll surrender to him.' "

Hargrove Bowles, a Helms schoolmate and later a Democratic political leader, called Mr. Jesse a grand old fellow. "Old Man Helms," he said, "used to catch me parking near the church cemetery. He'd tell me, 'Hargrove, if I catch you out here again, I'll have to take you to your daddy.' But he never did."

During his first senatorial campaign Jesse Helms stopped by Monroe to introduce his six-foot-five-inch, seventy-nine-year-old father to the press. "This is the original Jesse Helms," he said. Mr. Helms, Sr., was "erect and agile with strong facial resemblances to his son." On that occasion he had the town fire truck driven out of the station and persuaded his son to sit on the driver's seat for photographs. Helms did so with some embarrassment.

"Mr. Jesse"—or "Papa Jesse" as his children called him—lived until 1974. He saw his son sworn in as senator in 1973. Helms later wrote of that occasion: "My father died almost exactly a year after he sat in the Senate Gallery in January 1973 and watched me take the oath of office. If I should live to be a thousand, I'll never forget looking up at him as I returned to my seat. Tears were streaming down his face." "My father was a 'gentle' man," said his son Wriston. "He was always fair, and it took a whole lot to get him riled up. But he could be plenty firm. He always told us that when you take a stand, stay there unless you're really proved wrong."

Helms and friends of the early days have nostalgic memories of Monroe. They recall swimming in Richardson's Creek and attending movies at the Strand and Pastime theaters. They also showed up regularly at church on Sundays and at prayer meetings during the week. The social life of those days revolved around the church. (The Helmses attended First Baptist.)

Helms's classmates don't remember him as being especially gregarious. One of them described him as "very reserved, not outgoing even one little bit. He wasn't one of the boys, and he didn't do much talking as a kid."

If young Jesse had strong opinions, he did not express them much then. Nor was he interested in politics. He grew up during the Great Depression, when times were rough and people in Monroe had to use "scrip" instead of dollars when the banks failed. "I came up between the two world wars," Helms said in a recent interview. "All the people around me emphasized working and saving and personal responsibility. They spelled out in one way or another the uniqueness of America."

Helms was eternally energetic and hardworking. If he was not remembered in the sandlot baseball games, he did apply himself in school and took on odd jobs along the way. He played the violin and the sousaphone (a tubalike instrument) and practiced with the school band for hours.

He got along well with his teachers and was especially devoted to Ray House, a former textile worker who was a memorable teacher for several generations of young people in Monroe. "The original 'music man' man came through Monroe about the time Jesse was moving through high school," House recalled. "He sold the kids a lot of music instruments none of them could play. He left them with instructions, but then he vanished. It seemed to me we ought to use those instruments, so we got a high school band together, and it worked pretty well." Bowles, Helms, Henry Hall Wilson (later president of the Chicago Board of Trade), Bud Nance (later a Navy admiral), and Bill Hinson (today a High Point oral surgeon) were among House's music protégés.

House took the Monroe High School band to Greensboro and won the statewide music contest for eleven years. On one trip Helms won the sousaphone competition. House recalled how he did it. With Dr. James Christian Pfohl, music director of Davidson College, as judge, Helms stopped midway in his presentation, turned to Pfohl, and said: "Sir, I'm scared to death." Pfohl replied: "Well, young man, I'm scared too. Just proceed with your music." Helms won first prize.

Even then Helms was resourceful. House remembers Helms as being "as smart as he wanted to be. In those days the girls were supposed to be the smartest, and the boys didn't put much store by it. Helms was smart enough." As Helms graduated from Monroe High School, which finished at the eleventh grade, House urged him to pursue a college education. He encouraged Helms to enroll at a nearby Baptist junior college, Wingate, only seven miles from Monroe, and Helms did. "If Ray House taught us anything," Helms said later, "he taught us that we are personally responsible and accountable."

During his high school days Helms worked as a soda jerk at Wilson's Drug Store and served as a carrier for the *Charlotte News*. He swept floors at the *Monroe Journal*, where he wrote high school sports. Somewhere along the way he became interested in journalism and once wrote that he liked "journalistic work or the life of a pharmacist." The high school newspaper, the *Mohisco*, of May 1938 said Helms's ambition was to be a columnist. By 1940 he was doing just that—writing an essay, "The Vagabond Scholar," (at one dollar per column) for the *Monroe Journal*. Helms had a way with words, as his friend Bill Hinson recalled. He had a large vocabulary, and his work was full of human interest and folksy humor. He had a simple style, often on the sentimental side. This talent helped him later as a television commentator and politician.

After a year at Wingate, Helms decided to transfer to Wake Forest, another Baptist college, then located north of Raleigh. With the help of Principal House, who always looked out for "his boys," he made the change. House used to tell his students, "You're not going to make it sitting back whining."

Helms was no whiner. He set about working his way through Wake Forest. He paid his bills by washing dishes in his boardinghouse. He worked in the college news bureau and read proof for the *Raleigh News and Observer*. "Jesse was a shy young fellow in those days," a Wake Forest classmate, Jay Jenkins, recalls, "but he got over it." He served as part-time stringer for the United Press and the *Raleigh Times*. But Helms never finished at Wake Forest. During his third year he decided to cast his lot with journalism. He moved from the proof room of the *News and Observer* to the sports department. Then, striving to get on the straight news side, he accepted an offer from the *Raleigh Times* publisher John Park to become assistant city editor.

Ed Rankin, now vice president for public relations at Cannon Mills and at that time a reporter for the *News and Observer*, remembers Helms well. Along with David Howard of the United Press, they boarded together at the old Vance Apartments on Capitol Square. "We lived in one room with a double bed and a cot," Rankin recalls. "We flipped to see who would get the cot, and I was lucky. Nobody can say I ever slept with Jesse Helms."

But Rankin's report on Helms was positive. He found the young reporter fun to be with and good company. As fellow Baptists, they had an occasional beer, but "we didn't do much of that," Rankin recalled. Helms was arrow-straight, his contemporaries remembered, a "clean-cut Baptist type." Helms was still high on sports, and he also became high on Dorothy Coble, a *News and Observer* reporter, whom he met while working on the sports desk. They were married on October 31, 1942.

In the meantime World War II had broken out, and Helms decided to sign up. Because of poor hearing, however, the result of an infection suffered while at Wake Forest, he was not accepted. Later he managed to enlist in the navy and served for the remainder of the war as a specialist first-class in recruitment in North Carolina and Georgia.

Dorothy Coble Helms was the daughter of a wholesale shoe salesman and had graduated from Meredith College and the University of North Carolina Journalism School at Chapel Hill. Both the Helmses recall that her father, Jacob, got them interested in politics. "You couldn't be around him without talking about what was going on," Dot Helms told a reporter. Helms himself remembers listening to Fulton Lewis, Jr., and H. V. Kaltenborn on the radio. He says Jacob Coble was "the original conservative." Helms met another conservative in Raleigh who influenced his views. He was Alvin Wingfield, Jr., a salesman and radio commentator, who later committed suicide. Wingfield introduced Helms to the works of Austrian-born economist Ludwig von Mises (1881–1973), a proponent of libertarian economics. Helms cited von Mises's book *Human Action* as influential and recommended it to his friends.

After the war ended Helms returned to the *Raleigh Times* in 1945 as city editor; but he had become interested in radio. The following year he left Raleigh to become a reporter for station WCBT in Roanoke Rapids. Helms introduced innovations in the interviewing technique by broadcasting recorded remarks of people he interviewed. It was a prelude to television. Helms was a disk jockey for a while, but he found that uninteresting.

After two years in Roanoke Rapids, Helms made a move that influenced his future career. In January 1948 he returned to Raleigh to work for A. J. Fletcher, a feisty entrepreneur who loved classical music. He had just opened a small 250-watt radio station, WRAL, and he asked Helms to become its news director.

That was the start of an association that eventually projected Helms into politics. Fletcher, a man of strongly conservative views, had considerable influence on the young reporter. "They were damn near like father and son," said Superior Court Judge Pou Bailey, an early Helms friend. "Jesse had a tremendous respect, almost reverence toward A. J., and A. J. had tremendous confidence in Jesse. They made a hell of a team." Contemporaries remember Helms lugging his wire recorder all over town. Writing and broadcasting the news, he became intrigued by the power of the press and by his own ability to command attention. By the start of the 1950s he became known as the voice of conservatism in Raleigh and was turning, even then, to commentary rather than straight reporting.

It was during the acerbic senatorial campaign involving liberal University of North Carolina President Frank P. Graham and conservative attorney Willis Smith in 1950 that Helms came to the fore as an influential media figure. Helms covered the first Democratic primary struggle between Graham and Smith (which Graham won). It featured flamboyant charges of Communist taint and intellectual socialism against the former university president. Helms took a leading role in the runoff campaign.

"I went on the radio telling folks that supporters ought to get to [Smith's] house and encourage him to run," Helms said. WRAL ran announcements throughout the day about the rally. Several hundred people turned out. Smith, former speaker of the State House, a prominent corporation lawyer and chairman of the Duke University board of trustees, leaned toward bowing out. But after the crowd arrived, he announced he would make up his mind the following morning. During the period following the first primary three Supreme Court rulings involving desegregation had been handed down. That influenced Smith's decision to run.

Smith then went on to beat Graham in a bitter second primary in early June. The campaign focused on blatant and exaggerated racial charges against Graham. Smith supporters circulated handbills warning "*White People Wake Up*." Circulars asked such questions as, "Do you want Negroes riding beside you, your wife and your daughters in buses, cabs and trains? Negroes going to white schools and white children going to Negro schools? Negroes to occupy the same hospital rooms with you and your wife and daughters?" Some of the printed material, distributed in mill villages and at industrial plants, featured photographs of black soldiers dancing and drinking with white women. One pictured a Negro dancing with a woman who had the superimposed face of Mrs. Graham.

Helms denies that either he or Senator Smith knew about or sanctioned scurrilous campaign material. Others, however, have different memories. Judge Bailey worked in the Smith campaign too. He told one reporter that "Helms contributed to practically every ad that was run." After Helms denied having prepared advertisements for Smith, Judge Bailey said, "Maybe Jesse didn't create any of those ads, but I'm pretty sure he saw them all."

Senator Helms is indignant today when critics link him with racist publicity unleashed for Smith. He charges instead that Smith was the "victim of a horrendously improper campaign" that branded him a racist. "Time and time again [Smith] would reject the proposals made to him about a racist campaign," Helms said.

Helms also said that earlier he had a chance to work for Dr. Graham. He said that he and Dr. Graham were "close friends" and that Graham and Governor Kerr Scott, who had appointed the university president to the Senate, approached him about handling election publicity and a job in Washington if Graham won. "The hardest thing I've ever had to do," Helms says, "was to say, 'Dr. Frank, I love you to death . . . but I don't agree with you philosophically. I can't be in your campaign.'"

The emotional backlash of the Smith-Graham campaign polarized liberals and conservatives in North Carolina. Many considered it the ugliest political contest in a state which had rarely engaged in overt racism during the twentieth century. Whatever Jesse Helms's role may have been in it, the campaign upgraded his career. One year after the primary the young radio reporter went to Washington as an administrative assistant to newly elected Senator Willis Smith.

4. Br'er Rabbit in the Briar Patch

In the early 1950s, while Jim Hunt carved out an impressive high school record in Wilson County, Jesse Helms embarked on a short career as administrative assistant to Senator Willis Smith in Washington. After Smith's unexpected death in 1953, Helms remained briefly with newly appointed Alton Lennon, but then returned to Raleigh as executive director of the North Carolina Bankers' Association.

Helms got only a taste of the heady political life of Washington. It included involvement in Senator Richard Russell's unsuccessful effort against Adlai Stevenson for the 1952 Democratic presidential nomination and a friendship with Senator Richard Nixon. But that sampling broadened his horizon. It influenced his decision two decades later to run for the Senate and return to Washington.

As executive director of the bankers' association and editor of its magazine, the *Tar Heel Banker*, Helms received a full introduction to the corporate establishment of North Carolina. He and Dorothy, and their two daughters, Jane and Nancy, moved back to Dorothy's father's neighborhood in Raleigh and built a red-brick, quasi-colonial home next door. Jacob Coble, who had been a successful wholesale shoe salesman, was by then retired and a widower. Hayes-Barton, where they lived, was a pleasant middle-to-upper-class neighborhood in a still rather sleepy southern capital city.

Helms immediately brought liveliness to the formerly staid pages of the *Tar Heel Banker*. He wrote an editorial and a personal column each month. While the publication was a lobbying and personnel relations vehicle for the banking industry, Helm's comments roamed widely across the realm of public affairs. Bankers did not perceive Helms as ultraconservative then because he was constantly goading them to plunge more actively into politics, something many of them viewed with suspicion.

Helms insisted politics was an honorable business that should attract more able conservatives, but he maintained it should never be put ahead of principle. "Compromise, hell!" he wrote in 1950. "That's what has happened to us all down the line—and that's the very cause of our woes. If freedom is right and tyranny is wrong, why should those who believe in freedom treat it as if it were a roll of bologna to be bartered a slice at a time?"

Helms sharpened his developing conservativism, including a distaste for such governmental projects as tobacco subsidies (a viewpoint he altered after becoming a senator). In 1957 he saw signs of Communist involvement in racial turmoil at the Little Rock, Arkansas, schools and predicted that private schools would become fashionable if integration expanded.

Helms's editorials revealed his developing fears about racial integration, but they were never as bombastic as his television commentary became later. He included racial jokes and stories in his columns, including a lovable old dialect-speaking black. When a state civic club complained about such stories, including similar ones about Baptists, Catholics, and Jews, Helms protested that the club was overreacting. "To rob the Negro of his reputation of thinking through a problem in his own fashion," he wrote, "is about the same as trying to pretend that he doesn't have a natural instinct for rhythm or for singing and dancing."

More recently—last year—when a *Charlotte Observer* photographer prepared to take pictures in Helms's Raleigh study, Helms quickly pulled an illustration off the wall and away from the camera. "That'll get me in trouble," he told reporter Bill Arthur. The picture showed a smiling, toothy black man wearing a planter's hat, sitting in a rocking chair on a columned mansion porch. He was drinking a mint julep and the caption said: "This is what me and Martin Luther had in mind."

During those years Helms expanded his friendships with legal and business associates of the late Senator Smith, who remained his idol. He became a member of Judge Pou Bailey's every-other-Thursday poker club, which included bankers, businessmen, and lawyers. Bailey called Helms "one of the worst [poker players] I ever saw for the same reason that endears him to a lot of folks: He is completely honest. If Jesse throws his money on the table, it's because he's got the cards. He never bluffs." Bailey, a member of an established eastern Carolina family (his father had been Senator Josiah Bailey and his grandfather Congressman Edwin Pou), admired Jesse's conservative views, but came to feel he was far too rigid. "Jesse can't see any grays. Everything is black and white," Bailey said. "I've told him over and over he ought to give on some of the small issues." Jesse's reply to Bailey was always: "Well, Pou, which of my principles would you have me compromise first?"

In 1957 the lure of politics again enticed Jesse Helms. After joining the Rotary Club and the Masons, he decided to take his own advice. He announced for city council, was elected rather easily, and then won a second two-year term. A Raleigh newspaper said of him in those days: "On occasion [Helms] dressed down the mayor and other council members he was at odds with." He began to voice strong opinions and clashed at times with city manager William Carper. But Carper didn't consider Helms anti-government. "He was anti-government domination," Carper said. Others, however, considered Helms an unpredictable gadfly and obstructionist. He fought an urban renewal project and opposed a crucial annexation proposal in southwest Raleigh which was supported by conservative businessmen.

By the middle of his second term in 1960 the budding politician received a flattering offer from A. J. Fletcher: a chance to rejoin WRAL, by then a successful television station. Helms returned with the title of executive vice president and vice chairman of the board. The most inviting thing about the Fletcher offer, however, was an opportunity to resume his journalistic career with a television commentary five nights a week called "Viewpoint." During the next dozen years this presentation would make Helms's name a household word across eastern North Carolina. It was also broadcast on seventy rural radio stations and reprinted in some two hundred newspapers. It paved the way for Helms's Senate career.

"Mr. Fletcher didn't want merely a television station," Helms once wrote.

"What he really wanted was a voice that would speak loud and strong for free enterprise." Helms became, in effect, another son to the freewheeling Fletcher. "The old man thought the sun rose and set behind Jesse's left ear," observed Judge Bailey.

"Viewpoint," a five-minute "editorial," was a ready-made vehicle for Helms's journalistic talent. According to Bailey, Fletcher put Helms on the air and "told him to give 'em hell. It was just like putting Br'er Rabbit in the briar patch." Helms plunged in with gloves-off attacks on some of his favorite targets—Communist sympathizers, sexual perverts, left-wing do-gooders, pornography, crime in the streets, liberal professors, and secular humanists. He never was at a loss for colorful, acerbic language: on civil rights—"The movement has an uncommon number of moral degenerates leading the parade"; on Social Security—"Nothing more than doles and hand-outs"; on female anti-war protesters—"stringy-haired, awkward young women who cannot attract attention any other way"; and on Medicare—"A step over into the swampy field of socialized medicine."

Helms's broadcasts—2,761 of them over the next twelve years—caught the state's attention. Often dipped in acid, occasionally sentimental, and always lively, they preached all-out libertarian conservatism with a vengeance. One newsman described the WRAL-TV commentator as "folksy, low key, mannerly and good at story-telling." But Helms was rarely bland and often mean. Either he delivered a sharp uppercut to the chin or a teary accolade for one of his conservative heroes.

Helms devoted one "Viewpoint" to lauding Fletcher, who as chief executive of Capitol Broadcasting Company, had made a New Year's Eve appearance on WRAL-TV. "The gentleman," Helms declared, "obviously belongs to a vanishing breed in America—perhaps not so much in philosophy as in spirit. Plenty of men still cling silently to the notion that America's greatness was built on the principle of free enterprise, personal responsibility and faith in God, but not so many are willing to fight at great personal risk, in defense of those ideals. The 81-year-old executive who delivered our 2,000th editorial on New Year's Eve has not been merely willing, but constantly eager, to participate in the battle." On his death in 1979, Fletcher left Helms a one-hundred-thousand-dollar bequest of stock in Capitol Broadcasting Company.

Another "Viewpoint," in 1969, applauded Governor Ronald Reagan of California for getting the best of a reporter who tried to say that "right-wingers" took over Germany for Hitler. Reagan's reply was that it was the left-wingers who helped give rise to Hitler. "The blame," as Helms quoted Reagan, "belongs to the wrong-wingers—those who call themselves 'liberals.' They have indeed been 'liberal' in giving away America's heritage."

Like Reagan, Helms had a knack for colorful phraseology. "A liberal," he said, "is a person who likes to give away somebody else's money—after he has feathered his own nest."

Helms once called Walter Cronkite a "hysterical crybaby" and chastised a University of North Carolina professor for assigning his pupils Andrew Marvell's "To His Coy Mistress" because it involved seduction. The thrust of his commentaries went a good deal further to the right than the conventional conservatism of those tumultuous years following the Kennedy assassination and the rise of Lyndon Johnson's Great Society. Racial violence and campus disruptions made ready fodder for Helms's outrage. His televised blasts attracted a large audience across rural North Carolina. Even his critics began to watch "to see what Jesse had to say."

Often Helms found himself at odds even with his fellow conservatives. In one "Viewpoint" broadcast he declared that Richard Nixon "seemed mysteriously and pathetically swept up in the expediency of professional politics," had "lost his boldness and imagination," and "fallen short of statesmanship." He spoke of Nixon's paradoxical political career and was suspicious of his trips to Russia and China.

Helms defended such attacks on individuals who might seem his allies by saying he believed in principles and not people. During Watergate, when he was slow to abandon Nixon, Helms recalled that at the time of Nixon's popularity he (Helms) had been criticized for "having been critical of the President." Now that Nixon was unpopular, "I'm accused of defending him," he said. "I'm not defending him. I'm defending principles."

Not all those who heard Helms approved. Helms got thousands of laudatory letters; others, though, saw his attacks on such institutions as the World Council of Churches ("in favor of violence and revolution") and the Civil Rights Bill ("something the communists would very much like to see enacted") as pernicious and unfair. The Federal Communications Commission received enough complaints to cause it to investigate WRAL-TV in 1964 before renewing its license. The renewal followed, but accompanied by a warning about complying with the agency's fairness doctrine.

Helms had attracted a fanatically loyal television audience. It grew during the strife-torn sixties. As protest groups marched in the streets and entrenched power brokers gave up some of their prerogatives and feared revolution, Helms made a defiant call for a return to Old South verities and conventional, Anglo-Saxon folkways. No voice like that had been heard, much less heeded, in North Carolina since the roughest years of Reconstruction. Helms stuck doggedly to those views. If he seemed an anachronism to some, he was a voice in the wilderness to others.

One of the more flamboyant aspects of Helms's personality appeared during his hard-fought campaign against Nick Galifianakis in the 1972 Senate campaign. It was at a Charlotte political rally featuring Vice President Spiro Agnew. A large crowd had assembled at a city park recreation center. Among them were about twenty-five long-haired anti–Nixon-Agnew demonstrators parading outside the center. Inside a smaller group had taken their positions.

During the hour before the vice president's arrival, state political candidates, party officials, and dignitaries joined the crowd in listening to patriotic songs from a well-scrubbed group of teenagers. After Agnew's arrival each state candidate was introduced, and each received some abuse from the demonstrators; but they saved the worst for Helms. Shouts of "racist" echoed through the hall. Helms, according to one newspaper report, "became flushed with anger as he attempted to respond. After a while he paused, glanced at the neat singing group to his left and said, 'Isn't it nice that the majority of young people are represented by them.' Then looking in the direction of the demonstrators, he added, 'Instead of by that!' The crowd roared its approval. Helms stood peering at the demonstrators, his face scarlet. The second the applause subsided, he again attacked the hecklers. 'And that one with the real long hair,' he yelled, pointing to a disheveled youngster among the chanting group, 'That's George McGovern!'" Helms showed he was quick to anger under attack and not hesitant to lash out at any adversary, traits which marked his senatorial career.

When incumbent Senator Everett Jordan thought about retiring in 1966, a group of Helms's friends, mostly Democrats (since Helms was still a member of that party), had visited him to urge him to run. Those Tar Heel conservatives were seeking, as one later put it, "fire insurance" in case Jordan decided to retire. At that time the group sent out a letter asking support for Helms and got fifteen thousand favorable responses in three weeks. Later Jordan decided to seek reelection, and nothing came of the 1966 visit.

But six years later—after Helms, on the urging of his daughter Nancy, had switched his registration to Republican—pressures on him to run intensified. Helms spoke of not being willing to be run "through the meatgrinder" of politics. "He didn't want to run," said his emerging political adviser, the shrewd Raleigh attorney Tom Ellis. "But we shamed him into it."

5. Too Proud to Be Proud

Before Jim Hunt, North Carolina's "progressive plutocracy" had produced in the twentieth century two dominant figures, Senator Furnifold Simmons and Governor O. Max Gardner. Between them they ruled the political establishment for almost half a century (1900–1948).

But Gardner's death in 1947 marked the start of serious factionalism inside the Democratic Party. Although the Republicans failed to win a major statewide office until twenty-four years later, no single Democratic organization prevailed for long between 1948 and 1972. Kerr Scott, the "Good Roads" farmer governor, announced he was "letting in a little fresh air" when he defeated the Gardner machine's last candidate, Charles Johnson, in 1948. Scott later went to the Senate, but he never succeeded in entrenching his "branch-head boys" (although in 1968 his son, Bob Scott, won the governorship). Governor Luther Hodges, a moderate conservative industrialist, dominated the 1950s. The 1960s were split between Governor Terry Sanford, a moderate liberal, and Governor Dan Moore, a moderate conservative.

By mid-century North Carolina had moved some distance from what Judge Robert Winston had called her in 1923—a "militant mediocracy." Winston described the state as populated by plain people, neither rich nor aristocratic but rather provincial and proud of it. Indeed, it was said of North Carolina that it was a state "too proud to be proud." A Virginian who called the Tar Heels a tail of Jefferson's kite criticized their aggressiveness in declarations of modesty. "The trouble with you people," he concluded, "is that you're so damned proud of your modesty."

But times were subtly changing. The University at Chapel Hill had helped dilute some of the provincialism, and new forces were stirring. Some of the self-abasement of the past had begun to dissipate. The strict conservatism of what had once been called the Rip Van Winkle State had given way to the flux of progressive ideas. Scholars have noted that the South delayed longer than the rest of the nation in reconciling its traditions and culture with revolutionary changes wrought by Darwin, Freud, Marx, and Einstein. North Carolina's awakening came late too; but it came in a hurry.

Because of Chapel Hill and its cult of new leadership, the state's political structure had begun to reflect new influences too. Because it had never succumbed to the blandishments of the kind of extremist white demagogues who flourished in the Deep South, North Carolina was perceived nationally as "the most liberal southern state." Generally, Tar Heels preferred the moderate middle. Dr. Frank P. Graham, president of the University of North Carolina, and a coterie of influential social scientists led by Howard W. Odum accounted for much of this reputation. But such varied governors as Luther Hodges, Kerr Scott, and Terry Sanford added to it. For whatever reasons, North Carolina seemed to be a state where important economic and social changes were in progress. Even Arnold Toynbee, in his *Study of History*, found occasion to view North Carolina as different. "In North Carolina," he wrote in 1946, "the visitor will find up-to-date industries, mushroom universities and a breath of the hustling 'boosting' spirit which he has learnt to associate with the 'Yankees' of the North."

Young Jim Hunt identified with this blossoming liberalism in the early 1960s, the Kennedy years, when he joined the gubernatorial campaigns of Terry Sanford and Richardson Preyer. But even then Hunt was sensitive about political nuances. He soon ran up against the perils of liberalism in an essentially conservative state. "You can't put two liberals back to back in the Governor's office," a wise political observer said of the unsuccessful effort to make Judge Preyer Sanford's successor. Hunt learned that lesson thoroughly and capitalized on it later with the help of his mentor Bert Bennett.

Bennett and Terry Sanford had been classmates at Chapel Hill in the late 1930s. Out of their personal friendship sprang an enduring political alliance. They managed the Democratic Party's newly emerging progressive organization, and its road was rocky. Bennett saw in Hunt an attractive heir in the Sanford mold. By 1970 the liberalism that was late in coming to North Carolina had begun to lose favor on the national scene. Camelot was dead in the wake of student riots and the catastrophe of Vietnam. Many Democrats who thought they could win in its afterglow were disappointed.

Planning politics for the new era, Bennett and Hunt observed that Bob Scott, Kerr's son, had parlayed his occupancy of the lieutenant governor's office into the governorship in 1968. Previously that post had been a dead-end street, but Scott had used it to stay in the public eye until he was ready to move on. The office included presiding officer duties in the state senate. Scott had successfully lobbied to make it a full-time position as he finished his four-year gubernatorial term in 1972.

Hunt and Bennett saw it as the ideal way station for an ambitious young politician. In 1971 Hunt was asked why he didn't strike for the governorship. "I don't think I'm prepared to be governor," he said. "I've simply not had the experience to make that race."

Hunt's hunch appeared accurate. While he won the lieutenant governorship with ease the following year, both the governorship and one of the state's senatorial seats fell to the Republicans for the first time in seventy years. A conservative movement had materialized with stunning impact in North Carolina.

After Hargrove ("Skipper") Bowles, the Greensboro businessman and former childhood friend of Jesse Helms, lost the governorship to Jim Holshouser, Hunt, at thirty-five, became the Democratic Party's leader. In so doing, he won the backing of diverse Democratic factions—those of former governors Dan Moore and Bob Scott as well as the Sanford-Preyer wing. Under duress, the party sought to reunite.

As a coordinating and coalescing figure, Jim Hunt remained sensitive to North Carolina's changing climate. Even before his election he had begun to break away from his conventional "liberal" moorings, becoming more centrist. In 1971 he had endorsed Nixon's handling of the economy. In a Greensboro speech he said: "I believe we are on the right course in trying to correct the problems. All of us must stand behind the President and be willing to make personal sacrifices to get our economic house back in order." In the same speech Hunt declared: "The free enterprise system has two obvious advantages over any state enterprise system. These are efficient production of goods and services and compatibility with individual freedoms and liberty."

Hunt also emphasized a favorite Helms theme: the decline of morality and sobriety in America. Neither a smoker nor a drinker himself, Hunt never tried to force his personal views on others; but he did sound off on them occasionally. A decline in traditional values, he told a veterans' meeting, has undermined the nation's system of laws, education, and family life. We must "help rebuild America from within so it will continue to be a country worth fighting for. . . . We must have change where it is essential but change with stability."

"Both Helms and Hunt are essentially moralistic," a political veteran said of them recently. "But there's a difference. Helms thinks all the nation's ills come from moral deviations. Hunt is clean as a whistle himself, but he separates morality and the law. He wouldn't go as far in trying to force his personal views on others. And he knows that all politics involves the art of compromise."

Just as he had planned, Hunt's four years in the lieutenant governor's office became a staging area for the governorship. The office had become "full time" (at a salary of thirty thousand dollars a year). During Hunt's tenure the position required a delicate touch, for there had not been divided government in North Carolina for seventy years. The conscientious but boxed-in Governor Holshouser tried to manage the executive department without partisan turmoil, but Democrats in the legislature naturally chipped away at executive prerogatives as time wore on. Since the governor had no veto, considerable power lay in the General Assembly, where the Democrats had overwhelming majorities in both houses.

Hunt wore the velvet glove of the natural diplomat. He tried to maintain a surface harmony, but underneath contentiousness and frustration prevailed. Governor Holshouser charged that the "legislature has not set goals or direction." Lieutenant Governor Hunt replied that the charge was "unwarranted and unjustified." He said the executive branch lacked "leadership and commitment. . . . I don't think you can stand apart. . . . If you're governor, you've got to lead and I don't care if it's tough."

Out of this battle came stalemate and a trend in the Democratic General Assembly toward placing more curbs on executive power. Governor Holshouser began to find it difficult to discharge his duties. With the fall of Nixon after Watergate, Jim Hunt's chances for winning the governorship in 1976 brightened perceptibly. Under the shock of the Republican insurgency the state's Democratic Party had solidified. Its various factions saw in Hunt the vehicle for regaining executive power.

Hunt had proved his ability to attract varied groups to his standard. He had a natural appeal for farmers in the largely agricultural state, but he was also popular with teachers, blacks, and state employees. He made a major pitch for the support of old-line industrialists and businessmen, who had previously been cool to the progressive wing. Hunt knew there were more conservatives than liberals in North Carolina. Constantly protecting his right flank, he carefully drew a line between himself and old-line liberals. When a senatorial candidate criticized the General Assembly, he said, "He represents a point of view that is generally considered 'quite liberal' for this state . . . not the viewpoint of the majority."

Jim Hunt constantly played to the majority, wherever it might be. Early in his campaign for governor, he organized and held the Citizens' Conference on Sex and Violence on Television—which were similar to the hearings Senator Helms staged in Washington during the same period. "It's been designed," said an annoyed television official, "to catapult Hunt into the Governor's office." During the energy crisis, Hunt criticized the State Utilities Commission for giving power companies "a 35 million dollar bonus" at the expense of the consumer. He said he intended to make the commission more responsible to the rate-paying public. By that time Hunt had emerged as the strongest political leader North Carolina had seen in a generation. "He'll run for governor unless a Trailways bus runs over him," mused State Senator Ralph Scott, "and even that would have to be fatal to stop him."

On April 4, 1976, Hunt announced for governor. His platform ran the gamut from crime deterrence and judicial reform to elevating reading standards in the public schools, giving the public a "fair shake" on electric costs, and raising manufacturing wages. Hunt's opponents were Ed O'Herron, a wealthy Charlotte businessman; George Wood, a legislator from Edenton; and State Senator Tom Strickland, another businessman from Goldsboro. They scarcely had a chance. Hunt had extended his political organization into every county of the state. He rode a tide of reaction against Watergate, which subtly but surely damaged everyone connected with Richard Nixon. O'Herron had contributed to both Nixon's and Helms's campaigns in 1972, and when that became known, it hurt Hunt's most formidable Democratic opponent. He carried the August primary, getting 53.2 percent of the vote in the four-man race.

In November Hunt racked up an astonishing 65 percent of the vote against his Republican adversary, David Flaherty. The thirty-nine-year-old Hunt amassed the largest margin in the gubernatorial race since Luther Hodges ran largely unopposed in 1956 during the desegregation controversy. North Carolinians gave Jimmy Carter 56 percent of their vote over Gerald Ford in the same election.

Jim Hunt was a rising star in a Sunbelt state vigorously on the move. His personal popularity outweighed any questions of liberal or conservative. At the very time Jesse Helms began making his weight felt in Washington among New Right Republicans, a fresh political force had revived the Democrats back home.

Naysayer and Pragmatist

6. The Lone Ranger

Vermont Royster, the retired *Wall Street Journal* editor, found Jesse Helms, after six years in the Senate, a "phenomenon in search of an explanation." Helms, he wrote, had first appeared in Washington in 1973 as a "sort of oddity . . . a congenital naysayer standing somewhere to the right of Barry Goldwater and Ronald Reagan." After a while, though, and especially after Helms rolled over his opposition again in 1978, Royster admitted that "he must be taken seriously" as a national political figure.

Helms's senatorial colleagues had reached the same conclusion soon after the tall, stoop-shouldered figure with the graciously disarming Old South manner had appeared in their midst. Helms first came to the fore as a skilled parliamentarian. He was befriended by the late Senator James Allen (D-Ala.), a visceral conservative and a master of parliamentary procedure. Allen had more than once so confused his senatorial opponents with the intricacies of his maneuvers that they found themselves voting for legislation they condemned or against new laws they favored. Helms proved an adept student. In October 1973 he won the Golden Rule Award as the first GOP senator to preside over the Senate chamber for more than one hundred hours. He was present for 96 percent of the Senate votes in 1973, and he nearly succeeded during his freshman year in getting a bill approved abolishing forced busing to achieve school integration. Helms modestly explained that he was "just a country boy trying to live up to what I promised I would do."

What that was, Helms's colleagues soon learned, was to keep things constantly stirred up. The new North Carolina senator spoke in dulcet tones when seeking favors or greeting friends. One of his favorite expressions, especially among women and children, was "Bless yo' heart." But Helms could strike furiously in rhetorical combat. He was a master of the sharp retort. His shrewd way of sensing the vulnerabilities of an opponent, and with a phrase or an offhand comment wounding him to the quick, aroused anger among many and in the liberal camp, blind fury.

Helms was also full of endless energy. He seemed to savor standing alone at the storm center of hopelessly unpopular causes. He provoked his own GOP associates by forcing them to vote on delicate political issues that most of them would have preferred avoiding.

From the outset Helms planned strategies for enacting his key social programs. They included an anti-abortion amendment, removal of the federal courts' authority to render decisions "denying or restricting as unconstitutional voluntary prayer in the public schools," and slashing social welfare programs, especially food stamps.

Helms's colleagues on both sides of the aisle felt the buzz saw of his dogmatism, his capacity for embarrassing them. What set the North Carolina senator at greatest odds with his Republican associates, though, was the way he placed his deep-seated conservative philosophy ahead of his loyalty to the GOP. Among politicians, loyalty ranks high. But Helms always insisted his "principles" came first. Almost immediately he turned his criticism and invective against his own partymen.

In early 1975, after Gerald Ford had succeeded Richard Nixon, Helms castigated both parties, saying they had "failed miserably to give voters clear choices." "I say that we need two parties, a liberal party and a conservative party," he said. Nixon, Helms maintained, was elected in 1968 not so much because he was a Republican as because he "articulated views that appealed to a majority of voters without reference to party affiliation."

Helms had a stubborn conviction that many voters favored right-wing views but seldom found party platforms or candidates to espouse them. "We need to organize conservatives into a more coherent structure," he said, one that would include "not only our trusty band of ideological conservatives" but also nonpolitical citizens who were concerned about such issues as "pornography, the right to life, school textbooks, community control of schools and economic interests." Riding what he saw as a new wave of conservatism, Helms sought to give what he called the "Silent Majority" a chance to be heard. Similar strategies had been tried earlier by such presidential hopefuls as Barry Goldwater and George McGovern, but without success.

Senator Helms's chief lieutenant, the affable and shrewd Raleigh attorney Tom Ellis, felt even more strongly that Republican moderation should be vigorously opposed. But in 1975 Ellis said that Ronald Reagan (whom both he and Helms had supported) should bide his time until the prospects for challenging President Ford were brighter. Senator Helms was one of Reagan's earliest backers. Soon after his election to the Senate in 1972 Helms visited Reagan at the governor's mansion in Sacramento.

On the state level Helms and Ellis opposed the moderation of GOP Governor Jim Holshouser. Their anti-Holshouser vendetta began in 1973, but built to a crescendo when Holshouser supported President Ford for the nomination in 1976. Differences that had earlier seethed underground broke into the open when the Helms forces denied the retiring governor an invitation to attend the 1976 Republican National Convention as an official delegate.

Helms's opposition to Gerald Ford had appeared even earlier. By March of 1975 he was saying that President Ford's statement that the Republican Party had to be "broad based" was a "bunch of hokum." If the "Republican Party continues trying to be all things to all men, it will come out a poor second choice. . . . The Republican Party can win only if it appeals to people who want to bring stability back to the government."

During the spring of 1975 Helms also sounded off against Ford's secretary of state, Henry Kissinger. Helms demanded Kissinger's resignation because of his "fixation" on détente and because he was a "proven failure." Simultaneously he pumped for his constitutional amendment to ban abortion and also introduced a bill that would dock the pay of congressional members every time Congress failed to balance the federal budget. The Senate voted the latter measure down overwhelmingly.

All these ploys began to attract national media attention. At first Helms had been perceived as an eccentric nobody. But his energy and persistence touched sensitive nerves. In an article in June 1975 entitled "The Helms Gang," John H. Averill of the *Washington Post–Los Angeles Times* Service called Helms "a hard-line reactionary out of cloth torn from the racist shirt of the Confederacy." Averill quoted one admiring politician as saying that "Jesse is so conservative that he makes Goldwater and Thurmond look like liberals." He noted the Helms belief that compromise is unthinkable and that losing in defense of a principle is a matter of honor—that is, "victory achieved by compromise is akin to heresy."

Helms, along with Senator James Buckley (R-N.Y.), had been instrumental in helping Senator Carl Curtis (R-Neb.) form what they called the Steering Committee, a conservative counterpart to the Wednesday Club, a group of liberal and moderate Republicans. Quickly this group of a dozen GOP senators became known as "The Helms Gang."

In June 1975 Helms formed what he called the Committee on Conservative Alternatives. It was designed to determine how a third-party presidential candidate could be put on the ballot in each state. The group pondered either Ronald Reagan or George Wallace as "possible alternatives" to Gerald Ford. After Helms's blast at Ford, Senator Goldwater replied: "Gerald Ford is President of the United States and he is a Republican and I think any talk of a third party movement at this time is wrong. . . . I believe a third party would hurt rather than help the conservative cause." But Helms and his senatorial seatmate, Buckley, continued to push their alternative plans. Helms once bragged that he never "let Buckley forget that he sits to the left of Jesse Helms." Together they had their eye on making Reagan their third-party candidate if Ford failed to endorse their rightist stands in the 1976 election.

In early July 1975, however, Helms abandoned his third-party plans and announced his support for Reagan as the 1976 GOP candidate for president. In the meantime President Ford had appointed Governor Holshouser as his southern campaign manager. This set the stage for a bitter battle between Helms and Holshouser in the North Carolina presidential primary on March 23, 1976. Helms organized the campaign for Reagan in North Carolina and became its chairman. He charged Holshouser with campaigning for Ford at state expense. He predicted that Reagan would win the Tar Heel primary—and he was right.

The victory came at a crucial moment for Reagan. He had lost to Ford in four previous primaries, the most recent in New Hampshire, where he polled 49 percent of the votes against Ford's 51 percent. As the North Carolina contest approached, Reagan was considering withdrawing from the campaign. His North Carolina victory, in which he won twenty-eight delegates to Ford's twenty-five, kept him in the running. Steadily he began to gain on Ford.

Jesse Helms went to the Republican National Convention in Kansas City that August as an obscure freshman senator from the South. He left as a national political figure who had led a campaign that almost upset the Ford bandwagon. "Just suppose we were dealing with incumbent Reagan and challenger Ford," said Tom Ellis afterward. "Have you ever thought how long Ford would have lasted? Not long."

As it turned out, Helms got a chance to make a convention speech on national television. Helms's supporters pushed his candidacy as Ford's running mate and distributed five thousand "Give 'Em Helms" lapel stickers. Helms's name was placed in nomination for the vice presidency, but he withdrew it. Nevertheless he got ninety-nine votes and an unprecedented amount of mail for a freshman senator.

Word abroad at the convention was that Reagan was leery of Helms's support in North Carolina and told his backers that "you can't run a national campaign from that state [North Carolina]." Both Helms and Ellis were highly critical of John Sears and other Reagan strategists at Kansas City. "It just seemed to me they blew it," Helms said. "They don't have any policies or good strategies," echoed Ellis.

As the convention ended, Senator Helms agreed to support Ford after he promised to "run on and abide by" the GOP platform. "I will help the Republican Party any way I can—until November," Helms declared. And he did. At a ribbon-cutting ceremony opening the GOP headquarters in Wilmington in October, Senator Helms, as guest of honor, said: "We will imagine this is Jimmy Carter's neck. How 'bout that!" Then after Democratic candidate Carter made a confusing statement about a proposed cut in defense spending and repeal of the right-to-work law, Helms sounded off again. Carter, he said, is "like the Cheshire cat—whenever you try to get a straight answer out of him or pin him down to something factual, everything disappears but the grin."

That turned out to be prophetic about the Georgia governor. Jimmy Carter won the 1976 election, but failed against Helms's candidate four years later.

7. A Touch of Camelot and Carter

On a blustery day in January 1977 Jim Hunt, the farm boy from Rock Ridge, set several precedents as he was sworn in as North Carolina's ninety-sixth governor.

Dressed in a business suit instead of the usual formal wear, he walked the two blocks from the gingerbread Governor's Mansion to Bicentennial Square, where the outdoor inaugural ceremonies were being held for the first time. When it came time for his inaugural address, the new governor delivered a 450-word oration, the shortest on record, written by himself. In it he quoted John White, governor of Sir Walter Raleigh's second Roanoke Island colony, and paraphrased Charles B. Aycock, the state's famed "Education Governor" (1901–4).

That night at an inaugural ball featuring actor Andy Griffith, the Grandfather Mountain Cloggers, and the North Carolina Symphony, two thousand guests attended along with eight thousand spectators at North Carolina State University's Reynolds Coliseum. The fare was turkey sandwiches, ham biscuits, cheese straws, and pastries but no champagne or hard drinks. The new governor and his wife danced briefly (a waltz); this, however, was to be no traditional debutante-style affair. "The Governor wants this ball to be one for all the people rather than just for the socially and politically prominent," a ball official said.

A newspaper reporter described the affair as "Carter country chic with a taste of courtly Camelot." Another identified the evening's beverage as a "wretchedly sweet potion called Meirs Sparkling Catawba grape juice." The celebration continued until a late hour.

Hunt's emphasis on education came to have great significance during his governorship. The new chief executive had been no brilliant student. He had struggled hard to maintain a good B average in college, and he flunked the state bar exam on his first try. But he remembered his schoolteacher mother tutoring the "hard-headed boys" in Rock Ridge when he was growing up. Although he reached maturity at a time of widespread cynicism about the faltering goals of education, Hunt retained a messianic zeal about its possibilities.

The new governor had an infectious enthusiasm about a "reading program" in the grammar schools. If young people were stumbling in high school and college because of poor training in basic learning skills, the solution was to launch a massive attack on those deficiencies where they originated. "We must stop cheating our young people, pretending they have learned when they haven't," he said. "We must give extra help to those who need it."

Hunt set about rearranging the educational furniture in North Carolina. When he had finished campaigning for legislative funds and public volunteer assistance, he had set in motion a program with three main points. First, the "Governor's Reading Program" had been phased into most of the classrooms in the first, second, and third grades across the state. This provided each teacher with a half-time aide, limited classes to twenty-six pupils, and carefully monitored progress. Second, almost simultaneously, the state began requiring students to pass a minimum competency exam to earn a high school diploma and put in place a $15 million remedial assistance program designed to help those who might have trouble meeting this requirement. Third, additional science requirements were added to the high school curriculum to coincide with tougher admissions standards throughout the state's university system.

To set an example, Governor Hunt served one day a week as a teacher's aide in his own elementary school system in Raleigh. This was part of a program to encourage others—particularly former classroom teachers, recent graduates of technical institutes, and those with a special interest in reading—to become voluntary aides across the state. Hunt sought some thirteen thousand volunteers to work with over seventy-three thousand young people. Help was not slow in coming. By the fall of 1978, for example, Greensboro's schools had sixty-one reading aides, Guilford County schools fifty-nine, and High Point schools twenty-five.

At the same time Hunt supported the movement for what became in 1980 the North Carolina School of Science and Mathematics. This state-funded public school for the gifted (at Durham) brought four hundred eleventh and twelfth graders to a residential campus for specialized, rigorous training. Hunt recalled hearing about one high school graduate, voted most likely to succeed, who "couldn't figure up the sales tax on a new car."

As a result of Hunt's dust-stirring, by the end of 1982 the average second grader's reading scores had risen almost a full grade level, five to seven months ahead of the national average. Similar gains had been achieved in spelling, language, and math at all grade levels. During the first five years of the minimum competency exam program the failure rate in the state's schools had fallen from roughly 11 percent to about 2 percent. At the Science and Mathematics School, where half the staff held doctorates and the rest master's degrees, results were impressive. By 1982 the school had turned out fifty-one National Merit Scholarship finalists. Most of the graduates of its first-year class won scholarships and advanced placement at top universities.

By 1983 Jim Hunt's education initiative had begun to attract national attention. During a time of educational trouble it was identified as a bright spot. The governor had shown that his missionary zeal, combined with political skill, could get results.

Similar success greeted Hunt in other endeavors. Nobody quite believed he could entice stubborn North Carolinians to relax their attitudes about the single-term limitation for governors. Political observers were even more skeptical that he could achieve it during his first year in office—and especially make the change applicable to himself. Yet during 1977, when his popularity was highest and the danger of opposing him greatest, Hunt goaded a reluctant legislature to allow the people to amend the state constitution. "Legislators weren't voting on a principle, which most of them opposed," said a long-time political observer. "They were voting on a popular governor with 45 months to go in office." In November, utilizing his powerful "keys" organized in all the state's one hundred counties, Hunt pushed through a favorable popular vote, which later allowed him to become the state's first full two-term governor in the twentieth century.

In other areas Hunt implemented his "New Beginning." He appointed Howard Lee, the former mayor of Chapel Hill, as the state's first black cabinet member (secretary of the Department of Natural and Economic Resources). Lee had been an unsuccessful candidate for lieutenant governor the year before. "We must eliminate the last vestiges of discrimination that hold us down," Hunt said in his inaugural address. "Change must come in our hearts." Hunt also appointed two women to his cabinet—Dr. Sarah Morrow as secretary of human resources and Sara Hodgkins as secretary of cultural resources. His mother had been the first woman on the State Board of Health, an appointee of Governor Kerr Scott thirty years before.

In keeping with his emphasis on education Hunt championed what he called "the final link in our human investment"—an act providing fifteen prenatal clinics for high-risk pregnant women and day-care assistance for over six thousand children by 1981. "The most rewarding investment we can make with public funds today," he said, "is in our youngest children." This would mean "billions of dollars more each year in production, wages, profits and public revenues." This program, though, was labeled "socialistic" by his critics and eventually deemphasized.

While Hunt pushed education and social welfare, he also bore down heavily on his other major goal: attracting industry and creating new jobs. To do this he made overtures to the state's business and financial leaders and involved them in the effort. Several delegations of Tar Heel businessmen accompanied him on trips to foreign countries to woo industries. He called for a national constitutional convention to require a balanced federal budget similar to North Carolina's. Focusing on the Research Triangle, created during the regime of Governor Luther Hodges twenty years earlier, he proposed state help for the budding electronics industry, but he also put forward a "balanced growth" concept, in which industry would be guided to less wealthy, rural areas and not to the state's major urban centers.

Hunt's enthusiastic initiative won support from the business sector. There he was perceived not as a liberal but as a hard-headed pragmatist who understood the economic underpinnings of the state. An essential pragmatism had been reflected in Hunt's outlook from the beginning. "I don't like labels," he once told a reporter. "I try to be pragmatic. I try to look at alternatives and choose the best solution for problems."

Hunt applied that judgment in the controversial "Wilmington Ten" case. He refused to parole nine black men and one white woman convicted of firebombing a grocery store in connection with racial unrest in 1971. The case had created considerable stir because of the weakness of the evidence and the severity of the sentences. A widespread campaign was mounted among liberals to get the Ten pardoned. But Hunt demonstrated his determination to travel the middle road. He simply reduced the sentences, thus disappointing the advocates of pardon and the opponents of all leniency.

Hunt also championed a vigorous program of crime control. He favored a uniform sentencing law, merit selection of judges, toughened penalties for domestic violence, lightening the load in superior courts, and increased power for district courts.

At the same time the governor championed the movement to ratify the Equal Rights Amendment. By 1979 it had been defeated in three legislative sessions. Hunt's help was not enough. The ERA went down for a fourth time.

After he took office, the governor, who had earlier supported former governor Bob Scott's efforts to impose a tobacco tax, vigorously defended the federal tobacco program. The anti-smoking campaign had stirred deep fears among North Carolina leaf farmers. Both Hunt and Helms were aware that the issue was political dynamite as they curried farm support in the late 1970s. The issue grew in importance as they moved toward the 1984 senatorial race.

Toward the end of his first term some of Hunt's rivals in the Democratic Party began referring to his administration as a "political dynasty" and a "vast network of appointees who see to it that the Governor gets his way." That was the comment of Lieutenant Governor Jimmy Green, who had clashed repeatedly with Hunt and had aspirations to succeed him in 1980. Green ultimately chose to run again for lieutenant governor, although he had opposed the idea of second terms in 1977.

"Hunt's political style," observed one newspaper, "smooths over differences, offers a little something for everyone, takes the middle and least offensive course whenever possible." That tendency appeared in Hunt's growing interest in fighting inflation. As Jimmy Carter's administration ran into trouble, Hunt moved steadily in a conservative direction. He opposed increasing taxes and advocated a balanced budget. Bob Scott, the former governor who was to run against Hunt in 1980, took several jabs at Hunt's increasing conservatism. He charged Hunt with a lack of leadership that would "place heavy burdens upon taxpayers in the next decade or two." He spoke of the "politics of retrenchment" and criticized those politicians who were "trying to outdo each other in how much they can cut back."

Yet despite these murmurings and snipings, Jim Hunt approached the end of his first term as North Carolina's most popular twentieth-century chief executive. In a state where governors traditionally wore out their welcome by the end of four years in office, he triumphantly announced for a second term at the Vance-Aycock Dinner, an important party ritual, in Asheville in October 1979.

Most of the programs he espoused had been enacted—in education, closer regulation of public utilities, industrial development, judicial reform, and crime control. As inflation rose and the recession deepened, Hunt had sparred with classroom teachers who sought more than the 7 percent raise proposed by the 1979 General Assembly, and he had shown he could cuss in delicate negotiations involving a truckers' strike at Greensboro. "I can't wave a magic wand and make your problems go away, but let's get started toward a solution, dammit!" he told a mass meeting of picketing truckers. They voted to relax their protests and allowed tankers to resume hauling gasoline at the fuel terminal.

Some politicians, though, thought Hunt's "wobbling tendencies" would prove his Achilles' heel. He was the consummate politician, adept at appraising political crosscurrents, and he seldom got caught in over his head. He utilized some of Jimmy Carter's pragmatism, but he also knew how to seize the initiative and set his own agenda. Some critics said he left too many decisions to others (such as his budget chief, John Williams). He kept his political juices flowing almost twenty-four hours a day, and his enthusiasm for meeting and talking to people was boundless. One associate introduced him as a man who "cares about people, a man who has not spent his time making money or accumulating wealth, a man who has dedicated his talents to helping people." Hunt once released his income tax returns which showed he earned only seventy-five hundred dollars in one year from his Wilson County law practice. But it also showed income from sale of cucumbers from his home garden, which his children grew, harvested, and sold.

A reporter once said of him that "his passions for the topics he discusses are evangelistic. . . . He looks persons straight in the eye when he meets them and likely as not knows them, something about them or knows somebody who knows them. He carries texts for his speeches in his pocket, but is so familiar with them and emotionally wrapped up in them that he doesn't bother to look at the texts."

As a young man Hunt was described by one friend as "intense." But as his gubernatorial career flowered, he loosened up. He even began telling jokes on himself. Hunt's wife, Carolyn, the first lady from Iowa, experienced some of the same transformation. "The woman crossing the parlor of the Governor's Mansion," one reporter wrote in 1977, "was a far cry from the tense campaigner of October 1976 or the somewhat stilted first lady who waltzed at the inaugural ball in January." Hunt had found a formula most Tar Heels respected. "He is not afraid of new ideas," observed the *Greensboro Daily News* on the eve of his second inauguration. "But he also possesses a keen sense of the possible. He is as much at home in a corporate board room as jumping furrows on a Coastal Plains tobacco farm."

Hunt also was increasingly visible on the national scene. A rumor in the late 1970s had it that Governor Jerry Brown of California was considering him as a possible vice presidential running mate. That proved untrue. When Hunt visited President Carter at Camp David, as he shook up his cabinet at midterm, word got out that Hunt had been offered a cabinet post, which, he said later, he declined. When Hunt presided over the National Conference of Democratic Governors in 1979, an aide to the governor of New Hampshire commented: "[Hunt's] very smooth, a very polished character. I don't mean he's slick. No, not that. He's just very polished."

In his reelection campaign during the spring of 1980 Hunt had no trouble trouncing former governor Bob Scott in the Democratic primary. In November he defeated his Democrat-turned-Republican adversary, State Senator I. Beverly Lake, Jr., by a substantial margin. Like his popular predecessor Governor O. Max Gardner in 1928, Hunt was voted in while others of his party, including the state's junior senator, Robert Morgan, fell under a Republican onslaught, this one spearheaded by Ronald Reagan and Jesse Helms.

8. The Money Machine

A key victory in Jesse Helms's rise to national prominence occurred on November 7, 1978, when he successfully defended his seat against John Ingram, the Democratic state insurance commissioner. Ingram, a folksy populist, had whipped the Democratic establishment in much the same manner as Congressman Nick Galifianakis beat Senator Everett Jordan in 1972. In the spring primary Ingram defeated Luther Hodges, Jr., the banker son of the former governor, who had the support of mainline Democrats.

Ingram did it mainly by posing as a David against the Goliaths of wealth and privilege. He had won the insurance commissioner's seat by criticizing the business establishment, especially the insurance and utility companies. Hodges lacked political experience. He also had no knack for loosening up on the barbecue circuit. Ingram out-campaigned him at the crossroads.

But when autumn arrived, Ingram's attempt to characterize Helms as "The Six Million Dollar Man," referring to his fund-raising prowess, failed to score. Helms had set about encouraging an already widespread Democratic disillusionment with Ingram. Democrats generally viewed Ingram as a maverick. Only party loyalty kept many of them in line. This attitude of lukewarm support extended even to Governor Hunt's office.

Helms knew precisely how to lure dissident Democrats. In a state where Democratic voter registration outnumbers Republicans three to one, he needed those votes. His approach was to soft-pedal differences with every Democratic leader except the one he opposed. Helms even quieted his criticism of Jimmy Carter. He went out of his way to praise Governor Hunt. A week before the election he told reporters he believed Hunt would support his reelection bid if Helms were a Democrat. "We've had a good working relationship," he said. "He's been a very effective governor."

Then after Helms had been invited to appear at a joint press conference with Hunt and Bob Morgan, the Democratic junior senator, announcing a new agreement between the state and the Farmers Home Administration, Helms praised Hunt again. He said he'd been told by a high-level official in the Hunt administration that the governor had said he was "between a rock and a hard place" over whom to support in the Senate race. Then he reported a conversation with Hunt in which he told the governor he "understood" that he'd have to support Ingram. "I told him not to worry about it and say what he felt he had to as titular head of the Democratic Party."

That condescension annoyed Hunt. At a hastily called press conference he complained that Helms had tried to "misrepresent my position in this election." Helms, he said, was "totally wrong in suggesting that I support him in any way. I enthusiastically support John Ingram, and I do not support any Republican. . . . Helms's record is not consistent with the needs of North Carolina."

Helms, though, had already cemented his victory with disaffected Democrats. He had assembled an imposing group of what one newspaperman called "Jesse-crats." There were "Ladies for Jesse," including wives of former Democratic governors. There were "Athletes for Jesse"—mostly native Tar Heels who had risen to fame in the sports world—Richard Petty, "Catfish" Hunter, Gaylord Perry, Mike Caldwell, and Dave Rose. There were "Students for Jesse," "Farmers for Jesse," and "Veterans for Jesse." Dr. Lennox Baker, a prominent Duke University surgeon, headed the statewide "Democrats for Jesse" organizations.

Although hospitalized for three weeks by a back operation in September, Helms returned to the hustings as the election approached. He campaigned actively in more than eighty of the state's one hundred counties. Earlier he had called Ingram "too liberal" for mainline Democrats and "a hand-picked candidate of the AFL-CIO." By the last week of the campaign he stepped up the rhetoric. "Ingram has been throwing stink bombs with both hands," he said. "I've gone out of my way to be nice to the guy. I've had a lot of criticism for not doing it. But it's not my style. I've overlooked John's aberrations."

When journalist Elizabeth Drew asked a conservative Republican senator about Helms's shrewdness, his reply was emphatic: "He has an innate craftiness and cleverness that's stunning to watch. You can't box him in—he'll defang you when you get close. Anyone who sells him short is going to lose—and has. He's amazing and formidable."

Helms demonstrated that skill in his reelection campaign. He found Ingram's weaknesses and exploited them, all the while displaying a confident serenity. In October he appeared on the PTL Evangelical Hour and talked about his religious beliefs (adding a bit about foreign policy and domestic issues). He told about flying across the state in the early morning darkness during the 1972 campaign. He was almost exhausted from campaigning, he said, and began to pray. "For the first time in the campaign," he said, "I asked the Lord to help me because I needed it. I don't know how long I prayed. All of a sudden I realized the sun was coming in the window and I felt a sense of serenity I had never before realized."

On the Sunday before the November 8 election, Senator Helms attended church with the Reverend Billy Graham in Charlotte. Ingram's hometown newspaper, the *Asheboro Courier-Tribune*, endorsed Helms, saying Ingram's stands were "unbelievably shallow." So did many of the state's major newspapers. The *Raleigh News and Observer* and the *Charlotte Observer* refused to endorse either candidate. The *Observer* called Helms "an articulate, informed advocate of a political viewpoint we don't share." It called Ingram "arrogant, bullheaded, erratic, disorganized, disdainful of good advice."

Less than an hour after the polls closed Tuesday night, ABC News had proclaimed Helms the winner. This set off frenzied demonstrations in Helms's Raleigh campaign headquarters, where hundreds of his supporters had gathered to celebrate. Raised into the air were placards reading "Senator No Is on the Go!" (This referred to the name the *Raleigh News and Observer*, an implacable Helms foe, had given him earlier.) Other signs pushed Helms for president in 1980. When the victorious senator descended from his hotel room to thank his cheering supporters, he greeted them simply: "I'm Senator No, and I'm glad to be here."

It had been an overwhelming victory. Helms took 54 percent of the vote —the same amount he had taken in whipping Galifianakis six years before. But in 1978 Helms made inroads in many Piedmont industrial counties he had failed to win in 1972. Ingram carried thirty-eight of one hundred counties, but, excluding Durham and Orange, they were located in the northeast black belt and the far western part of the state.

Yet Helms failed to carry other Republicans on his coattails. The Democrats won nine of the state's eleven congressional seats. Helms won Wake County, site of the state capital, but Wake also elected a black Democratic sheriff and the state placed another black Democrat on the state's court of appeals.

From the start Ingram had been a loser. "When Ingram won the primary," one Democrat had told a reporter during the summer before the election, "it was like having your daughter come up pregnant. You don't like it, but you try to make the best of the situation." The Helms sweep, even against a weak opponent, had important implications on the national scene. It dramatized the remarkable extent to which, as one observer put it, "Helms had transformed his Senate seat into the engine of a unique political and legislative machine."

The reference was to the National Congressional Club, which had begun modestly in 1972 as a fund-raising group to pay off Helms's one-hundred-thousand-dollar campaign debt. Under the leadership of Helms's old ally, Raleigh attorney Tom Ellis, that goal was easily accomplished. Helms and Ellis began to see broader possibilities for the organization. Following the 1972 election they retained the services of Richard Viguerie, the direct-mail entrepreneur allied with right-wing candidates. Out of that association grew what became a national fund-raising combine that by 1981 had expanded into the nation's largest political action committee (PAC).

Gradually the Helms group enlarged the club's purposes to support other GOP "conservative" candidates running for Congress. To cope with changing national election laws they hired the prestigious Washington law firm of Covington & Burling to help spin off other corporate entities and assist candidates more extensively. Helms's forces established some half dozen conservative foundations and "think tanks" to offset what Helms viewed as liberal domination of federal decision making. "Their main benefit to me as a senator," Helms said in a 1982 interview, "is that I have almost immediate answers to questions that are on my mind. . . . If you're going to win on issues you've got to help elect the candidates who will vote your way."

The corporate spin-offs came rapidly after the 1978 reelection victory. They included Jefferson Marketing, a political advertising and consulting company which supervises direct mail and offers counseling service for political candidates. Jefferson owns "the list"—some 180,000 names of people across the nation who are all proven givers to the Helms cause. Further broken down by issues—those who oppose gun control or abortion or favor increased defense spending, "the list" produces millions of dollars in contributions every year.

Jefferson owns another Congressional Club corporation—the Campaign Committee. The company, which has more than two dozen staffers, provides campaign planning, advertising, press relations, and organizing services—even down to travel schedules—for conservative candidates, mostly in North Carolina. Each campaigner is supplied with an executive director and press secretary. The committee bills its clients by the hour. "It's sort of like an accounting, advertising or law firm that has three or four clients and is billing out its time to all of them," Carter Wrenn, Congressional Club treasurer, explained.

The committee's clients in the 1980 campaign included John East, who defeated incumbent Democratic Senator Robert Morgan; I. Beverly Lake, Jr., who lost to incumbent Governor Hunt; and Bill Cobey, who lost to Lieutenant Governor Jimmy Green. Rick Miller, Jefferson Marketing's chief, said the company also did a small mailing in 1979 for Democrat Jimmy Green, pitted in a primary race for lieutenant governor against house speaker Carl Stewart.

Senator East told a reporter that the involvement of the Congressional Club was a "vital part of a broad-based political coalition that is supportive to me." Before his victory over Senator Morgan, East said he probably stood to gain most financially from the club because he was running for the Senate. Wrenn reported that the club directed much of the fund-raising effort for East across the nation, using Senator Helms's endorsement.

Jefferson also owns another company, the Hardison Corporation, which handles computerized accounting. Besides these nuts-and-bolts corporations, Helms's conservative think tanks include the Institute of American Relations (IAR), the Centre for a Free Society, the Institute on Money and Inflation, and the American Family Institute—all tax-exempt organizations located in Washington. The IAR Foreign Affairs Council and the Congressional Club Foundation are tax-exempt lobbying groups.

Helms described the Congressional Club and its allied organizations as vehicles for uniting conservatives. They thrive on Helms's flair for igniting and publicizing right-wing social causes in the Senate and forcing liberal opponents to take stands on controversial issues, such as busing, school prayer, and right to life, which will stir up their constituents back home and make it difficult for them to explain their voting records. Among conservative candidates outside North Carolina who received funds in 1979 were Republican Steven Symms (R-Idaho), Senator Gordon Humphrey (R-N.H.), and the late Congressman Larry McDonald (D-Ga.), who died in the Korean Airlines plane shot down by the Soviet Union in 1983.

Much of the club's funds goes for expenses. In the last quarter of 1979, $250,000 went for such purposes, $107,000 to Jefferson Marketing, the Campaign Committee, and the Hardison Corporation, according to Wrenn. "It sounds like a lot of money and it is," he said. "But a lot of it goes for overhead, and training people to be active in political campaigns."

Tom Ellis, head of the Congressional Club, called it "unique in the nation. I don't know anybody who's done what we've done." Most Democrats look on it with foreboding, and even some Republicans are leery. "I think it's a political machine," said Bill Hiatt of Mt. Airy, the 1976 GOP candidate for lieutenant governor. "It's drawing some of the money that could otherwise go to state candidates." "The question will be," said Gary Pearce, Governor Hunt's press secretary, "Do you want the Congressional Club running North Carolina?"

Senator Helms's success at money raising grew enormously as the 1980 election neared. After having raised nearly $8 million against Ingram in 1978, the Congressional Club prepared for the presidential campaign and an effort to knock off North Carolina's junior senator, Democrat Robert Morgan. Helms told journalist Elizabeth Drew in 1979: "People are critical of the money I raise. What they don't realize is that we're able to get 200,000 people ready to move on any issue we decide is important."

Viguerie's skill at direct mailing complemented Helms's adroitness at dramatizing the issues. Viguerie said of the club: "Helms and Tom Ellis saw real quick what you could do with direct mail. Jesse has an organized army. If he sees something he doesn't like he's now got nearly a half-million people he can appeal to, and they'll follow his lead. There isn't another politician in the country who has that."

The 1978 election energized the Helms money-making machine. John Ingram tried to exploit the "Six Million Dollar Man" theme and failed. North Carolina voters, who had earlier responded negatively to big-money candidates and outside influence, returned to office the largest money raiser in history. If money was the name of the game, Helms and Ellis had tapped a vein of gold, and they knew where to get more.

9. Jesse Wept

"Without Helms the 1980 Republican National Convention would be a snoozer," a North Carolina reporter wrote to his newspaper from Detroit in July. Helms agreed. "I am unintentionally the only game in town," he told a newsman.

Until the last day of the convention, when Ronald Reagan failed to get Gerald Ford as his running mate and turned to George Bush, the proceedings had been dull and predictable. Reagan had arrived in Detroit with the presidential nomination won, but behind the scenes tension between

Reagan and Helms flourished. Differences in emphasis and style became more apparent as Reagan's chances for victory grew in November and as his instincts about how to win clashed with Helms's.

Even at the 1976 Kansas City convention Helms and Tom Ellis had differed sharply with Reagan's platform pragmatism and his belief in a balanced ticket. The two men had helped Reagan win the crucial North Carolina primary earlier that year by flooding the state with television spots. "They talk about the master strokes and all that," Helms said of that affair. "The only masterstroke was raising the money to put Reagan on TV."

So after his own reelection in 1978, Helms was slow to endorse Reagan's drive for the presidency. He had opposed Senator Richard Schweiker (R-Pa.) as a vice presidential running mate in 1976. Reagan, he concluded, had ignored television in order to get rid of his show-business reputation.

Helms's entourage arrived in Detroit determined to force Reagan to accept a "real conservative" on the ticket. Only in March 1980 had Helms endorsed Reagan's candidacy and launched an independent fund-raising effort for him through the Congressional Club. Helms taped one- and two-minute television commercials to run two days before the primaries in Florida, Georgia, and Alabama. This was an "independent effort," Ellis explained, and did not count against Reagan's $17.7 million campaign ceiling.

Helms made his first impact at Detroit as a busy member of the platform committee. He immediately charged managers of the committee with using "hardball tactics" to deny conservatives a voice. He balked at the traditional GOP endorsement of women's rights and fought vigorously to include an anti-abortion plank. The committee ended up approving general language to leave ERA for the states to decide and waffled on anti-abortion. "As opposed to the economy, energy, defense and big government issues," declared Senator John Tower (R-Tex.), committee chairman, "ERA and abortion raise constitutional and moral questions on which Republicans quite frankly are divided." Helms said his only purpose was to see "that Reagan's positions are reflected in the platform." He was partially successful.

The larger issue at Detroit, though, was the vice presidency. Helms had received ninety-nine votes for that nomination four years earlier. He had no intention of accepting a "moderate conservative." Thus he had allowed his name to be filed as a vice presidential candidate in the New Hampshire primary. In late June the Raleigh-based Helms for Vice President Committee mailed out ten thousand letters asking conservatives across the country to sign a petition urging Reagan to choose Helms at the convention.

Those efforts failed, but not before the candidacy had provoked a minidrama. Helms's name did not appear on a list of eight vice presidential choices being considered by Reagan on the eve of the convention, and

Reagan's managers tried to keep Helms at arm's length. Helms announced he would "fight" if the nominee were George Bush, but spoke favorably of Senator Paul Laxalt. He said his own candidacy was "serious" and it was "highly probable" his name would be presented.

That circumstance produced squirming among the forty members of the North Carolina delegation. They had arrived in Detroit united behind Ronald Reagan, even though ten of the forty were pledged to George Bush on the first ballot. But after Helms and Ellis announced their plans, Tar Heel delegates told reporters their ranks were split. Delegate Jim Godfrey, an ally of Governor Holshouser, put it to Helms this way: "I find myself in the position of not wanting to make Ronald Reagan mad and not wanting to make you mad." To that Helms replied: "Jesse Helms is not going to get his nose out of joint. You do what your conscience tells you."

Helms and Ellis never relinquished their pressure. They claimed to have one hundred delegates already. "They are our friends," Helms said of the Reagan camp. "I am theirs." But then he went on to insist they had a "hang-up" about that "balanced ticket thing. . . . If it's so bad to be a conservative, why is Reagan where he is now?"

Meanwhile the national media, unable to find anything else newsworthy, concentrated on the Reagan-Helms split. Helms was invited to all the talk shows. Networks sent limousines to pick him up. The *New York Times* bought him lunch and CBS bought coffee. Network newspeople waited outside his door for opportunities to get his comments. *Time* Magazine interviewed him for an hour. The *New York Times* called Helms "the spiritual leader of the convention." Helms replied he was "overwhelmed by all the fuss."

On the evening of Reagan's nomination, word got out that Gerald Ford would be the vice presidential nominee. At that point Ellis announced the Helms vice presidential campaign was on hold. When the Ford proposal fell apart, Helms was in the CBS black booth being interviewed by Jack Kilpatrick and Bill Moyers. When Walter Cronkite informed Helms that Ford was out and Bush in, Helms was flabbergasted. He told a newsman later that at first he hadn't realized what had happened. "I thought, 'Gee whiz, unh,'" he said. "I was just stunned." When Cronkite asked for his comment, Helms waved his hand and demurred.

Later Helms said he didn't feel betrayed or deceived, but added that Reagan had led him to believe that Ford had "all but accepted" a place on the ticket. "Maybe it was Reagan who was led down the primrose path," he said. From their distant seating area in the Joe Louis Auditorium (called "deep right field") the North Carolina delegation cheered and applauded Reagan's speech announcing his choice of Bush. Helms was nowhere to be seen in the auditorium. The next day in closed caucus he told his state's delegates he was abandoning his fight for the vice presidency, but still wanted their votes on the first ballot. He also announced that the Reagan camp had invited him to address the convention for ten minutes.

After interviewing three delegates following the closed session, reporter Jack Betts of the *Greensboro Daily News* wrote that "emotions ran high. At one point Helms wept. Others cried aloud. One woman delegate burst into tears and Helms swept down from the podium to embrace and comfort her. Then after Helms swore the delegates to secrecy, he disclosed he probably would not have his name placed in nomination but would get a chance to speak in support of the Reagan-Bush ticket but with emphasis on his [own] conservative principles."

The delegates dried their eyes and joined in singing "For He's a Jolly Good Fellow." Helms declared himself happier with the Republican Party than at any other time since his switch from the Democrats in 1970. "If they'd passed the collection plate," said one delegate, "it would have been the perfect ending to a perfect prayer meeting."

The North Carolina delegation voted thirty-five to five for Helms. The five dissenters included former governor Holshouser. Some were miffed when Helms didn't sit with them during the polling of the states. "Look here, we supported him for vice president, gave him our votes and he wouldn't even come back to sit with us," said one delegate. J. A. Dalpiaz of Gastonia, a charter member of the Congressional Club, added his criticism. "There's no question that there's some resentment against the club and against Tom [Ellis]. Tom's the lightning rod for Jesse, and since the club took over the party's machinery in 1976, they've alienated some people."

During the roll-call vote that last convention night Senator Helms ducked out to get a snack at his and Ellis's special hideout, the Ponchartrain Hotel. Some of the delegates were particularly annoyed because Carter Wrenn, treasurer of the Congressional Club and not a delegate, occupied Helms's seat and tallied up the votes for vice president. "I wish the Congressional Club would go take a jump," one delegate was heard to say. "To continue to justify its existence," said Kinston lawyer Mac Howard, "they've got to produce some wins. It is sort of an awesome task they've got."

Precisely that kind of vindication lay ahead in the November election. One of the three Congressional Club–sponsored candidates for statewide office, an East Carolina University political science professor, John East, narrowly defeated the state's junior senator, Bob Morgan. That was frosting on the cake for Ronald Reagan's trouncing of Jimmy Carter and another victory for the rising Helmsmen.

10. A New Direction

On October 18, 1980, Jesse Helms went home to Monroe to celebrate his fifty-ninth birthday among hometown friends. In an informal talk that day he declared: "Consider this question: Is the Lord giving us one more chance to save this country . . . to return to Him and to restore the priorities of decency and morality and honesty?"

As if in answer to the senator's prayer, the United States electorate the following month swept Ronald Reagan to victory over Jimmy Carter and unseated twelve Democratic senators to give the Republicans their first Senate majority in two decades. The sweetest part of that victory—the part in which Helms played a significant role—was the downfall of North Carolina's junior senator, Robert Morgan, at the hands of a Helms-Congressional Club protégé, political science professor John P. East of East Carolina University.

East, whom some Helms critics called "Helms on wheels," arrived in North Carolina from his home in Springfield, Illinois, as a twenty-five-year-old Marine in 1955. Just after leaving the Marines at Camp Lejeune he contracted polio and was confined to a wheelchair. He returned to school at the University of Illinois, where he obtained a law degree. Then he practiced law in Florida for a year before enrolling at the University of Florida, where he got his master's and doctorate in political science. He then came back to Greenville, North Carolina, as a political science instructor in 1964. Almost immediately East became interested in Tar Heel politics. He ran unsuccessfully on the Republican ticket against Congressman Walter Jones in 1966. He followed that by winning 48 percent of the vote against longtime North Carolina Secretary of State Thad Eure in 1968.

The rise of the New Right in the 1970s encouraged East's interest in politics. Bright and ambitious, he became the North Carolina Republican national committeeman at a crucial moment in 1976. Then he became aligned with the Helms camp and decided to take on Senator Morgan in 1980.

A number of ironies surfaced in the East-Morgan senatorial struggle. Morgan, a small-town lawyer from Lillington, had taken over Senator Sam Ervin's senatorial seat in 1974 on the latter's retirement. He had won the Democratic nomination without opposition, an unusual feat in Tar Heel politics. Earlier, in the 1960s, Morgan had managed the gubernatorial campaign of segregationist Dr. I. Beverly Lake, Sr., and was a supporter of the notorious Speaker Ban Law, which banned "known communists" from state campuses. In 1980 Morgan won the accolade of the American Conservative Union as the most conservative Democrat in Congress. Yet Morgan protested. "I'd say, even as Democrats go in the Senate, I am moderate," Morgan said.

As the senatorial campaign unfolded, Associated Press correspondent William Welch recalled that when Helms ran for reelection in 1978, Senator Morgan wasn't much heard from. Like Hunt and other Democrats he supported Helms's opponent John Ingram, but "there was said to be an unspoken agreement that Morgan and Helms wouldn't openly go after each other's scalp."

If this was true, Morgan must have felt the victim of a double cross two years later, for Senator Helms led the attack on behalf of his protégé East. The campaign featured big spending by the Congressional Club, with a heavy emphasis on television. The issues pinpointed were Morgan's support of the Panama Canal treaties and his opposition to the B-1 bomber, but a major theme was the attempt to identify Morgan with Senator Kennedy and Senator McGovern and their "liberal" policies. The Congressional Club ads pictured Morgan with these Democrats and tied him, through his voting record, to "increased government waste," a "weak defense," "labor bosses," and "voting wrong 10 times on forced busing."

Simultaneously, Helms kept a close eye on Morgan's activities in the Senate and blocked him wherever possible. He led the fight in defeating one of Morgan's choices for a federal judgeship, Charles Winberry, and held up another, a black state court of appeals judge, Richard Erwin. When Morgan opposed Helms's bill to water down a National Park Services bill to enlarge the wilderness areas, Helms lashed out with a five-page statement, accusing Morgan of taking a different stand on wilderness legislation in other states. Morgan had the nominal support of Governor Hunt's Democratic machine, but the governor was busy with his own reelection campaign. Senator Helms showed up for rallies with East, saying "1980 is the year conservatives *must* take control of the U.S. Senate. We can do this by electing men like John East." East emphasized a "stronger national defense," curbing government bureaucracy and waste, voluntary prayer in the schools, a balanced budget, a return to fiscal responsibility, and "a pro-American foreign policy."

Morgan's forces seemed stunned by this offensive. Reflecting on his defeat later—East won by the narrow margin of ten thousand votes—Morgan expressed bitterness about how Helms had turned on him. "I should have attacked East," he said. "But that would have been unpleasant and if I'd done it, people would say this is the meanest, nastiest campaign."

Another irony, besides the obvious conservatism of both candidates, was the fact that for a number of years Morgan had been chairman of the board of trustees at East Carolina University, where East taught. It was a case of the university professor taking on the small-town lawyer in a largely rural, conservative state and defeating him. The craftsman behind the victory was the same Jesse Helms who had managed his own rise to power through judicious use of television and a barrage of conservative ideology. At his birthday party in Monroe that fall Helms declared, "Now I don't know much about politics, and don't heckle me because I really don't. I'm the most awkward candidate you ever saw, and I don't have sense enough to try to be all things to all men."

But Helms had proved to be a brilliant politician. As 1981 approached, he had positioned himself for even more impressive gains. The Democrats had lost their Senate majority, which placed Helms in a position both to approve the awarding of patronage at home and to increase his influence in Washington. In a careful move to attain greater sway in foreign policy, Helms had shifted from the Armed Forces Committee to the Foreign Relations Committee following his reelection in 1978. By 1980 he was third in line for the chairmanship behind Republicans Charles Percy and Barry Goldwater.

Even more dramatic changes had taken place elsewhere, however. The swing in the Senate proved almost as significant as Reagan's capture of the White House. The greatest losers were civil rights activists, environmentalists, and labor unions. Such powerful Democratic senators as Frank Church, Harrison Williams, George McGovern, Warren Magnuson, Birch Bayh, and Gaylord Nelson had fallen under the Republican onslaught. Herman Talmadge had lost not only the chairmanship of the Senate Agriculture Committee but his Senate seat as well, and it was there that Helms decided to move. He stood first in line to take over the chairmanship. As the top spokesman for an important rural state, he felt he could make his weight felt in matters important to North Carolina, notably the ailing tobacco economy.

Helms immediately announced that his chief objectives as head of the Agriculture Committee would be to reduce food stamps. The program, he said, might be trimmed by as much as 40 percent, "giving only to those who are truly needy. . . . It's got to be changed so you can't have so many freeloaders." When it became apparent that Helms would become chairman of the Agriculture Committee, the sensitive livestock futures market dropped dramatically. Analysts suggested that meat demands would fall if Helms were able to cut back food stamps as much as he threatened.

But if, reflecting his state's vested interest in tobacco, Helms showed much concern for agricultural matters, he often seemed even more interested in foreign policy. Beginning in 1979 Helms had put together what Washington observers called his "foreign policy cabinet." It included James P. Lucier, forty-five, a former Richmond newspaper editorial writer; John Carbaugh, thirty-three, a law graduate of the University of South Carolina and former Nixon staffer; Dick McCormick, thirty-eight, also a Nixon staffer and graduate of the University of Fribourg, Switzerland; and James W. ("Bud") Nance, a retired rear admiral who had been Helms's childhood friend in Monroe.

This team passed the ammunition for the senator on important foreign policy issues and in a sense set his agenda in such matters. McCormick helped Helms keep an eye on the new Marxist-oriented regime in Nicaragua. Lucier did research and shaped strategy on legislation for lifting United States sanctions against Rhodesia (Zimbabwe). Helms sponsored the United States trip of Zimbabwe Prime Minister Abel Muzorewa, who was petitioning President Carter to extend diplomatic and economic recognition to his government.

Helms conferred with Prime Minister Margaret Thatcher in London in 1979. He and the prime minister had exchanged correspondence "for years," and Helms once confessed, "My wife said if I was ever going to do any philandering, it would be with someone with a British accent."

Helms's principal target during those years was the SALT II agreement, which he called a "sell-out" to the Soviet Union. "It may well be time," he said, "for the U.S. to try a SALT-free diet." The new foreign policy team helped maintain a steady drumbeat of opposition to the treaty, which was never ratified by the Senate. Helms's foreign policy team kept him minutely informed about proposed staff changes in what Helms had always considered the left-leaning United States State Department. He routinely opposed appointees there who didn't suit his brand of diplomacy, usually without much success.

But Helms never got discouraged. The shifting political currents were moving his way. For example, as early as 1979 Helms predicted that Nicaragua would go Communist. He opposed a $75 million grant to the Sandinistas, who had overthrown the dictator Somoza, saying: "This money will go to a Communist regime. How can the United States send aid to set up another Cuba at a time when thousands upon thousands of people are trying to escape Cuban Communism?" Helms bragged about what some called his own "state department." "I've got three of the top men on Capitol Hill," he said. "Mainly because of them, I'm never challenged on my facts when it comes to foreign affairs."

During that time Helms's associates were often bitterly criticized by both Democrats and Republicans for their "personal diplomacy." Lucier, who made dozens of trips to Europe, was accused of encouraging Rhodesian Prime Minister Ian Smith to take an unyielding position on negotiations over the new Rhodesian constitution. But criticism never slowed the Helms offensive. While often losing in showdown fights, Helms never let up.

Many saw in the Republican victory of 1980, and the massive changes it wrought, one of those watershed elections in United States politics that occur periodically and reshape the national destiny. Columnist George Will described the GOP victory in these words: "An awesome shudder went through the Republic as through a stately sailing ship that is altering its course in heavy seas." Helms, though, knew how to explain such a victory in plainer terms. "I shall always be pleased that North Carolina kept the Reagan candidacy alive in 1976," he said. "Had it not been for North Carolina then, Ronald Reagan would not be the President-elect tonight. But I don't have to remind him of that. He's not that kind of fellow and he knows what we did for him." Helms also told reporters that when he needed something, it would be just a "telephone call away" and that he would go directly to Reagan and not through Bush. "I figure Bush will need me as much as I need him."

But Helms didn't win all his objectives in the political turnovers of 1980. Two of his three state candidates—Beverly Lake, Jr., and Bill Cobey—lost in their gubernatorial and lieutenant gubernatorial efforts. The House of Representatives remained Democratic. The Lake defeat sent the popular Jim Hunt sailing strongly into office for a second term.

Master Campaigner and Avenging Angel

11. Political Tarnish

When Jim Hunt announced for his second gubernatorial term at the Vance-Aycock Dinner in Asheville on October 7, 1979, the subject of his Republican opponent, Beverly Lake, Jr., came up at a press conference. Former state senator Lake had that week switched his party affiliation from Democrat to Republican. He had also shaved his moustache. Lake, Hunt said, was trying to avoid looking like Thomas E. Dewey, the New York governor defeated by Harry Truman in 1948. "He may not look like Thomas Dewey," Hunt said, "but when we get through with him next year, we're going to make him feel like Thomas Dewey."

Hunt made good on that promise. Lake, a Raleigh lawyer, emerged as an unimpressive campaigner, even with the help of Helms's Congressional Club. Hunt linked Lake with his father's segregationist racial views. Prior to the November election, on Hunt's initiative, the two staged a televised debate at Meredith College, where Hunt's high-level, positive discussion of campaign issues left Lake far behind.

In the debate Lake first tried to use graphics, unveiling a placard entitled "Hunt's Political Machine," which tied the governor to state AFL-CIO leader Wilbur Hobby. When the debate moderator ruled that out, Lake launched a slashing but poorly organized attack. Hunt concentrated on the achievements of his first term, ignoring Lake's charges. "Lake managed to say little about what his administration would do," observed the *Greensboro Record.* "He came across as incompetent and stupid."

Earlier, in the May Democratic primary, Hunt had taken on former governor Bob Scott and easily trounced him. Hunt and Scott had also staged a television debate in February. Scott attacked Hunt for increasing his office staff by 130 percent. The governor's overpowering political style, he charged, had sent a "wave of fear across Raleigh with state employees afraid to speak out about problems." But the Scott rhetoric seemed overwrought. Hunt calmly outlined the accomplishments of his first term and plans for his second and ignored Scott's criticisms.

Hunt's administration weathered several embarrassments that year, however, all outgrowths of the high-powered political tone of his regime. In the first, a Hunt appointee, Mather Slaughter, foolishly initiated a project evaluating the political loyalties of sheriffs whom he knew in connection with his alcoholic beverage control work. Both Governor Scott and the Republicans seized on this issue when somebody leaked Slaughter's memos written to Betty McCain, cochairman of Hunt's reelection committee. Republican Congressman Howard Coble of Guilford County charged that this political sleuthing "stinks to high heaven." Jack Lee, GOP state chairman, called the memos "evidence of a political spy network inside state government."

After McCain admitted she had requested the evaluations (without Hunt's knowledge), the governor ordered them halted and transferred Slaughter from his politically sensitive job. "I called Betty and let her know it was wrong," Hunt told the press. "She didn't mean anything by it. . . . You know Betty. She wants everybody to tell everybody something about politics."

The Republicans tried to keep the issue alive by appointing an investigative panel to probe what they called this "latest installment in Jim Hunt's scenario of gutter politics." Coble asked Hunt's reelection committee to reimburse the state for Slaughter's salary and related expenses. Lake told political rallies that Hunt used "political operatives" to "spy on duly-elected public officials to see who are loyal to Governor Hunt."

The issue never fully caught fire; but another, which had surfaced earlier, continued to command the attention of Hunt's critics. In 1979 the Department of Human Resources had awarded more than $1 million in job training contracts under the Comprehensive Employment and Training Act (CETA) to the AFL-CIO and two companies controlled by its state president, Wilbur Hobby. Hobby was known as a strong Hunt supporter, and the Republicans charged that this was "a political pay-off." Ultimately Hobby was indicted and lost his AFL-CIO post. "You shouldn't have to share your money with a union boss," charged a television commercial sponsored by the Congressional Club. "You'll never spend it. Wilbur Hobby will."

As it turned out, the state AFl-CIO in 1977 had reportedly obtained certain commitments from Hunt after supporting him in 1976. The union said it expected to be awarded job training contracts by the state. It also wanted a "friendly" chairman of the State Employment Security Commission. (Hunt later appointed a chairman recommended by the union.)

Finally, at about the same time, State Auditor Henry Bridges turned up fiscal irregularities in a CETA contract totaling five hundred thousand dollars. CETA jobs had been offered to two Hunt supporters, one the daughter of Hunt's mentor Bert Bennett. The governor himself was never directly associated with these episodes, but one of the memos publicized during the Slaughter affair advised cabinet secretaries to "take the blame for any unpleasantness in this election year and to let the Governor take credit for the good."

These matters received exhaustive exposure in the press, but they never achieved the status of full-blown scandals. "The memo episode," wrote William B. Welch of the Associated Press, "presented another side of the Hunt Administration, different from the earnest, serious-minded and above-reproach image Hunt so often seems to project."

While Hunt recognized that a gloves-off campaign wasn't necessary against Scott or Lake in 1980, he never relinquished the pressure. His campaign against Scott capitalized on the former governor's eleven-year-old remark that "tobacco is no longer king in North Carolina." It was during Scott's regime (1969–72) and with his support that the General Assembly levied a two-cent tax increase on tobacco. In 1980 Hunt simply said: "I am one governor that is pleased to be associated with tobacco."

Hunt also recognized that 1980 was a political year in other ways. After having favored only a 5.5 percent salary increase for teachers and other state employees in 1979, he plugged for a 10 percent increase in 1980. He had given nuclear power a ringing endorsement in 1977, but by 1980 he was mentioning only safety aspects of nuclear power and alternate energy sources. Hunt had also dropped his campaign for executive veto power, although he still supported the idea.

The governor showed he had closely observed Jesse Helms's strategies. When Beverly Lake approached "Catfish" Hunter, the Tar Heel–born major league pitcher, about making a television ad for him as he had done for Helms, he discovered that Hunter was already committed to Hunt. "I guess some of those Democrats down there [in Hunter's hometown of Hertford] got hold of 'Catfish' early," remarked Tom Ellis. "You win some, you lose some." Governor Hunt presented Hunter with a certificate of appreciation, calling Hunter "the most famous Yankee ever produced in North Carolina."

As part of his reelection effort Hunt arranged a visit with evangelist Billy Graham at his mountain home in Montreat several weeks before the primary. The two had long been friends, and Graham insisted that no politics was involved. He had similarly greeted Helms in Charlotte two years earlier on the eve of his reelection contest against John Ingram.

In the May primary Hunt beat Scott by a better than two-to-one margin. He won a majority in all North Carolina's one hundred counties, gaining seven of every ten votes. A newspaper headlined one of its postelection stories: "Hunt Backers Find It Hard to Be Humble." It was a sweeping affirmation. Scott was a good sport about his defeat, but the Scott name, traditionally magical in Tar Heel politics, had met its match. Hunt himself said the issue in the primary campaign was whether "the state wanted to continue to move forward or to look back in fear and doubt."

The governor thus unveiled the issue he intended to raise against Lake in the fall. In the meantime Hunt led the state Democratic delegation to the National Democratic Convention in New York in August, where fifty-six of the state's delegates were pledged to President Carter and thirteen to Senator Kennedy.

Hunt took nine bodyguards to New York. A security problem had arisen following a shoot-out in Greensboro between Communists and members of the Ku Klux Klan in which five members of the Communist Workers Party were slain. Blaming Hunt for complicity in the deaths, CWP members had followed him to the Denver meeting of the National Governors Conference, where they threw eggs at him and and heckled his remarks. Earlier they had been disruptive at a Hunt press conference in Raleigh, and the governor and his family had received anonymous death threats.

Hunt's bodyguards, and the interest they aroused, turned out to be one of the livelier aspects of a dull convention in which Carter was easily nominated over Kennedy. The North Carolina delegation voted against a Kennedy-sponsored proposal for an "open convention." Unlike Helms in Detroit, Hunt, cochairman of the delegation along with Senator Morgan, maintained a low profile in New York. The governor sat with his delegation much of the time, didn't attend many parties, arrived early and stayed late, and was available to anyone seeking him. Newsmen reported that he was a more effective chairman than Helms had been at Detroit.

By the end of September Hunt had adopted another Helms tactic. One of his Republican opponents in the lieutenant governor's race of 1972, Johnny Walker, announced he was organizing a Republicans for Hunt Committee. Walker, the managing director of a hardware company in Boone, said he was endorsing Hunt over Lake because Hunt was "a superb progressive and dynamic representative of our state in business and social functions." He said he couldn't support the "radical conservatism" embraced by Lake. Walker had once served as Richard Nixon's finance director in North Carolina and was North Carolina cochairman of the George Bush campaign in 1979.

In the fall race Hunt again became the master campaigner. At political rallies he demonstrated a phenomenal ability to remember names. His twenty-minute speeches were positive. He never failed to add personal details about individuals in the audience. One observer noted that he "thrives on working a crowd." Hunt himself admitted that he loved "one-on-one campaigning. . . . I wish I could do it every day." He could discuss Paul Tillich with college graduates and use "ain't" with blue-collar workers. As he moved from county to county, he invariably met with his "keys" before attending public meetings. Among his close associates was his staff aide, twenty-four-year-old John Bennett, son of his friend Bert Bennett.

One reporter observed that Hunt combined the activist zeal for education of Charles B. Aycock and Terry Sanford, the road-building skills of Cameron Morrison and Kerr Scott, and the economic development touch of Luther Hodges. The major criticism he encountered was his obsession with politics. "The governor is a very political animal," admitted one of his associates. "I'm sure people think everything is weighed in political terms. But you have got to have someone in office to do the important things for the state, and I think that is a worth-while trade-off."

Bert Bennett put Hunt's political skill in a different light: "He just loves it. He loves the game. He loves politics. He loves being governor. He's a natural and there's no person on earth who works harder at it. He's lucky as hell, but he makes a lot of his own breaks."

Hunt's staff noticed that the governor had loosened up the longer he remained in office. "He's grown with the job," said one staffer. "He's less preachy than he used to be, and he's relaxed a little bit and has more humor about him. But he still has his soft side. He finds it hard to clamp down on people when he should."

In late October Carter's campaign sagged in the wake of the television debate with Reagan and the Iranian hostage crisis. With his own campaign going well, Hunt plugged for the faltering campaigns of other state Democrats, appearing at rallies with Senator Morgan and Congressmen Richardson Preyer, Stephen Neal, and Ike Andrews. Invariably neat and conservatively dressed and with never a hair out of place, he jabbed at his opponents with unflagging enthusiasm. One observer thought his technique was superior "because he can make you feel he's traveled all day just to shake your hand for five seconds."

This political zest paid off, for even as several of Hunt's Democratic colleagues suffered defeat, he won 62 percent of the vote over Lake and carried ninety of the state's one hundred counties. His victory resembled O. Max Gardner's gubernatorial triumph of 1928, when Herbert Hoover's Republicans carried North Carolina. Afterward Tom Ellis credited Hunt's victory to "incumbency." "He had it won from the start." A subdued Beverly Lake complained that the split between GOP moderates and conservatives affected his campaign. "I had to get in at one time and pacify the warring factions," he said. "There was the effect of two organizations working in some counties, sometimes working in opposite directions."

That same complaint would arise later as the conservative and moderate wings of the Republican Party prepared for the showdown struggle between Helms and Hunt many felt would come in 1984. Meanwhile both men turned to a new year in offices they had learned to use with increasing dexterity and authority.

12. Catching Hand Grenades

Jesse Helms, the ideological outsider for the first eight years of his senatorial career, found the insider's role difficult to accept in 1981 as Ronald Reagan entered the White House and the Republicans took control of the Senate. The senator immediately reasserted his Lone Ranger status by speaking forty minutes on the Senate floor against the President's nomination of Caspar Weinberger as secretary of defense. Weinberger, he insisted, wouldn't be tough enough on the Soviets.

That was "only the first shot across Reagan's bow," one correspondent reported. Helms also opposed the appointment of Frank Carlucci as Weinberger's deputy. Then he declared full-scale war against State Department appointments by the new secretary of state, Alexander Haig. The senator also had to make what he called "a painful decision" when he supported Mr. Reagan's bill to raise the ceiling on the national debt by $50 million. This led Senator Spark M. Matsunaga (D-Hawaii) to observe wryly: "I understand we have a new liberal senator from North Carolina."

"Courtly even when flapping most furiously," wrote Helen Dewar in the *Washington Post*, "Helms sweeps down on the transgressors—from feminists and labor barons to errant diplomats and generals—like an avenging angel of old-time religion. And, to the extent that President Reagan departs from the scriptures, he, too, can expect thunderbolts. . . . He let no more than four hours of the Reagan Administration go by before attacking some initial appointments in order to make his case against any ideological backsliding by the new team."

Helms, of course, had always put what he called his "principles" ahead of everything else—party loyalty, personal friendships, and partial victories. Indeed, some of his colleagues had said with some exasperation that he "made a career of losing on principle" even as he, in the words of George Will, "set the outer limits on conservative activism." Yet the senator was not quite as comfortable doing this when his old friend Ronald Reagan was president as he had been when he could direct his thunderbolts at Jimmy Carter or even Gerald Ford. "It is a decidedly different feeling to be catching hand grenades instead of throwing them," Helms confessed to a North Carolina reporter. He never feared, though, that his opposition would destroy his relationship with the White House. "We have the kind of friendship that will endure," Helms said of Reagan. "He's not a yes man either. . . . We just like to send 'em a message."

Meanwhile, the courtly Helms was calling the President's wife "Miss Nancy" and telling pages in the Senate she was "the finest beauty in the land." He even began inviting liberal reporters, whom he labeled "nice fellows," to lunch in the Senate dining room.

Delaying the confirmation of Reagan's appointees was a fitting way to demonstrate principle, but Helms saved his real energy for the task of getting his social program enacted. To begin with, the senator wanted more spending cuts than Reagan's budget recommended: "We've got to demonstrate that we are for real in terms of what we have been talking about all these years, that we are not nervous nellies and that we will take actions that may not be popular with some pressure groups but that are mandatory if we are going to get this country straightened out." Beyond that Helms's prime objectives were what he called "profamily issues"—anti-abortion, anti-ERA, anti-busing, pro–school prayer.

It was on these points that he soon discovered Reagan had different priorities and would support the New Right more with "symbolic gestures" than "substantive concessions." Helms, on the other hand, vowed full steam ahead on all his pet social issues, which had so badly divided Americans.

On the issue of limiting school busing, Helms took pains to try to convince critics that he had in some ways altered his earlier, prosegregation views, which were very much on the record during the stormy years after the *Brown* desegregation decision. Helms had been slowly amending his pronouncements—or his memories of them. During the 1960s in his Raleigh television editorials Helms called segregation right for its time. By the 1980s he recalled that twenty years earlier his 1960 editorials were telling restaurant owners they could make more money by serving both blacks and whites. Helms told a North Carolina reporter that he favored "genuine freedom of choice" in the schools. If we had had it, he insisted, "we'd have never gotten into all this busing, hostility and deteriorating education."

Helms said he believed in states rights—not as a code word for segregation but as a valid principle: The federal programs had destroyed "something very precious in terms of the black man's hope of gaining his place in the sun. . . . For example, so many fine black schools have been destroyed in terms of pride by busing. We have a case in Raleigh where a black school used to have the finest band, the finest teachers, the finest choral groups, basketball teams, football teams. These people would have fought for that school. Now they don't care because it is all mixed up. It is a hodge-podge of kids going back and forth for no reason at all."

The senator became highly indignant when people charged he was racist or anti-black. "I don't think you will find a black citizen anywhere who knows me who will say I am anti-black, anti-yellow or anti-anything. I judge people on the basis of merit." Helms's sister, Mary Elizabeth McNeely, recalled that one of Helms's black friends, a former shoeshine boy during his youth in Monroe, always asked about her brother when she saw him. "He had black friends as a boy just as most Southern white youths did," she said.

Yet Senator Helms never supported any issue or movement designed to help blacks improve themselves. His record was much to the contrary, from the time of the school desegregation decision to the equal rights struggles of the 1960s. As one of his supporters admitted, "Jesse can be very strong for people as individuals and very hostile to them as groups."

The same was true in the realm of social welfare. Helms's desire to slash welfare spending, the senator said, should not be viewed as lack of compassion for the poor but rather an act of compassion toward taxpayers. "I don't think there is a soul in the world who would object to doing everything possible for the truly needy; the sick, the elderly, crippled, blind and so forth," he told a reporter in 1981. "But when you start talking about welfare programs for people who walk off their jobs, who absolutely will not work, that is not only a lack of compassion toward the taxpayer, it is a lack of compassion toward the people who are ripping off the government because they are being led into the swamps of irresponsibility. What we have to do in this country is pull together and everyone pull a load."

In March 1981 Helms began to reveal just what his social program would entail. Proposing that the food stamp program be slashed 50 percent, he called it "full of fraud." It included, he said, criminal rings that purchased stamps from the program's clients and sold them at a profit. Helms's cuts, which were even deeper than Reagan's, provoked a storm of opposition from the Democrats. Senator Patrick Leahy (D-Vt.) defended federal food programs: "[They] have worked. There is no question in my mind that hunger still exists in the United States. We may not want to admit it, but it's a shame on our country." Helms replied that hard-working Americans were fed up with food stamps. "Accepting benefits destroys their [the recipients'] initiative."

In March also Helms introduced his human life amendment. It overturned the 1973 Supreme Court ruling that sanctioned abortions before the third month of pregnancy, unless a mother's life or health was threatened. The amendment declared: "The paramount right to life is vested in each human being from the moment of fertilization without regard to age, health or condition of dependency."

By the end of March Senator Helms clashed with the differing priorities of the Reagan administration. The President had given lip service to Helms's ideologies, but decided that his own economic program—specifically cutting taxes—would be jeopardized if he gave primacy to the Helms-led social agenda. The Republican leadership joined the President in agreeing to pursue his economic program and postpone social legislation until 1982. That would put tax cuts and defense buildup ahead of anti-abortion, prayer in schools, and anti-busing. Helms sought to minimize this defeat. "We don't have the urgency that we had previously on these issues," he said, "because we have an administration that shares our view."

His social program blocked for the time being, Senator Helms turned his attention to foreign policy. With the help of his rambunctious young foreign affairs aide, John Carbaugh, he set about pushing for better relations with right-wing dictatorships, relations which had been downgraded by the Carter administration and its human rights campaign. Carbaugh, thirty-five, was a skillful lobbyist. He had, Washington reporters said, persistence, flair, an affable manner, and a sense of humor. Unlike Helms, he loved the sophisticated life—fast cars, good restaurants, classical music. "Every now and then I have to rein him in a little," Helms confessed. "But I'd rather have someone creative and an activist on my staff than someone who sits around waiting for instructions."

Carbaugh pushed a proposal to cut off aid to the new Nicaraguan government, which Helms had early perceived as Marxist and little better than the Somozan government it had supplanted. Carbaugh, who had been a member of Reagan's transition team, lobbied the White House and Congress for appointments for Helms conservatives to key policy posts in the State Department and opposed moderates associated with President Ford and Henry Kissinger. He also pushed Helms's pro–South African tilt and opposed resuming arms control talks with the Soviet Union.

Senator Helms had a long relationship with right-wing military regimes in Central and South America—among them Argentina, Bolivia, and Chile. He had visited the generals of Argentina prior to the Falklands War and supported them in that engagement. "These countries that my liberal friends are so concerned about, for all their faults, want to be our friends," Helms said in 1981. "They are anti-Communist. Now they certainly are imperfect. But they do at least have the quality of being opposed to Communist domination of this world."

But in one sensitive area—the tobacco price support program—Helms did not remain fixed and forward on his "principles." Early in his journalistic career he had railed against all government subsidies, from Social Security to welfare stamps; but after reaching Washington he changed his views about tobacco, more as a matter of survival than anything else. By 1981 the anti-smoking campaign was a force to be reckoned with. As newly installed chairman of the Senate Agriculture Committee, Senator Helms and other tobacco-state congressmen were embattled. In March he suggested that North Carolina tobacco growers would be willing to pay the grading and warehouse inspection fees, a move first proposed by the Carter administration and later endorsed by Reagan.

Helms declared he would not "preside over the dismantlement of the federal tobacco program," but added that there could be no exception to President Reagan's budget-cutting program. Across-the-board cuts were necessary to "save the nation from ruin." The tobacco industry could not expect "special treatment." It had to share in the effort to balance the budget. Through it all, though, he said he was still "concerned about the hundreds of thousands of North Carolinians who earn their living from tobacco."

The senator had every reason to be concerned. North Carolina produced 70 percent of the nation's flue-cured tobacco, and the industry employed 148,000 North Carolinians, one out of every seven jobs. As Agriculture Committee chairman, Helms had prime responsibility for guiding the complex four-year farm support bill, including tobacco, through the Senate.

Governor Hunt and other Democrats made sure that the senator knew the state would be watching his performance. Hunt already had expressed disappointment because President Reagan had not stepped forward to defend tobacco, as he had promised he would during the 1980 presidential campaign. "All the years the Democrats were in [control in Washington] we kept the programs," Hunt declared. "Now we do not have the leadership." In July North Carolina's Democratic Congressman Charles Rose noted pointedly that Helms's stand on some social programs, notably food stamps, had angered certain members of Congress, making the job of protecting tobacco and peanuts all the more difficult. "In this place, anytime you pick up a sword and go after somebody," he said, "you'd better be prepared to have that sword come back at you in a place where the wielder thinks you're most vulnerable."

Helms soon encountered that backlash. He and President Reagan had been less than enthusiastic about the size of the dairy support program and sought to reduce it. When Helms and other southern senators supported the peanut program but voted to hold dairy prices to their current level, dairy state senators rebelled and helped pass an amendment eliminating part of the peanut program. They were joined by grain state senators unhappy over the Agriculture Committee's compromise calling for lower subsidies on wheat. "In more than 12 years here, I've never seen senators from the major farm states fall apart like they did today," said Senator John Melcher (D-Mont.).

Suddenly Senator Helms found himself in a fire storm. By the time the tobacco program came to the floor, the farm bloc was badly fragmented. Tobacco state senators beat back an amendment that would have abolished the program or reduced its scope. When Helms moved to table Senator Mark Hatfield's amendment to eliminate the tobacco program, his motion passed 53–42. "Let the tobacco farmer stand on his own feet as we are asking the welfare recipients, the poor and the needy to do," Hatfield said. Helms replied: "If he [Hatfield] wants to see a large increase in the welfare program, let him succeed in destroying the tobacco program." Hatfield: "I've about come to the conclusion that tobacco is better than sex." Helms: "I don't remember."

That battle won, Helms and Senate Majority Leader Howard Baker (R-Tenn.) managed to ward off another assault by Senator Thomas Eagleton (D-Mo.). His amendment to reduce tobacco price supports for grades noncompetitive on world markets failed 41–40. Helms achieved his squeaky victory only by soliciting Baker to help him change four Republican votes.

After that encounter Helms charged that Governor Hunt had misled and confused Senator Eagleton, whom he had lobbied as a fellow Democrat. Hunt fired back that he hadn't talked with the senator about plans to change the tobacco program. Helms said he "accepted" the governor's reply, but Hunt responded by placing on Helms responsibility for losing a vote on the peanut program. The fight became stormy as the two Tar Heel leaders courted the state's farming constituency.

After the close vote Helms told reporters, "I was scared silly by the Eagleton amendment." In the course of the Senate floor fight both Senator Helms and his colleague Senator East had used all their influence. At one point Helms responded to critics of his food stamp reductions by saying that a leading tobacco opponent in the House, Congressman Frederick Richmond (D-N.Y.), who had been arrested for propositioning a male, had "a curious life style." Senator East remarked that Senator Eagleton, who had once undergone shock treatment, had "mental problems." Later, in a letter to a North Carolina newspaper, Helms apologized for his comment. "I regret the incident," he wrote. "It will not happen again." Senator East also apologized.

The controversy continued over whether Helms's tactics in pushing his social agenda had damaged his leadership in agriculture. Congressman Richmond called Helms "the worst liability you have in the state of North Carolina." Ward Sinclair, a *Los Angeles Times–Washington Post* reporter, observed that Helms "seemed willing to allow budgetary assaults on the dairy and grain support program while standing resolute against changes in the peanut and tobacco programs." Senator Robert Dole (R-Kan.) came to Helms's defense. "He is," said Dole, "a respected and hard-working member of the Senate whose actions are founded on strongly held principles. He is doing an effective job in standing up for the interests of his agriculture constituents." At the start of the fight in mid-summer Helms and East had sent a joint letter to other senators saying that destruction of the tobacco program "would create chaos in the farming sector where stability had prevailed." They warned that the issue goes to "the heart of all commodity programs in your state if the attack on tobacco succeeds."

Later that year in a High Point speech, though, Helms drew a distinction between tobacco and the other programs. He declared that tobacco price supports should survive because they did not cost the taxpayers, while the milk support program should be cut because it had cost at least $1 billion that year and would cost $2 billion the following year. The tobacco program had not been a heavy financial burden on government. Since its start in 1946 it had produced a $68 million profit on successful resales after repaying obligations to the Commodity Credit Corporation for all except seven crop years. It defaulted on loans for those seven years at a loss of $42.8 million. The profits, however, had been returned to tobacco growers, while the government had footed the losses. That procedure was changed in 1982, allowing government losses to be offset by profits as a step toward making the program completely self-supporting.

In the showdown the senior senator from North Carolina succeeded in saving the tobacco program, and, as it turned out, only minor changes were made in the peanut program. Initially Helms had been unwilling to play pork-barrel politics with other senators (the traditional "you-scratch-my-back-and-I'll-scratch-yours"). But he soon got over that. At one point he joined in opposing efforts to eliminate a law giving United States ships preference in hauling foreign aid food, thus gaining the support of Senator Daniel Inouye (D-Hawaii) and other shipping state senators. When the four-year farm program had safely survived rough senatorial waters, Helms suggested that "all of us, regardless of political affiliation, [should] let bygones be bygones and from this point on remove the tobacco question from the political arena."

But the controversy grew over adverse health effects of tobacco. By the following year Governor Hunt was testifying before a congressional subcommittee studying revision of the tobacco program. Hunt strongly opposed forced sale of allotments held by nonproducers. Critics said absentee landlords increased production costs, and in the long run made the program more costly, but Hunt warned against squeezing out small producers.

"Better financed and large land-based farmers are going to be in a better position to bid for allotments offered for sale," he said. "Many of our young farmers must rent and have limited equity. It would be tough for them. I want farmers to keep control of their programs. Where would support to make the program cost-free or even self-supporting come from? I would err on the part of farmers having control, even if it means costing us a little money."

The tobacco program, Hunt insisted, is not "a subsidy. . . . That's been a lie. If putting up our own money will put an end to it [the lie], I say let's do it and have it paid for by the farmers." Both Hunt and Helms thought farmers should contribute more to the support program. "They expect us to make some adjustments," Helms said. "We must make it a no-cost program."

Senator Helms's first year of "catching hand grenades" had accomplished little in the way of enacting his controversial "profamily" program. But he did manage to stave off damaging attacks on tobacco price supports. The senator's implacable assaults on President Reagan's State and Defense Department appointments seldom succeeded, but the stir he raised in the Senate caught the attention of the media. *Time* Magazine decided he merited a cover story, which traced his career and called him "a saint to his fans, a dangerous buffoon to his foes" and "the New Right's righteous warrior." *Time* concluded that he had a "born politician's ease with a crowd, a saint's generosity toward an individual in distress and a Malthusian indifference to human suffering on a large scale." In response Helms said that many people had told him *Time* had meant the story to be a "cheap shot" but that it had failed. He also criticized the magazine for not publishing more of the pro-Helms letters it had received.

Then the senator found himself "celebrated" in another publication, *Playboy Magazine*. He received a complimentary copy of the issue containing an article about him, minus the centerfold, along with an invitation to reply. Helms, as usual, was more than ready. "Well, ain't that nice?" he said. "I'm going to send them a picture of Patches [his dog] for their centerfold."

13. Against the Wind

Little more than a month after his decisive gubernatorial victory of November 1980, Governor Hunt announced that his second inauguration would be as down-home and unpretentious as his first: dress would be business or Sunday suits; the setting would be informal and outdoors; speeches would be brief. On Saturday, January 10, 1981, the governor's party walked in freezing rain the one block from the Governor's Mansion on Blount Street to the outdoor speakers' platform on the steps of the Archives and History Building, where before an audience of some four thousand Hunt took the oath of office administered by Chief Justice Joseph Branch.

After removing his chesterfield, Hunt delivered a ten-minute inaugural address. It vigorously sounded his theme for the eighties: "Across the nation the winds of retreat are blowing," he declared. "But North Carolina must sail against the wind." The reference was to the newly elected Reagan administration. Hunt noted paradoxically that the "role of the federal government is properly diminishing, and the states can again become the true laboratories of democracy." With the careful pragmatism that often characterized his rhetoric, the governor declared that while "it is time for government to reduce its burdens on the people," it is "not a time to turn back from progress." He insisted that North Carolina, which had become the tenth most populous state, was "poised to lead the nation."

But then he mentioned the state's obstacles—it was forty-first in per capita income and forty-seventh in infant mortality, its schools had high drop-out rates, and many of its rivers were polluted. He challenged the state to join the technological revolution, to volunteer to help a child learn to read, to protect neighbors against crime, and to give aid to senior citizens. In a reference to the Greensboro Klan-Communist shoot-out, he said the state would not tolerate "bigotry or hatred." He concluded: "We shall light the flame of human brotherhood."

Two days later, at the swearing in of his new cabinet, the governor expanded on the centrist theme of his inaugural address. "We must prove that we can be both conservative and progressive. We must prove that government can be both lean and compassionate." Hunt repeated the goals he had campaigned on in 1980: Economic development, education, energy alternatives, environmental protection, and crime control. "Inflation is our greatest problem," he declared. "We are going to be conservative in the use of the people's money. We are going to do some cutting back. . . . But we will also do some wise investing of the people's money."

These contrasting themes arose repeatedly in the governor's speeches. Later that month, in his state-of-the-state message, he spelled out his program. One top priority was a request for $24.4 million to build a microelectronics center in the Research Triangle to help lure high-tech industries. Another was a proposal to allocate funds to reduce classroom size and give state employees a 7 percent salary increase.

Turning to the subject of highway construction during a painful recession, Hunt foreshadowed what was to become a major struggle during his second term: hiking the state gasoline tax. Even though the governor's blue ribbon highway study commission had the previous year strongly recommended higher gasoline taxes, the governor refused to stake himself out on the issue. Two decades earlier Governor Sanford had sponsored the passage of a tax on food and other items, which quickly became known as "Terry's Tax." Hunt was determined not to have a similar label hung on the tax he had proposed. In the words of one critic, "He dropped back and punted." He said he was leaving the highway tax matter to the General Assembly and the "people."

As usual, though, Hunt had a game plan. He sought to broaden responsibility for a decision to raise the gas levy. Through shrewd appointments to the Advisory Budget Commission and other political alliances, he brought in influential legislative leaders to help package and sell the tax. By late April, when Hunt finally produced a highway improvement bill, including a three-cent-a-gallon gasoline tax hike, he had rallied an impressive team to share the burden.

On April 28, as one correspondent put it, "amid all the trappings of a political campaign," Governor Hunt asked the General Assembly to approve a $200 million revenue package, including the gasoline tax increase, to maintain the state's ninety-one thousand miles of roads. In a carefully staged television speech managed by his campaign advertising consultant, Hunt proposed an eight-point package. In addition to the tax increase, it included hikes in other tax fees on auto use, shifts of certain revenues from the general to the highway fund, and increased taxes on liquor, mining, and vacation house rentals. It also provided a slim and complicated tax rebate for "necessary driving" to offset the tax impact.

Months before, Hunt had recognized he was approaching an important political fight. In the midst of a severe recession the people and their legislators were in no mood for increased taxes. Yet the governor and other state officials perceived that sharp cuts in highway maintenance could endanger the state's future economic health. "It's not easy to pay more taxes," Hunt said. "But my job as governor is to explain to you the problem as I see it and to recommend not the popular thing, not the easy thing but the right thing for North Carolina's future."

Another politically dangerous issue hovered over the highway tax fight. During the 1980 campaign a bid-rigging scandal had erupted. Four highway construction firms were indicted on charges of rigging their bids for highway contracts, and they pleaded guilty. Just prior to the election Hunt had promised not to accept campaign contributions from contractors doing business with the state, but some funds had already been accepted (five hundred dollars each from Nello Teer and W. T. Phillips). "We will return them," said Hunt aide Stephanie Bass. "The Governor said we would not take them, but we made a mistake. We will not keep them."

The full scope of the bid-rigging scandal emerged after the November election, when six paving companies were fined and six of their executives given active prison terms by a federal court in Charlotte. Eventually fifteen companies were found to have been involved in the practices, which had been transpiring for years either without detection by or in collusion with highway officials. One contractor told the federal court such activities had been common for the thirty-five years he had been in business. Until 1980, when the rigging became public knowledge, state highway officials had regularly accepted the hospitality of industry trade associations at resort hotels, and construction companies had made their private planes available to gubernatorial candidates without question.

Suddenly in 1981 corruption in highway affairs became a volatile issue. Federal Judge Franklin Dupree, Jr., said of these matters in open court: "Our officials in the State Highway Department have either been completely remiss in uncovering it [bid-rigging] and bringing it to light, or what is far worse turned their backs on it."

This controversy boiled over on the eve of Governor Hunt's campaign to hike the state gasoline tax. Newspapers recalled that Terry Sanford flew to the 1980 Democratic National Convention in a Dickerson Company plane, that Nello Teer, another prominent contractor, had made his plane available to Governor Dan Moore during his successful gubernatorial campaign of 1964, and that Hunt had access to a company plane owned by Seth Wooten, a Wilson contractor, during his races for governor. Wooten was among those contractors convicted of bid rigging. A Hunt spokesman was careful to point out, however, that the governor had always paid the normal rental fees when the Wooten plane was used.

"Coziness between highway contractors and top state officials has for many years been as common as the blacktop on the state's 91,949 miles of highway," wrote reporters for the *Greensboro Daily News* in a lengthy story on "paving and politicking" published in April. "The words highways and politics have been virtually synonymous," they quoted Governor Hunt as saying at swearing-in ceremonies for members of the State Board of Transportation in 1977. "The time has come to break up their relationship."

Yet according to the newspaper, shortly before that ceremony Hunt's organization had collected almost seventy thousand dollars in campaign donations from highway contractors. Hunt officials told contractors to "make a good impression" on President Carter's officials attending a Carter-Mondale fundraising dinner at Asheville in October 1979. Former governor Bob Scott told reporters that he always turned to contractors when he needed money for functions not covered by state funds. "There are things a governor just has to do, like going to party conventions, or attending a conference of Democratic governors."

Hunt's opponents enthusiastically hopped on the issue. Helms's National Congressional Club proposed a gas tax debate (which Hunt declined) and called the hiked taxes a "reward for government waste." It criticized the North Carolina Travel Council, a supporter of Hunt's program, as an organization backed by "fat cats, national banks, a power and light company and wealthy Department of Transportation members." Democratic State Senator Marshall Rauch (Gaston), a Hunt critic, declared that "so many legislators are in absolute awe of the governor that they want to stand in line to receive his adulation."

But the Hunt forces were undaunted by this onslaught. They retaliated by calling the Congressional Club's charges "lies and insults" paid for by contributors from "oil companies and other special interests." By June 3, after a delay to lobby for more support, Hunt's legislation, in somewhat amended form, passed the Senate by a two-to-one margin. It was an easier victory than the governor's supporters had anticipated for the "Good Roads Package." The three-cent tax increase had been reduced by one-quarter of a cent and minor revisions made in other items by the time the package got through the House, but the total revenue raised came near the figure originally sought by Hunt's blue ribbon study commission.

Milton Heath, an Institute of Government staff member, called the gas tax controversy "the biggest legislative fight in 20 years." The governor's backers and critics debated whether it had damaged his reputation. "I think [Hunt's] gotten what he went after," said Senator Rauch, "but I'm afraid he'll suffer a tremendous political loss and follow in the footsteps of Terry Sanford and Bob Scott." Both won new taxes—Sanford on food and Scott on soft drinks, cigarettes, and gasoline. But neither got very far in later campaigns.

"I think [Hunt's] been strengthened," said John A. Williams, the governor's budget officer. "He's advocated a program against tremendous odds and he's won. And people love a winner. He's a stronger man today than he was three months ago." "It won't help him," said Bert Bennett. "But it's a lot better that he won approval of the tax than lost it. That would have been worse. I don't think the gas tax will be as serious for Hunt as the food tax was for Sanford."

Helms's chief lieutenant Ellis said, "I don't see how it's a plus [for Hunt]." Some Hunt partisans, though, believed the Congressional Club opposition had helped consolidate Democratic support for the governor. "The appeal was that we need to prove to these people right now that we're going to stick together," said one legislator.

Hunt himself said he considered it the toughest fight of his life, even tougher than the second-term campaign, and he probably saw the battle in the clearest perspective. "I'm going to have eight years in office," he said. "By the time I'm through, and there are many more things to do, I will be judged on all of them." Bob Scott echoed that theme and added, "One thing in Hunt's favor is that we live in a time of high interest rates with everything going up, and three cents a gallon may get lost in the shuffle."

Hunt's supporters were betting that would happen. Even as the campaign faded, some decided to respond to the Congressional Club's ad charging the Hunt administration with "cronyism." They printed up a batch of T-shirts bearing the words: "I'm one of Jim Hunt's cronies." They also obtained T-shirts for the governor and Mrs. Hunt with the words "No. 1 Crony" and "No. 1 Crony's Wife."

14. Helms at Bay

In September 1981 Hugh Morton, a public-spirited entrepreneur, asked Jesse Helms and Jim Hunt to help save the Cape Hatteras Lighthouse. The 110-year-old landmark on North Carolina's Outer Banks had been losing its battle with erosion and was about to fall into the sea. Hunt and Helms accepted cochairmanship of the Save the Lighthouse Committee and launched a $1 million campaign. The press promptly tagged it "The Jim and Jesse Show."

At a Raleigh luncheon publicizing the drive Hunt and Helms appeared together as good sports to josh each other and make as much capital out of the event as possible. "I don't care which party straightens out America just so long as one of them does," Helms said. "I don't care which one save the lighthouse, as long as one of them does." Hunt was less sure they could get results: "I doubt that the ocean would listen even if Senator Helms and myself went down there together," he said.

The lighthouse luncheon proved to be one of the last congenial public meetings of the senator and the governor before their titanic senatorial battle. During 1981 Hunt had won what he called the toughest political fight of his life—raising highway taxes during a serious recession. The senator had struggled in vain to get his "profamily" social programs enacted in Congress and had seen his pet bills killed or postponed. In April of 1982 the senator again found himself very much in the national spotlight. The subject was the Falkland Islands War.

"I have difficulty understanding how he could side with a dictatorship which has violated international law and fail to side with a democratic ally who has been our strongest ally over the years. It strikes me as an aberration."

The speaker was Retired Admiral Elmo Zumwalt. The subject of his criticism was Senator Helms, who stunned even some of his most ardent backers by supporting Argentina after its invasion of the Falkland Islands.

Helms's interest in Argentina went back to his earliest years in the Senate. He had cultivated the country's military leadership and had visited Buenos Aires three times. Helms's immediate reaction to Prime Minister Margaret Thatcher's spirited response to the invasion had been to urge Great Britain to give up the Falklands. "The best policy is to recognize Argentine sovereignty," Helms declared. "The United States should put pressure on both parties to withdraw from this confrontation."

As Secretary of State Alexander Haig conducted his unsuccessful mediation between London and Buenos Aires, Helms offered his own advice, saying that President Reagan had asked him to use his influence with Argentina. Helms's recommendations followed the line of the Argentine generals: a compromise giving Argentina sovereignty over the islands but maintaining British customs and laws for its citizens, with dual citizenship and passports. "I think the British bit off more than they can chew," Helms said. "The crisis could result in military disaster for the British and the Argentines. It could harm United States relations with Latin America and provide new opportunities for Communist insurgencies." Britain, he said, "in my judgment" cannot win. "I think I'll prove to be right."

Helms, of course, proved to be wrong. As the British pressed their invasion, the senator changed his tune. Haig had been an inept negotiator, he said. His own position had been misunderstood; he didn't favor Argentina, but only thought history was on its side on the sovereignty question. He was, he said, simply asking both nations "to back up and cool off."

Whatever embarrassment the senator felt over the accuracy of his prediction was soon forgotten in unfolding events that spring, when Helms became engaged in bitter combat with other members of Congress on such issues as busing, voting rights, anti-abortion, a tobacco tax hike, gun control, school prayer, and the death penalty. Helms even clashed with his fellow conservative Senator Strom Thurmond (R-S.C.), chairman of the Senate Judiciary Committee, when he attached a gun control and death penalty amendment to Thurmond's carefully nurtured legislation to streamline criminal laws and ultimately contributed to its defeat.

President Reagan, too, came in for some strong words from Helms when he backed legislation requiring a strong cigarette health label. The senator called it "Califanoism" in the Department of Health and Human Services. His reference was to Joseph Califano, HEW secretary in the Carter Administration, who had taken a strong stand against the health hazards of smoking.

As the recession deepened, Helms suggested a 5 percent pay cut and a salary freeze for members of Congress and other officials. This was designed, the senator said, to gain support for cuts in other parts of Reagan's budget. "We have the perception of throwing 20 widows out in the snow every day and protecting ourselves with tax breaks," Helms said. "It's time to re-establish some credibility with the people." He also supported a two-thirds' reduction in cost-of-living adjustments for Social Security recipients and other entitlement programs. Then Helms charged that his own state, North Carolina, had one of the nation's worst records for handling food stamps, a 15.8 percent error rate compared with a national average of 13.3 percent. He recommended that states pay the full cost for improperly issued stamps.

Overcoming a spirited filibuster by liberal senators headed by Senator Lowell Weicker (R-Conn.), Helms and Senator J. Bennett Johnson (D-La.) persuaded the Senate to vote to weaken busing as a tool for racial integration in the schools. It was a long and bitter fight, starting with a typically

Helmsian tactic, an amendment attached to a bill authorizing funds for the Justice Department. Its purpose was to prohibit the department from spending funds to pursue discrimination cases that could lead to court-ordered busing. Senator Johnson offered an amendment that would bar federal courts from ordering busing plans that transported school children more than five miles or fifteen minutes from their homes. It also allowed the department to ask courts to overturn existing busing plans that exceeded those limits.

Congressional sentiment had begun to lean toward curbing busing, because, among other reasons, its record of success was spotty. Senator Johnson declared that it had driven middle-class families of all races out of the public schools. "[It] is a leech on the educational system. . . . What good is a remedy if it doesn't work? . . . The overwhelming social science evidence is that busing has failed across America and increased racial isolation."

Senator Weicker, who had earlier mounted one filibuster, threatened another. But at that point sixty senators had already voted cloture (debate cut-off) and seemed ready to do it again. Ultimately the Senate set a 100-hour limit on debate and then by a 63–33 vote passed the Helms-Johnson legislation. It was the final Senate chapter of a stormy eight-months' battle. Helms and Johnson had won a considerable victory, but passage in the House was far from certain. The legislation remained bottled up in Congressman Peter Rodino's Judiciary Committee and never got to the House floor.

If some had viewed Helms as a "political Don Quixote tilting at the windmills of change" or a maverick senator who "made a career of losing on principle," many were beginning to think otherwise. The Helms right-wing initiative popped up everywhere. The senator was a master of parliamentary rules, and he had an efficient staff that was enthusiastically loyal, well organized, and quick to research complex issues and help constituents. The Jesse Helms who had flirted with a third-party movement in the 1970s was strategically located now to put pressure on his friend Ronald Reagan whenever he wandered too far from Helms's conservative agenda.

In late spring the senator launched the first of a series of campaigns on various issues in which he defied the dominant sentiment in the Senate and the House. By the end of the year his efforts would leave bitterness and hostility among contending factions and isolate Helms and his fellow Tar Heel senator, John East.

The Senate approached the end of a year-long drive to renew key provisions of the 1965 Voting Rights Act, which was credited with encouraging registration of more than one million blacks. By early June sixty-eight senators had endorsed an extension approved in May, over Helms's strenuous objection, by the Senate Judiciary Committee. It would maintain federal supervision over states that had poor minority voting records. Support for the bill, a compromise suggested by Robert Dole, came from liberals, moderates, and conservatives, including the Reagan administration.

All this failed to impress Helms, however. He wrote letters to fellow senators announcing that unless changes were made, "I am obliged to oppose [the bill] to the maximum extent possible." Helms said it was unfair to make the legislation applicable only to some dozen states (including North Carolina) and sought to make its application nationwide. He also aimed at making it easier for states then covered to escape Justice Department scrutiny.

When Helms's efforts at amendment failed to draw support, he organized a filibuster and said he was prepared to block consideration by talking on the Senate floor "until the cows come home." Joined by his junior colleague, East, Helms spoke, often to a deserted floor. He focused his attack on Senator Ted Kennedy (D-Mass.), charging him with pushing voting rights to further his political career. "We live in an intimidated society," Helms said. The bill is "punitive and degrading" to the South. A black leader, the Reverend Leon White, head of the North Carolina–Virginia Committee for Racial Justice of the United Church of Christ, said: "The failure of the Republican Party . . . and the senators from North Carolina to vote for extension of this act is solely based on racism."

At one point Helms announced he had in mind at least forty-one amendments, including some on such unrelated topics as school prayer and abortion. "This ball game would be over," he said, "except for the intransigence of the senator from Massachusetts who apparently is running this railroad train." "Nobody is railroading a bill that has 76 sponsors," replied Senator Charles Mathias (R-Md.). "If that's a railroad, I want to buy into it."

On June 15 the full Senate voted, 86–8, to take up the bill. On June 17, after more than thirteen hours of almost continuous debate, some lasting into the early morning hours, Senator Helms abandoned his filibuster. "Many senators appeared exhausted," an Associated Press reporter wrote, "some slouching in their chairs and resting their heads on their hands." Senator Dole reported afterward that "restless" Republicans pressured Helms to give up because delay might have jeopardized other issues of greater importance. They also feared that the bill's failure would hurt the Republican Party in the South, where they had made key electoral gains.

On June 19, after breaking the filibuster, the Senate passed the Voting Rights extension, 85–8. Senator Helms, still feisty, said he had obtained guarantees from Howard Baker that, in exchange for abandoning his filibuster, the Senate would take up his pet social legislation—anti-abortion and school prayer—before the November election.

The voting rights struggle in June was mild compared with the controversy Helms and East found themselves in when President Reagan's controversial $99 billion tax increase bill came to the Senate floor. The North Carolina senators had firmly supported the 1981 White House tax reduction program. They were startled when the President reversed course, in the midst of growing recession, and endorsed tax enhancement. Helms and East initially opposed the bill, not only because they disliked tax hikes generally but also because the legislation doubled the federal tax on cigarettes from eight to sixteen cents a pack. That hit home.

Yet they felt the pressure to support the President. After the Senate had debated the bill all night, it was defeated on the first vote 49–47. At five in the morning Helms and East informed Senator Dole, the bill's chief sponsor, that they were changing their votes. After that the bill passed 50–47, with Senator Harrison Schmitt (R-N.M.), who had not voted earlier, joining Helms and East in an affirmative vote. "I realized if I didn't switch and John didn't switch, the bill would go down," Helms said afterward. "My intent had been not to support it because of the increase in taxes over the three-year period. I think that's the wrong way to go. . . . If the bill had been defeated, they would have had to start all over again and [have] a delay in any action by Congress that would have been harmful to any hopes for reviving the economy."

Later that morning Helms was awakened by a telephone call from President Reagan aboard Air Force One thanking him for his vote, but news of the switch had already reverberated in North Carolina. Helms said he thought Tar Heel tobacco farmers would understand "the politics of the situation." By the time he got home to explain his vote at the opening of the flue-cured tobacco market, though, he realized he had given his opponents a major political issue.

State Democratic Party Chairman Russell Walker said the Republican senators' vote change could mean the loss of thousands of jobs. State Agriculture Commissioner Jim Graham said he believed the tax legislation had something to do with lower tobacco prices on the opening market. Governor Hunt declared: "This is a repressive tax. The middle-income people have been hurt enough already by the Republican economic policies. A lot of states have taxes so high that this on top of everything else will hurt." Congressman Charles Rose (D-N.C.) said he was "shocked." A Nash County farmer, Grady Pridgen, said: "I remember back in the thirties when grown men were sitting around on piles of tobacco with tears running down their cheeks." Horace Kornegay, chairman of the Tobacco Institute, said the Helms and East votes were a "disappointment."

Helms lost no time replying. Speaking in Rocky Mount, he said his critics were dividing pro-tobacco forces and were themselves endangering the program. "There's no room for partisan politics where the tobacco program is concerned."

By August 6, as Congress worked to shape the final tax increase bill in conference committee, North Carolina Democrats sensed they had a potent issue. They published a newspaper advertisement labeling Helms and East the "Tobacco Tax Twins" who had "betrayed the interests of North Carolina." Dave Flaherty, GOP state chairman, accused the Democrats of "again playing demagogues" and added: "Every one of the Democratic congressmen from North Carolina voted for the same tax package when they voted to send it to a conference committee."

But Helms and East had already begun to back away from their support of the tobacco tax increase. Helms proposed a compromise, raising the tobacco tax by two cents and putting more tax on beer, wine, and alcohol to make up the difference. He said he would vote against the conference bill unless the tobacco excise was changed. East said that "having honored the presidential request, I am now in a position to reaffirm my original position."

Ultimately both Helms and East voted against the final conference bill, but the political damage had been done. Ironically the Democrats could be accused of having used the same kind of oversimplified assault on Helms and East that the latter had used in 1980 against incumbent Democratic Senator Robert Morgan on the B-1 bomber. Morgan had supported the B-1 on every vote until President Carter dropped it from his budget. Then he followed the party line and in one last balloting voted against restoring it to the budget.

Helms knew he had been stung badly. "I'm sure [Hunt's] fine hand is in the ["Tobacco Tax Twins"] ad. I'll tell you right now, they're making a mistake on this one. Those tobacco farmers who might be misled now won't be misled when we go to bat. If I don't return to the Senate, you know who'll be chairman of the Senate Agriculture Committee? Senator Richard Lugar of Indiana. By jolly, if that happens, you can bet there won't be any more tobacco program."

The tobacco tax controversy was important for North Carolinians and would follow Helms for some time; but in the Senate it was quickly forgotten when, in mid-August, debate began on his anti-abortion and school prayer legislation. Helms pondered the toughest bill that would still attract enough votes to clear the Senate. One bill that he judged would not survive would have declared a fetus to have constitutional rights under the Fourteenth Amendment, thus making abortion illegal. Ultimately the senator's bills were introduced as amendments to a measure increasing the federal debt ceiling, which Congress had to act on before the start of the next fiscal year on October 1. The amendments sought to restrict access to abortion and would bar the Supreme Court from reviewing state laws permitting public school prayer.

These amendments provoked a storm of opposition. "We have before us the greatest constitutional crisis since the Civil War," declared Senator Daniel Patrick Moynihan (D-N.Y.). "If the court is to be a subordinate branch of the United States government, of the United States Congress, then we are no longer the republic founded at Philadelphia in 1787."

The key vote on school prayer came fairly early. Senator Weicker offered an amendment to reaffirm the authority of federal courts to enforce the Constitution, notwithstanding other provisions of the prayer proposal. Helms moved to kill Weicker's amendment. His motion failed by 59–38.

After the Labor Day recess Helms's anti-abortion legislation got a boost from President Reagan. He sent letters to Capitol Hill urging lawmakers to support it and praised Senator Baker for pushing for cloture. "We must never become a society in which an individual has a right to do away with inconvenient life," the Reagan letter said. But the President's intervention failed to secure the necessary sixty votes for cloture. On September 15 an angry Jesse Helms declared he would attach amendments to other spending bills if the liberal filibuster wasn't ended. "If I don't get a vote on my two proposals, all bets are off," Helms said on the ninth day of the filibuster. "We will not be saying goodbye to this issue if we are denied a vote."

On the following day the Helms forces failed for a third time to invoke cloture. The vote was 50–44. Then Senator S. I. Hayakawa (R-Calif.) moved to table the Helms amendment. Initially the vote was 46–46, with Majority Leader Baker, who opposed abortion, withholding his vote. Then Senator James Sasser (D-Tenn.) provided the decisive vote against, after the issue seemed stalemated, making it 47–46.

Finally on September 23 the Senate refused to cut off debate on Helms's prayer proposal by a 53–45 vote, short of the 60 votes needed. Senator Baker called it "legislative gridlock." The following day the Senate voted to strip the prayer amendment from legislation increasing the federal debt ceiling and approved the debt ceiling extension.

After using all his resources, Senator Helms had met defeat on all fronts.

"We needed more horses," he said, admitting that by agreeing to delay the social issues battle for one year he "may have made a tactical mistake." When all the dust had settled, Helms's watered-down abortion bill had been set aside by the Senate, his anti-busing bill was still stuck in the House, and his prayer bill had been rejected.

Was it Helms's style and tactics that doomed his social legislation? Bill Peterson of the *Los Angeles Times–Washington Post* Syndicate quoted one senator as saying: "It's not any one single thing. It's not abortion. It's not school prayer. It's his tactics. It's what he did on tobacco. It's his fight with Tom Eagleton. It's his Congressional Club and how he makes you vote on emotional issues and then sends a bunch of money into your state and tries to beat you."

Helms, though, was defiant. After the *Wall Street Journal*'s Albert Hunt wrote a front-page story quoting a senator as saying "Jesse is reeling up here," Helms sent an unusual letter to the homes of his fellow senators. In it he said that an "honest faith" error by one of Senator Howard Baker's staff members had caused a misunderstanding about attaching the anti-abortion legislation to the debt ceiling bill. He expressed dismay about media charges that he had broken promises on how his legislation would be handled. "I am not a dishonest man. I don't renege and I haven't reneged," Helms said. "Jesse isn't reeling up here. Senator Packwood, Senator Weicker and Senator Kennedy are reeling because they find themselves in a corner."

The *Wall Street Journal* stood by its story, in which it also quoted senators as saying there was a "clear backlash building against Helms in the Senate" and that the overwhelming issue was personal pique against Helms and his "political grandstanding."

Helms remained the hero of the New Right. "He's absolutely still the generalissimo of our movement," said Peter Gemma, executive director of the National Pro-life Political Action Committee. "He's gotten us what we wanted: recorded votes."

But Senator Goldwater expressed the views of most senators after the bitter controversy had ended. "This is my 48th wedding anniversary. My wife is mad as hell, but I gotta be here worrying about what Jesse wants me to do. I don't think [Helms] has helped the conservative cause a bit. I have very serious doubts about whether the Senate ought to try and solve all the social and moral wrongs in this country." When asked to comment on Goldwater's statement, Senator Helms replied: "I admire Barry Goldwater."

Finally the *Greensboro Record*, commenting on the congressional fight and its chief protagonist, declared: "Helms is not a handsome rascal nor is he charismatic in any ordinary way. But he does have strong convictions and the courage to defend them. He is a national figure for a number of reasons. He is stridently and inflexibly conservative, which makes him a minority in a minority. In other words he sticks out in a crowd and doesn't in the least mind the exposure. He is a winning politician."

15. A Family Spat

While Jesse Helms spent most of 1982 struggling in vain to enact his New Right social programs in Congress, Jim Hunt's organization back home began gearing up for the political battles of 1984.

Hunt's people were vastly encouraged by the outcome of the 1982 general elections. Helms's National Congressional Club had invested heavily in seven Tar Heel congressional campaigns. None succeeded. Bill Cobey, the GOP hopeful from Chapel Hill, spent more than five hundred thousand dollars trying to unseat Congressman Ike Andrews, damaged by a drunken driving conviction two weeks before the election. Instead of winning additional congressional seats the Tar Heel GOP lost two of its four incumbents.

The Helms camp blame dthe poor results on the nation's pocketbook nerve. The election was not a referendum on Jesse Helms, observed Tom Ellis. It was a referendum on unemployment and the Reagan administration's economic program.

Hunt agreed that the "Reagan recession" had been a plus factor, but he also thought the voters were concerned about negative GOP campaigning. Hunt's own lieutenants even then agonized over how hard-hitting Hunt's own campaigning should be as they struggled to build a fund-raising mechanism to offset Helms's formidable money machine. One newspaper noted that Hunt himself had indulged in a bit of negativism by accusing the Fifth District congressional candidate, Anne Bagnal, of "lying" in her contest against Congressman Steve Neal.

Former congressman Richardson Preyer, a cochairman of Hunt's upcoming campaign, answered somewhat tentatively when asked about the newly organized North Carolina Campaign Fund's first nationally distributed fund-raising letter. The fund, a Hunt money mechanism, called Helms "a dangerous right-wing demagogue" engaged in "racial bigotry." "We don't want to come out on the other side of the coin to the Congressional Club," Preyer said. "I will say, on fund raising you do have to give some wheat. The direct mail people say this is the way to raise money, and sometimes the way they do it strikes you as a little tough. We are concerned and want to be very careful that we don't end up savaging people and talking in terms of anger."

In December 1982 the North Carolina Campaign Fund held its first fundraiser in Raleigh—a $250-a-couple dinner. An initial fifty-thousand-letter direct mail campaign during the summer produced twenty thousand dollars. Hunt's team hired the Falls Church, Virginia, fund-raising company of Craver, Matthews, Smith & Company to perform these duties. Also on board were pollster Peter Hart and media adviser David Sawyer.

As the behind-the-scenes organization fell into place, the Hunt group disagreed often on how much their campaign tactics should differ from those of Helms. Some advocated fighting fire with fire. Others thought matching tactics with Helms would be counterproductive. Already Hunt's organization perceived it could no longer criticize Helms's nationwide money-raising efforts. To offset the expected television blitz from Helms would require raising big money. That meant moving beyond the boundaries of North Carolina.

While juggling several projects at home, including a high-profile industry procurement trip to the Far East, the governor was becoming deeply involved in national Democratic politics. In March 1981 Democratic National Chairman Charles Manatt had appointed Hunt chairman of a sixty-nine-member national commission to study the presidential nominating process. The Hunt Commission held its first meeting in July and announced as its agenda shortening the primary period, making future conventions more deliberative, and insuring greater participation of established officeholders. This was seen by many as a reaction to the reforms that the party had made after the 1968 national convention at Chicago to open more convention seats to women and minorities. The 1980 convention, and the party's defeat that November, had convinced many Democrats that "openness" had gone too far.

By early 1982 the Hunt Commission had finished its deliberations and unveiled a detailed blueprint for party reform. The proposals restored more power in the nominating process to officeholders and party officials. They also shortened the presidential primary season from twenty to fifteen weeks and authorized states to stop using proportional representation to select delegates. Finally, the proposed reforms scrapped the "faithful delegate" stipulation and allowed delegates to attend the convention committed but not hog-tied. Some speculated that these changes would produce an outcry from special interest groups inside the party. But the recommendations were adopted by the Democratic National Committee with hardly a whisper of protest.

Hunt obtained the national exposure his press secretary, Gary Pearce, had foreseen when he urged Hunt to take the chairmanship in 1981. "I think at first there was some skepticism of him because he was from the same state as Jesse Helms, he was a big Jimmy Carter supporter and nobody knew what to expect," Pearce said. "I think he's dispelled a lot of that skepticism."

As for Hunt himself, he was delighted with the outcome. He did not disagree when a reporter suggested that the commission's recommendations had moved the party from the left and constituted a "centrist coup." The proposed changes, Hunt said, "will help us win and help us govern. They will make the convention more representative of the main stream of the party" and particularly help in more conservative states.

"I was extremely impressed with [Hunt]," said Senator Patrick Leahy (D-Vt.). "He was handling everybody from environmentalists to feminists to labor people."

In the fall of 1982 a Raleigh correspondent wrote for his newspaper that "confidence, bordering on cockiness abounds these days in the Hunt camp." The year had unfolded in a series of calamities for Senator Helms. On top of the deepening Reagan recession, the two North Carolina senators had voted to double the federal tax on tobacco in an effort to rescue President Reagan's revenue bill. All Helms's New Right social programs struck out in Congress. And seven GOP congressional candidates had been defeated in North Carolina.

As the Ninety-seventh Congress shuffled to a finish, Senator Helms, remembering his daddy's dictum never to give up, took up one more lost cause. He organized a filibuster against the Reagan-backed five-cent-a-gallon gasoline tax increase. "It's another dumping on the consumer," Helms said, "taking money out of the economy." On a similar gas tax hike his own Congressional Club had fought Governor Hunt in Raleigh the preceding year. The Helms effort involved a small group of senators who, in the words of one reporter, "used every twist within the Senate rules to delay or block the inevitable at a time when exhausted senators and House members were eager to get home for Christmas." At one point, as the filibuster droned into its second week, Senate Majority Leader Howard Baker pulled the bill from the floor. It appeared Helms and his associates had won. But then, according to reports, Baker decided that if Helms won on the gasoline tax, he would be able to paralyze the Senate at will in 1983. He returned the bill to the floor.

Toward the end President Reagan called Helms urging him to drop the filibuster. Helms said of the call later: "I reminded the President that he once said it would take a palace coup for him to support a tax bill like this. 'Mr. President,' I said, 'when did the palace coup occur?'" Finally, late one night, after Helms had voted to keep his colleagues in Washington over Christmas if that was what it took, Senator Baker filed his cloture petition. The Senate voted 81–5 to cut off debate.

After cloture had been invoked, Senator Helms walked over to Senator Alan Simpson (R-Wyo.), who had earlier called Helms's unrelenting efforts to kill the tax bill an "obdurate, obnoxious performance." "Let's be friends," Helms said. As other senators watched, Simpson refused to get up from his chair or seal the handshake in the accustomed fashion. He stared at the man standing over him for several seconds without saying a word, and soon Helms turned away.

Other strong criticism came from both sides of the aisle. "Going to these extremes was a serious mistake," said Senator Lloyd Bentsen (D-Tex.). "I think Helms and East hurt themselves. I can't recall a time when personal feeling was that intense." "There will be a veritable phalanx of opposition against farm measures and other legislation of direct interest to North Carolina," Senator Simpson said. "The Helms group was a minority within a minority within a minority."

But Helms was as defiant as ever. "I didn't come here to win a popularity contest among senators," he said. "It is not unheard of for a senator to be the subject of wrath. The Senate, when all is said and done, is a family. There are spats. I admit it was a heated one last night." Helms said his opposition was not intended to inconvenience anyone, but the tax increase is "bad legislation that will cost more jobs than it will create."

Governor Hunt, who had had his own troubles over a gasoline tax hike earlier, refused to be drawn out on the Helms filibuster, even though the entire North Carolina Democratic delegation voted against the hike. Hunt knew that North Carolina's highway system needed the money. "I will not take a position," he said, "because I'm not up there."

As 1982 ended, Senator Helms's fortunes had sagged. One poll taken by the University of North Carolina Journalism School in October showed 51 percent of North Carolina voters would favor Hunt in a senatorial race against Helms; 35 percent preferred Helms. A year earlier Hunt's lead had been narrower (46 percent to 38 percent).

After the November election the *Raleigh News & Observer*'s cartoonist Dwane Powell, a belligerent Helms foe, portrayed the senator with lumps on his head and Senator East in his pocket, saying: "Tell me again, John, about the time I made the cover of *Time* Magazine."

Yet Helms's backers were undismayed. Paul Taylor, writing for the *Los Angeles Times-Washington Post* Syndicate, noted the paradox of Helms's New Right: "One of the secrets of the Congressional Club style of fund raising on 'hot button' or emotional social issues is that the harder its champions fall—Helms took some massive spills on abortion and school prayer in the Senate last month—the faster the checks pour in." And down in Raleigh Tom Ellis took a philosophical view. "The papers claim Jesse Helms is an embarrassment to the state," he said. "Hell, Claude Sitton [*News and Observer* editor] is an embarrassment to me. That's just another way of saying you don't agree with someone."

Congressman Henry Hyde (R-Ill.) put it stronger: "If Jesse Helms was crusading for liberal causes, they would have erected a stained-glass window in his honor at the Brookings Institution. He is reviled because he is unyielding in his fight on behalf of traditional values. One Jesse Helms is worth a thousand political opportunists." Howard Phillips, director of the Conservative Caucus, agreed: "Jesse Helms is unique. The only battles we lose are the ones we fail to fight, and Jesse can never be accused of failing to fight. That's why he's our most valuable player."

As for Jesse Helms himself, he acknowledged that the Republicans "took a beating." But then he added that despite the year's misfortunes it "would be no cakewalk" for Jim Hunt to unseat him in 1984.

16. "The Old Jim Crow"

As 1983 arrived, the *Washingtonian Magazine*, a sophisticated journal of the capital establishment, concluded that Jesse Helms's defiant Senate performance as the "Grinch Who Stole Christmas" had wrecked his career. It labeled the senior senator from North Carolina as the "luckiest candidate not to have been running in 1982." The *Washington Post* followed by putting Helms on its "out" list for the fading year while citing Helms's Tar Heel colleague, Elizabeth Hanford Dole, as definitely "in." But all this publicity about the senator's fading influence only enhanced what President Reagan called Helms's "lonely crusader's role."

The new year had scarcely begun before the senator unveiled his own plan to rescue the financially troubled Social Security system, even though President Reagan's own bipartisan commission looking into its problems had just announced its recommendations. In a "major" statewide television address, Helms differed sharply with the commission. He proposed a plan that would allow everyone to set up his own "individual retirement security accounts," similar to the new Individual Retirement Accounts, or IRAs. Individuals would invest their money in savings and loans, banks, or other private financial institutions. The current compulsory Social Security system would be slowly phased out so that by 1984 employers and employees would be paying part of their Social Security taxes to private accounts instead of to the federal government. "In the long run," Helms declared, "we want to replace what is now a taxation system with a private savings system where participants would own their own accounts."

Helms said his plan would give recipients roughly three times the benefits that the existing program offered and let their families inherit the remainder when they died. The bipartisan commission's proposals, Helms said, reflected "a total absence of creativity and imagination and, worse still, a lack of understanding of where they would lead the U.S. economy."

The senator's attempt at "creativity" ran into heavy opposition, however. The main criticism centered on the revenue short-fall which would result. Helms offered elaborate suggestions for spanning the cost gap—bringing all federal employees under the umbrella, delaying and pro-rating cost-of-living adjustments, and even borrowing sums from the general fund. Harsher criticism came from those who charged that Helms sought to wreck Social Security and substitute an uncertain "voluntary" package. "It would throw the nation's elderly and widows to the mercy of the money markets and make the U.S. government guarantee the results," charged Congressman Charles Rose (D-N.C.). Other critics said the program was "designed for the better educated citizen" who had a knowledge of banking and investments and that it could be catastrophic if economic conditions darkened.

The criticism was so heavy that by mid-March Helms acknowledged that he could muster only ten to fifteen favorable votes in the Senate. He withdrew the plan on the condition that it be "studied" by the Treasury Department. Meanwhile the Social Security study commission's proposals passed the House and eventually the Senate.

Still, though, Helms remained undismayed. In June President Reagan showed up at a major thousand-dollar-a-plate fund-raising dinner in Washington, and lavishly praised the senator. Helms was once a "lonely crusader but his army of conservatives has grown steadily," the President said. "He grew into a lion-hearted leader of a great and growing army."

Almost simultaneously Governor Hunt launched his own big-money solicitation outside North Carolina with a thousand-dollar-a-plate dinner at the Georgetown home of Mrs. Averill Harriman, chairman of an organization called Democrats for the Eighties.

In early summer the Helms camp began an elaborate media advertising campaign aimed at Hunt. It was designed, Tom Ellis explained, "to dim the glow of Hunt's image as a saint." Citing the governor's nascent fund-raising activities outside North Carolina, it labeled him a hypocrite for earlier criticizing Helms's out-of-state soliciting. It also identified Hunt as one of a crowd of "rabid liberals" and linked him with the black registration drive of the Reverend Jesse Jackson. The general impression was that "Jim Hunt is a real sweet fellow and Jesse's a real mean fellow that votes no a lot," Ellis said. "If you didn't stop to look at the bits and pieces, you'd think he ain't never done nothing wrong, that Hunt's a saint."

In mid-July a Helms advertisement, published in 150 small daily and weekly newspapers outside urban areas, featured a photograph of Jackson visiting in Governor Hunt's office along with the comment by Jackson that he hoped to register two hundred thousand black voters in North Carolina. "Ask yourself," the ad said, "Is this a proper use of taxpayer funds?"

Governor Hunt blasted the ads. "They are mud-slinging in its worst sense. They appeal to the worst. They appeal to fear."

"Who's the racist?" responded David Flaherty, state GOP chairman, "the guy out trying to register black voters so they can elect him to the Senate or the guy who's just saying what's going on?"

The Helms organization did not confine its efforts to blasts at Hunt on the race issue. That same summer it initiated its own voter-registration drive, featuring the Reverend Jerry Falwell, the Lynchburg, Virginia, head of the Moral Majority. In June Helms, Falwell, and Lamarr Mooneyham, leader of the North Carolina Moral Majority, conducted a two-day, five-city foray across North Carolina promoting the registration of two hundred thousand new conservative voters. The barnstorming campaign, coordinated through cooperating fundamentalist churches, included press conferences and receptions. "We happen to feel that Senator Jesse Helms is a national treasure, not just the property of the North Carolina electorate," Falwell said. "We're out to register everybody who breathes."

"The only way to keep a political blackmailer like the Reverend Jackson from acquiring the kind of political clout that he needs to implement his racist agenda," said Mooneyham, was to mount a conservative drive.

Senator Helms played the role as genial, supportive host. He wore a "Senator NO" watch with a red-white-and-blue watchband on his right wrist and generally avoided mentioning Hunt or any major issue except abortion. Rather he concentrated his attacks on the biased "major media" and urged a return to morality, usually to ringing cries of "Amen" and "Praise the Lord" from his enthusiastic audiences.

Falwell got more specific by denouncing AIDS as the scourge of homosexual sinners and the "20 million cases of herpes." "If the Lord does not punish America for some of the things going on," Falwell said at one stop, "and we do not correct them, we ought to apologize to Sodom and Gomorrah." Comments on other subjects were equally scorching; he denounced Harvard (which he called the "Kremlin on the Charles"), Hugh Hefner, "Hanoi Jane" Fonda, the Sandinista government of Nicaragua, Cuba, union bosses, Vietnam protesters, and "kooky outfits" like the American Civil Liberties Union.

Both registration drives compiled impressive statistics. Falwell said that since its founding in 1979 the Moral Majority had registered 4.5 million Americans. During 1982 the Democratic-controlled election boards in North Carolina registered almost seventy thousand new black voters, boosting black registration by 17 percent. But election officials said that only 63 percent of eligible blacks were registered, even after that.

In September Helms played a peripheral role in a dramatic international incident. He narrowly missed being on the ill-fated Korean Airlines jumbo jet flight 007 shot down by a Soviet fighter when it strayed into Soviet airspace. The incident bolstered his anti-Communist crusade because it seemed to confirm what he had been saying about the Russians.

Helms was on his way to represent the United States at a conference observing the thirtieth anniversary of the United States–South Korea mutual defense pact. Only a scheduling conflict kept him off the doomed aircraft, which carried other members of the congressional delegation. Helms's plane was on the ground at Anchorage, Alaska, at the same time as KAL 007 and took off eleven minutes behind it.

In Seoul Helms condemned the Soviet attack as a "barbarity" that cannot be tolerated. "If it's not an act of war," he said, "it'll do till the real thing comes along." The senator stopped short of suggesting United States military response, but he recommended a series of economic and diplomatic sanctions that went considerably beyond President Reagan's.

Some one hundred supporters met the senator and his wife at Raleigh-

Durham Airport as they returned from Seoul. Helms had already made dramatic headlines in the world press by describing a touching encounter with two passengers on the doomed flight. They were young sisters, ages five and three, whom he met with their parents during the refueling stop at Anchorage. "I have never seen two more lovable little children. They were just beautiful. We talked and I played a silly little game on their arms—the kind of game I play with my grandchildren. They loved it." The last time Helms saw the children, he said, they were "blowing me kisses. . . . It's hard for me to think of what happened to them," he said, his voice choking with emotion. "I've been on a rollercoaster of emotions since then."

Even fourteen months before the 1984 senatorial campaign the black-voter sensitivity drive spawned by Jesse Jackson had begun to emerge as a key issue. A bitter encounter between diametrically opposed forces in the same area occurred in the fall of 1983. Senator Helms, as usual, was right in the middle of it.

By mid-September the senator had decided to lead a major campaign against a bill making Dr. Martin Luther King's birthday a national holiday. Similar legislation had emerged periodically since the civil rights leader's assassination in 1968. All during the early sixties in his television editorials, Helms had blasted King, ostensibly because of his "widespread Communist connections" but also because Helms identified him as a racial troublemaker.

The holiday issue was a typically volatile vehicle for Helms's maneuvers. Many Americans had argued that, all racial considerations aside, the country already had too many national holidays. "Martin Luther King was a great American," said Omaha, Nebraska, Mayor Mike Boyle. "His memory should be commemorated in some way, but holidays are expensive. It's too bad there is not another way to remember someone, besides giving government workers another day off."

Washington Post Writers Group Columnist Edwin Yoder, Jr., a longtime Helms foe in his native North Carolina, wrote: "Dr. King was a prophet, a man of good works, a thoroughly wholesome influence in American life, and the years may some day ratify the view that he should stand with Washington and Lincoln. But before John Adams and Thomas Jefferson? The time is not yet. . . . National holidays should be strictly reserved for figures, long gone, of absolutely undebatable magnitude."

So Senator Helms had an opportunity this time to "stand on principle," as he put it, without going to the extreme. He could take a position which satisfied many of his critics and never resort to more sensitive objections to the legislation which his opponents might label "racist." But Helms was never an individual to avoid head-on collisions or modify his rhetoric to mollify moderates.

As a start, he organized a full-scale filibuster on the floor of the Senate, seeking either to attach amendments to the holiday bill or send it back to committee. In the process he assailed King's reputation in searing language. "The legacy of Dr. King," he said, "was really division, not love.... Dr. King's action-oriented Marxism, about which he was cautioned by the leaders of this country—including the President at that time [John Kennedy]—is not compatible with the concepts of this country." Without referring directly to the race issue Helms insisted that the holiday would cost taxpayers $962 million in lost productivity by government employees and would generate a $4.3 billion loss in the private sector.

Helms had been warned by some advisers that opposing the King holiday could be "political suicide." Helms himself said afterward that Ellis had "serious reservations" about his offensive on the floor of the Senate. But he waded right in, glad to get another chance to needle his favorite adversary, Senator Ted Kennedy.

At the start of his filibuster Helms put 350 pages of FBI documents about King on the desk of every senator. Senator Daniel Patrick Moynihan (D-N.Y.) promptly labeled them "trash" and threw them to the Senate floor. Senator Kennedy accused Helms of making "false and inaccurate" statements. Helms responded by invoking a Senate rule against personal attacks on colleagues. When Senate Majority Leader Baker intervened, Kennedy agreed to drop the word *false*. Later Helms said of this: "I thought I would teach him [Kennedy] a little something about the rules of the Senate."

A more dramatic collision between Helms and Kennedy came later. As his filibuster proceeded, Helms requested that raw FBI files on King, which a federal judge in 1977 had ordered sealed for fifty years, be made available to the Senate. He initiated a lawsuit to open the files, which contained illegal bugging and wiretap transcripts of the slain civil rights leader's telephone and motel conversations, authorized by Attorney General Robert Kennedy. Helms insisted the files would sustain his charges that King was a Communist sympathizer, but Judge John Lewis Smith refused to unseal the evidence. A congressional committee which had reviewed the sixty-five thousand pages of files in 1978 had found no evidence that would label King a Communist sympathizer. David Garrow, a professor at Chapel Hill who had written a book about King and the FBI, reported that the sealed tapes contained only "off-color humor and other utterances that, while embarrassing if put on public record, would in no way impinge on Dr. King's basic moral character."

In mid-October, in his final effort to derail the bill, Helms reported that several senators told him they would vote for it only because they were under "political pressure." Helms also attacked Senator Kennedy for his prior criticisms and added that Kennedy's brothers, John and Robert, had tried to warn King about his Communist associations. Of Senator Kennedy's criticisms, Helms said: "His argument is with his dead brother who was President and his dead brother who was attorney general and not with the senator from North Carolina." Kennedy's face reddened, and he bristled in his seat. Senator Baker hurried over to speak with him. Then the Massachusetts senator, his voice cracking with emotion, accused Helms of using his late brothers as "part of a smear campaign. . . . If Robert Kennedy were here today, he would be the first person to say it was wrong to wiretap Martin Luther King. . . . He would be the first to stand for this holiday."

When the Helms motion to return the King holiday bill to the Judiciary Committee finally faced the Senate later that day, it failed 76–12, thus foreshadowing passage. On his sixty second birthday, October 18, Jesse Helms continued to criticize the federal court for its failure to open the sealed files. The Senate, he said, needed the documents prior to voting to make Martin Luther King "a role model for future generations."

As the King legislation came up for approval, Senator Kennedy again took the floor. "I am appalled," he said, "at the attempt of some to misappropriate the memory of my brother Robert Kennedy and misuse it as part of this smear campaign. Those who never cared for him in life now invoke his name when he can no longer speak for himself."

As these dramatic confrontations unfolded on the Senate floor, President Reagan, who had earlier promised to sign the bill if it passed, refrained from comment. Finally in his press conference he was asked to comment on Senator Helms's allegations that King was a Communist sympathizer. "We'll know in about 35 years, won't we?" the President replied. "I don't fault Senator Helms's sincerity with regard to wanting the records opened up. I think that he's motivated by a feeling that if we're going to have a national holiday named for any American, when it's been named for only one American in all our history until this time, that he feels we should know everything we should know about an individual."

But then the President went on to acknowledge that the "record cannot be opened because an agreement was reached between the family and the government." Reagan said he would not "set a precedent" by breaking "agreements of that kind." He said he would have preferred a day in honor of King "similar to, say, Lincoln's birthday, which is not technically a national holiday. King's birthday is symbolic of what was a real crisis in our history and a discrimination that is pretty foreign to what is normal with us. . . . I think the symbolism of it is worthy of this." He concluded that he would "sign it [the bill] when it reaches my desk."

The issue was settled, but Helms supporters and critics continued to weigh the significance of his performance. In the Senate itself the bipartisan reaction was emotionally negative—including such comments as "demeaning," "filth and obscenities," "nauseating," and "race-baiting." Senator Bill Bradley (D-N.J.) sounded the most caustic criticism. He likened Helms's image to that of "Bull Connor and his dogs" and said he was playing up to "the old Jim Crow."

Back home in North Carolina the response was milder and more cautious. Gubernatorial Press Secretary Gary Pearce said the governor would have no comment on Helms's Senate role, but added that Hunt supported the King bill, along with President Reagan. So did the overwhelming majority of the North Carolina General Assembly. The House voted 107 to 3 and the Senate 44 to 0 to make King's birthday a legal holiday in North Carolina.

A Raleigh reporter interviewed a number of Tar Heel political observers who thought Helms's high profile on the King issue would further mobilize black support for Governor Hunt. Others thought Helms had solidified his support among bedrock conservatives, particularly in eastern North Carolina, where the race issue remained sensitive. "It is probably a wash-out," said one conservative Democrat with no ties to either Hunt or Helms. "It ends up as neutral. It did ignite the black vote. It may also have firmed up his conservative support." Others thought it was a shrewd move on Helms's part because he had "nothing to lose" and "polarization works to his advantage," helping with money and recruiting volunteers.

Senator Helms himself was spirited in his critique. The King bill passed, he said, "in an atmosphere of political intimidation and harassment. People were scared to death of political retaliation." He himself, he said, had "acted on personal beliefs about what he thought was right. . . . Now I think the black citizens are shooting themselves in the foot by not playing one party against the other. . . . I face reality. They [blacks] have a history of voting Democratic down the line."

Throughout his career Senator Helms had insisted he always put principles first, but the Martin Luther King controversy showed signs of the political shrewdness that usually accompanied his strategies. Early in October Helms had agreed to drop his filibuster if Senate Majority Leader

Baker would allow a vote on a vital Senate Agriculture Committee farm target-price support bill. When Helms dropped the filibuster, Baker brought the much-lobbied bill, which included tobacco price supports, to the floor, where it was promptly passed. Helms called the bill a delicate compromise and said following its passage: "We have taken a giant step toward reducing [farm] surpluses." Helms said later: "I did not propose the quid pro quo. I just worked out the window of opportunity." Back home in North Carolina, David Flaherty put it another way. The senator dropped the filibuster, he said, because "he still puts North Carolina first. . . . The obvious priority is our farmers."

Tar Heel-born newspaper columnist Yoder had a different view. "[Senator Helms] has prospered before on negativism," he wrote "Depend on [him] to contaminate a serious argument with debating points from the gutter. . . . For Helms it is a matter of political survival, cost what it may in racial division. Divide and conquer has been the Helms way for 35 years."

Both Tom Ellis and Helms responded sharply to charges by State Democratic Chairman David Price that the senator was engaged in "the politics of red-baiting and racial innuendo." "What Price is doing," Ellis declared, "is the same thing [Senator] Kennedy is doing, and that is to intimidate our political leaders by saying if you disagree with a holiday for Dr. King, you are a racist. I don't think that is fair or correct. I think you can be against the holiday without being a racist or a red-baiter or anything else." Helms himself said in a Washington news conference: "I am not a racist, and I am not a bigot. Ask any black that knows me, and they will tell you I am not."

Opinion remained divided on King and the holiday issue. But the furor raised by North Carolina's senior senator one year before his re-election struggle proved that the race issue, while seemingly dormant at times, always lay just beneath the surface, ready to be energized.

17. That Old-time Religion

Hodding Carter, Jr., wrote thirty years ago that "the South may be described as the Bible Belt in the same offhand derisive way that the Eastern Seaboard can be identified as the Barbiturate Belt, the roaring, raw cities of the Midwest as the Tommy-gun Belt and the West Coast the Divorce Belt." Time has moved on in all these regions. Changes have eroded the stereotypes. But the South, including North Carolina, still clings to the old-time religion, and any politician who ignores that does so at his own peril.

Much of the grassroots strength of Helms and Hunt could be traced to their religious roots. One Baptist minister went so far as to note that both Jim Hunt and Jesse Helms were "almost peas in a pod" when it came to theology. "They're both pious, they believe in personal morality, they're very duty oriented. They're based in the same religious tradition. But it comes down to the kind of social consciousness they've developed off the theology."

Helms, who grew up in the First Baptist Church of Monroe and became a member of the Hayes-Barton Baptist Church after moving to Raleigh, constantly sprinkled his politics with religious themes. His enthusiastic alliance with the Reverend Jerry Falwell and the Moral Majority gave him a strong wedge among fundamentalist church members, many of whom had not been politically active in the past. But when Falwell decided to push politics from the pulpit, he provided Helms an ideal vehicle for his moralistic crusading.

Helms established close contacts with conservative ministers who shared his alarm about "atheistic socialism." In the senator's book *When Free Men Shall Stand*, he outlined how Christianity is incompatible with "political liberalism" and explained how the United States was founded for "the glory of God and the advancement of the Christian faith." At one point Helms's book is explicit about why he fights "liberalism" so zealously: "Atheism and socialism—or liberalism which tends in the same direction—are inseparable entities. When you have men who no longer believe that God is in charge of human affairs, you have men attempting to take the place of God by means of the Superstate. The all-provident Government, which these liberals constantly invoke, is the modern-day version of Baal."

At a prayer breakfast at Greensboro's First Baptist Church in 1977, Helms expounded on this theme: "We cannot walk the streets of our cities without being assaulted by pornographic and obscene literature. We cannot watch a movie or television without fear that our children will be exposed to all that is low and base in life. We cannot enter the public schools of this country without noticing the total absence of any religious influence in the classroom."

These themes tied in directly with Helms's campaign to install organized prayer in the public schools and to outlaw abortion. They also gave his political rallies, often held in connection with prayer breakfasts, a Billy Sunday evangelistic aura and a vision of Armageddon. At a Raleigh dinner in 1978 a speaker told the audience how Jesse Helms had brought him closer to Christ. "For a moment," a reporter wrote, "Helms was choked up and bowed his head to compose himself as the crowd thundered its approval."

Governor Hunt likewise took his Marsh Swamp Free Will Baptist upbringing seriously; but he emerged with a different emphasis. He grew up in a rural family where church-going and praying were as natural as day and night, but his religion gave him a social consciousness. The influence of a book about a medical missionary had led Hunt and his wife to spend two years in Nepal. Hunt grew up among Methodists and Baptists, but he and Carolyn joined the Presbyterian Church after they returned to Wilson.

Hunt once spoke of his religious beliefs at a United Church Ministries meeting in Goldsboro: "We are the agents of God's will on this earth," he said, and that forms "the core of our beliefs in this country, our spiritual, our social and our political beliefs. We can no longer remain complacent about the hunger of our children and elderly right here in our own backyards. The family of man not only shares the same planet. It now shares the same house. Hunger concerns me as a Christian."

Hunt's religious beliefs also influenced his work as governor. In February 1982 when he named a statewide task force to study drunk driving, a key appointee was Southern Baptist editor Marse Grant, who had waged a life-long crusade against alcohol. When that task force recommended strengthening the criminal laws against drunken driving, the governor invited fifteen hundred religious leaders from across the state to join his campaign. Some three hundred attended meetings held at the Governor's Mansion and in Asheville.

Grant recalled that at the meetings "the governor took the bill just like a schoolteacher and explained it." Then, after a question-and-answer period, Hunt led the closing prayer at each meeting. "One of our most conservative pastors, Wendel G. Davis of Fairview Baptist Church in Statesville, said, 'Governor, I just want to tell you that I'm glad I've lived to see the day when my governor can preach and pray like a Baptist preacher.' "

Hunt linked the campaign against drunken driving with the church's social outreach. Out of his task force report and the meetings with ministers came the essential proposals of what later became the governor's Safe Roads Act. Hunt called on the ministers to work with their congregations to change attitudes about driving and drinking. We must dole out "swift, sure and severe punishment," he said. "We will seek stricter enforcement and stiffer penalties to save lives. It is time to say that this business of getting into an automobile after somebody has been drinking and become impaired is unacceptable conduct and . . . we as citizens are no longer willing to overlook it." The legislation also proposed raising the drinking age from eighteen to nineteen.

Five months later these ideas from Hunt's task force were incorporated in the Safe Roads Act, which passed the General Assembly. Hunt had again used his political acumen, this time combined with religious zeal. The legislation contained controversial provisions, among them mandatory jail sentences, and the constitutionality of certain aspects was questioned. In essence, though, Hunt's main points prevailed.

In the 1983 General Assembly Hunt also endorsed additional appropriations for community colleges, for his micro-electronics program, and for upgrading mathematics and science instruction in public schools. Goaded by increased grumbling from state employees, especially teachers, the governor recommended lifting the salary freeze mandated by worsening economic conditions. But in his state of the state message the governor noted that "cold winds of a national recession [are] blowing through every home in North Carolina." He called his budget "the most austere this state has seen in a decade. . . . There is a limit to our financial resources, but no limit to our hopes."

In February 1983, shortly before Governor Hunt collapsed during a speech and was rushed to a hospital for an appendectomy, he advanced another cause about which he felt strongly, combatting mounting crime. In releasing the recommendations of the Governor's Commission on Crime, Hunt declared: "We cannot rest until every single person in North Carolina is safe from the young hood on drugs, the rapist who lurks in the shadows and the violent criminal who is out on bail."

Senator Helms did not ignore this activity. He knew that such issues had political appeal. After Hunt supporters published a full-page advertisement in state newspapers charging that Helms and East were "trying to cut Social Security benefits of one million North Carolinians," Helms challenged Hunt to a series of debates on subjects ranging from Social Security to America's moral priorities. Hunt replied that he would make a decision on debates after he had decided whether to run for the Senate.

By this time partisans on both sides analyzed every emerging issue for its potential political fallout. The governor surprised some supporters by opposing the widely publicized nuclear freeze. "We should negotiate from a position of strength," Hunt said. When his pronouncements were criticized, he added: "I'm taking a stand I believe is right. We have to be strong in this world to keep peace."

From the Helms camp Tom Ellis recalled that Hunt in 1982 had identified himself with nuclear freeze activists and declared "Ground Zero Week" in North Carolina. Ellis noted that this observance was supported by the National Council of Churches, the United Auto Workers, and the New World Foundation—all "ultra-liberal bodies." "I can't blame Governor Hunt for trying to put a lot of distance between himself and some of the people who thought up 'Ground Zero Week' promoting the nuclear freeze. . . . Governor Hunt mystifies us again with somehow popping up on both sides of an issue—a tough act but one that pleases everybody if you can get away with it."

In March 1983, at the National Governors' Association meeting in Washington, Hunt again put distance between himself and the traditional "liberal" posture. He voted against a resolution to reduce the federal deficit by cutting the defense budget in half. A Hunt spokesman in Raleigh explained that the governor agreed that the deficit had to be reduced, but thought it a mistake for the governors to "sit down and write the defense budget for the President. They just don't have enough information to do that."

About that time Hamilton Jordan, not long retired from his Washington post with Jimmy Carter, noted that Ronald Reagan would be tough to beat in 1984. "I think we can beat him," Jordan said. "But we won't defeat him if we nominate a candidate that looks like a doctrinaire liberal." He thought Hunt had the necessary mainstream qualities. "Jim Hunt is the most important Democratic governor we have in the country. He's built this centrist philosophy in the South that we need nationwide."

While aides implied that Hunt was a "closet hawk" on defense, other Tar Heels were bemused by Hunt's political slipperiness. Of the nuclear freeze issue one generally pro-Hunt newspaper editor wrote: "This is typical of the way Hunt works. He seizes a few fights he thinks he can win and goes to the 15th round, if necessary. But woe to those who may be looking to the governor for vocal support on other issues, such as the nuclear freeze if they don't conform to his agenda."

The Helms camp was alarmed enough by Hunt's efforts to increase its already heavy television ad schedule. In the spring the theme centered again on the governor's earlier castigation of Helms for taking political contributions from outside North Carolina. In 1982, these ads charged, Hunt had been saying that such contributions created "obligations that you ought not to have." Noting Hunt's current out-of-state fund-raising, they charged he was a hypocrite. "What obligations does politician Jim Hunt now have to these out-of-state liberal special interests?"

The governor's camp responded by saying that Helms was waging a "negative campaign" and avoiding issues. Richardson Preyer, chairman of Hunt's North Carolina Campaign Fund, observed that the fund would like to raise all its money in North Carolina but that doing so was impossible. It couldn't scrape up enough money to fight the Congressional Club, which "last year raised $9 million, most of it from out of the state." Preyer also said he regretted the first fund-raising letter of the North Carolina Fund, which had castigated Helms personally. "There are some things we've done that we're not going to do again."

By mid-year Hunt's senior counselors had concluded that the North Carolina Fund was more trouble than it was worth. On July 1 1983 its leaders announced it would disband on August 1 without attaining its $3 million goal through fund-raising and direct mail. Judge Preyer explained that a recent opinion of the Federal Elections Commission precluded the fund's publishing anti-Helms advertising unless it classified funds to pay for the ads as contributions (and this came under rules which limited such contributions by a group or individual). "I welcome the FEC ruling, even though it contributes to our decision to cease activity," Preyer said. "I believe it makes for a better political process by strengthening the role of the political party and limiting the role of the independent committee. We challenge the Congressional Club to play by the new rules."

As soon as Hunt recovered from a gall bladder operation in September 1983, he speeded up his campaign planning. At the Vance-Aycock Dinner in late October he unveiled a program called the "Four E's"—the economy, education, the elderly, and the environment. "I want you to talk about the Four E's," he said. "That is what it will take to carry us to victory in 1984."

In late October Hunt met with key leaders to plan the 1984 campaign. In meetings at Asheville and Burlington he conferred with about one hundred supporters to "touch base with our people in the counties," to urge them especially to meet their fund-raising quotas. Hunt's goal was $1.5 million by the end of 1983 and another $1.5 million by March 1984. All his senior advisers, including his wife, Carolyn, accompanied Hunt on these trips.

Simultaneously both the Helms and the Hunt organizations began new media blitzes to encourage their supporters. Helms's re-election committee dispatched letters to several thousand Democrats charging that Hunt was too close to organized labor. (The AFL-CIO had endorsed the governor in October at its Asheville convention.) Signed by the "Democrats for Jesse Committee," retired Superior Court Judge Albert Cowper of Kinston, chairman, the letter said: "Ask yourself would Jim Hunt stand up to the union bosses who have given him so much support? I think you know the answer." The governor's press secretary, Gary Pearce, replied: "Hunt's labor support is based on the governor's economic development record in North Carolina and comes despite his strong support of the state's right-to-work law."

In late November 1983 the state Democratic Party launched its first anti-Helms media drive. In part it was designed to boost the morale of frustrated Hunt supporters, who had watched the Helms television campaign for months. In part it was an experiment to sample the waters. "What we wanted to say," said Democratic State Party Chairman David Price, was "here are some economic issues that need to be raised." One ad said: "If you make more than $50,000 a year, then you've got a senator in Washington working for your needs. . . . If you worry about Social Security . . . then you ought to be worried about what your senator is doing in Washington." Another ad attacked Helms for voting to double the federal tax on cigarettes and making enemies for farmers. "Who is Jesse Helms working for?" it asked.

The Hunt ads created a furor in the Helms camp. Helms's press aide, Claude Allen, appeared at a Democratic press conference to distribute copies of a letter Helms had written Hunt accusing him of hiding on the issues. "Jim, stop trying to hide. Let's discuss the issues man-to-man." This was a reference to Helms's call for television debates. "Where does Jim Hunt stand on forced busing? School prayer?" The Helms forces then threatened to make formal complaint to the Federal Communications Commission about inaccuracies in Hunt ads.

The Hunt camp was elated. "I don't understand why Senator Helms is so upset that the Democratic Party is using ads on the issues and his record," Hunt said. "He has been criticizing me for eight months."

In mid-November Senator Helms began joshing his opponent. In a Winston-Salem speech he claimed to be puzzled. He used to receive business letters from a certain man in Raleigh, he said, who often added flattering handwritten postscripts saying such things as "I admire the kind of man you are" or "I admire the kind of life you lead." But Helms said he hadn't received any of those letters lately. "What's changed?" he asked. "What's changed is that he [Hunt] means to run for the Senate. He's been very complimentary until he got the Senate bug."

By Thanksgiving Hunt was no longer making a secret of his intention to run for the Senate. When pressed, however, he added that a formal announcement would come early the next year.

In the meantime George Bush visited the only state whose GOP delegates had refused to give him its votes for vice president in 1980. He came to pay his respects to the man who got those votes. At a $250-a-ticket dinner in Greensboro, Bush endorsed Helms and said he and Reagan would win next year. In response, the senator called Bush "a darn nice guy," which, he added, is "the highest compliment one politician can pay another."

In its December 31 issue the *Economist* of London listed Jesse Helms as one of six Republicans likely to seek the presidency if Reagan stepped down. When asked to comment, the senator modestly said: "I'm not at all interested. I love the Senate and its traditions. I enjoy the work and I know a little about it. If I leave, I'll leave public life altogether."

Epochal Battle or Mud Fight?

18. "I'll Carry It"

As the 1984 election year dawned, the national press sensed either an epochal battle or a mud fight brewing in North Carolina. They sent some of their best reporters to find out. In January the *Wall Street Journal* led off a page-one dispatch from Greenville: "The evening offered barbecued chicken, corn sticks, iced tea and Jesse Helms. Catfish Hunter couldn't make it, but for the North Carolina senator the evening was still a sentimental journey back to the Moose lodge where he began his first Senate campaign on a rainy night 12 years ago."

The *Journal* called the Carolina campaign a showdown between Old South and New South. But North Carolinians knew better. Helms, the small-town police chief's son, had few of the trappings of patrician Old South culture. His brassy, often pious conservatism lauded the nostalgia of the good old days; but it mainly offered a mixture of anti-Communist, anti-government rhetoric with occasional evangelistic religious overtones. Helms, however, never hesitated to use government power in his own behalf where it suited his purposes (for example, tobacco subsidies and organized prayer in schools).

Hunt, on the other hand, dealt cautiously with the conventional liberal symbols of the New South, even though his roots were in FDR's New Deal. From his earliest days Hunt had protected his right flank—a lesson he learned in the Sanford and Preyer gubernatorial campaigns of the 1960s. National reporters wanted to call Hunt "liberal"—since New South versus Old South made the image simple and dramatic. Yet Hunt always leaned toward the middle, so much so that he often straddled the fence. His moderation, which seemed liberal to some Tar Heels, was occasionally called "metooism" by newspapers like the *Raleigh News and Observer.*

From the start Senator Helms's strategy had been to push Hunt into far left field. His attacks identified Hunt with "limousine liberals," black activists, labor bosses, and gay liberationists. But the governor constantly dodged these associations. Sometimes this made him appear waffling and fuzzy. On occasion Helms described Hunt as the windshield wiper candidate: "first one way and then the other"—but Hunt's closest associates knew he had always been centrist, which made him both appealing and vulnerable.

Helms's expensive television campaign ten months before the election centered on one question: "Where do you stand, Jim?" Originally his strategists had hoped to come down hard on such issues as school prayer, national defense, Reagan's Central America policy, and the nuclear freeze, but in all these areas Hunt refused to be penned into a "liberal" position. The Helms people were reduced to ridiculing Hunt's fund-raising rallies in such out-of-state spots as Georgetown, Park Avenue, and Hollywood. They linked him with sinister liberal forces, but found it difficult to document specifics.

When Hunt supported the Martin Luther King holiday, Helms made what capital he could of it, even though the issue was a double-edged sword in the South. Some of the senator's backers worried about writing off the black vote so dramatically, but Helms had long ago taken his stand on that subject. He had no intention of changing.

The steady drumfire of anti-Hunt television and radio commercials had begun to yield spectacular results by early 1984. There had been a marked shift in voter sentiment, as measured by public opinion polls. Whereas Hunt led by 20 percentage points in early 1983, the race had become about even by spring of the new year. Phil Meyer, a journalism professor at the university at Chapel Hill, thought the King holiday issue itself had been a major factor. "We checked a number of issues," he said. "The Martin Luther King holiday was by far the strongest." Governor Hunt had something to say about that. "Don't think that his [Helms's] position on Martin Luther King was done at great personal sacrifice," he observed. But the governor stopped short of saying that Helms was running a racist campaign.

The Congressional Club television-radio offensive and Helms's rising fortunes alarmed Hunt's organization. Doubting that they could match Helms's fund-raising prowess, his strategists pondered how to marshal their own less lavish funds and somehow offset the monetary advantage. With both campaigns already geared up and running aggressively, the official announcements of candidacy in 1984 were anticlimactic.

Senator Helms had become increasingly critical of the press as the formal campaign opened. During the late fall of 1983 he refused to be interviewed by certain newspaper editors. He and his staff usually returned telephone calls from reporters, but he cut off editorialists whom he identified as hostile. The senator had always charged he was unable to get his message to the people because of "biased" media gatekeepers. That was why, he said, he needed so much money to buy television time. Helms's running feud with the *Raleigh News and Observer* reached a new peak in January when he described the newspaper as a "suck-egg mule."

Other Helms associates, including Tom Ellis and Carter Wrenn, also became inaccessible to the press as the campaign tightened. It was during this period, in mid-January 1984, that Helms refused to release information about his plans for re-election filing. A Republican source leaked the information at the last minute, but Helms's aides would neither confirm nor deny it. Thus it was that the senator walked quietly into the State Board of Elections office on the morning of January 18 at eleven o'clock in the morning, accompanied by a single aide, to pay his filing fee. There to greet him was the capital press corps, packed in a conference room. "My intention," the senator said with mock surprise, "was to come by and have a cup of coffee with [elections board director] Alex Brock. I don't even know how you people knew I was coming."

But Helms remained long enough (forty-five minutes) to answer reporters' questions. They ranged widely. Helms sought to make the point that his opponent was a political opportunist and that the survival of the country was at stake. Helms complained that Hunt wouldn't debate him. "All I get is remote-control responses from one or more of that battery of press agents he has."

Helms also got in additional licks at the press. He said his gripe was not with the reporters. "It's the editors and some of those people who sit up in those ivory towers, and who, as Senator Sam Ervin once said, 'He don't know nothing and he got that tangled up.'" Helms added that he was forced to run against the liberal media as well as his Democratic opponents. "The only way we can really get the story across to our satisfaction is to buy the time to make the case as we see it."

Following this policy, the Helms group sponsored a twenty-eight-minute speech by the senator, broadcast on Eastern Carolina stations during the week he filed. In it Helms emphasized issues he had supported or opposed during his twelve years in Washington—from anti-Communism and tougher import restrictions to opposition to the King holiday and support of school prayer. He again charged Hunt with hiding behind campaign spokesmen and reiterated his support for Tar Heel tobacco farmers. "Now you've always known where I've stood these past eleven years," he said in conclusion. "And you probably didn't agree always. But I wanted you to know where I stood and I always will and that commitment, my friends, still stands."

By contrast Governor Hunt's filing announcement party on February 5, one reporter wrote, had "all the trappings of a presidential visit combined with the jubilation of the Fourth of July." The ceremony took place at the yellow-brick James B. Hunt High School, five miles from the governor's childhood home in Rock Ridge. The carefully orchestrated party attracted some two thousand of the governor's neighbors and supporters from across the state. Three high school bands packed the school gymnasium, which was festooned with five sets of state and national flags. Banners fluttered across the gym saying, "Jim, We Love You" and "Pride in Our Native Son." On the platform sat members of Hunt's family and his senior advisers. The governor's spirited speech was interrupted twenty-one times by cheers and applause. At one point a band broke into the Democratic battle tune "Happy Days Are Here Again."

In his speech, which never mentioned Helms by name, the governor developed the theme that "it's time we took the North Carolina approach, that makes things work, to our nation's capital." "My friends, this election is about the kind of future we are going to create. And I intend to look forward." Hunt said he would be a senator "who works for a healthy, competitive economy that creates jobs and opportunities . . . who works for a fair economy where tax cuts go for working families and the middle class and not just loopholes and tax shelters for the rich."

Hunt went on to say: "I know we can balance the budget in Washington because I have balanced North Carolina's budget every single year. I know when to spend and when to cut. I know how to say 'yes' to the people's interests and 'no' to the special interests." Hunt ended by pledging to work for lower interest rates, environmental safeguards, and military strength. As he finished, and on a signal from a Hunt aide, one of the bands struck up "The Stars and Stripes Forever."

Later at the Wilson Recreational Center hundreds of Hunt friends and supporters attended a five-dollar-a-ticket barbecue lunch and heard other speeches about the governor's campaign needs. A grizzled tobacco farmer appeared as one of his champions. The day's activities ended with a fifty-dollar-a-ticket fund-raising buffet at Greenville.

Throughout the day Governor Hunt emphasized his rural roots. Everything about the rally built on the themes of family ties, devotion to home and church, and straight-arrow living. His audiences were a diverse mixture of farmers, housewives, corporate executives, blacks, teachers, small entrepreneurs, and workers. When asked whether he'd be able to carry the vote in eastern Carolina, Hunt showed no hesitation about answering. "That's where I'm from," he said. "And I'll carry it."

19. "Helms Can't Win"

"Barring an act of God, Helms can't win," Richard Whittle, a former North Carolina reporter, wrote for the *Los Angeles Times–Washington Post* Service in late October 1983. Whittle's statistics about Helms's "fluke" victories in 1972 and 1978 and the animosities he had stirred in Congress seemed impressive on paper. He portrayed Jim Hunt as unbeatable in down-home North Carolina: The governor "is a non-smoking, teetotaling, clean-shaven Christian whose immaculately coiffed hair and prim demeanor would suit him for a career in TV evangelism. He isn't known for cutting deals. He's known for wooing industry, boosting education and backing tobacco."

Whittle went all the way: "The roar of the battle indeed promises to be titanic. But if the volume implies doubt about the outcome, it shouldn't. It's all over but the shouting."

Whittle unveiled his predictions while the polls still showed Hunt running as much as 6 percentage points ahead of Helms. By the following spring that margin had been wiped out. Most pollsters thought Helms's massive television campaign launched in April 1983 had been responsible. Others saw the Martin Luther King holiday controversy as the major factor in the turnaround. The senator felt that way too. In a Raleigh speech before two hundred businessmen, Helms said: "I see a lot of 'Jesse in '84' buttons. I think we need a little ribbon on these that says 'Helms.' Jim Hunt's got another Jesse, and he's got [Hunt]."

Both candidates were aware of the potential impact of the Reverend Jesse Jackson's meteoric rise on their own fortunes. Helms tried to link Hunt with Jackson in a negative way, much as Willis Smith's supporters had linked Dr. Frank Graham with blacks in 1950. The Helms group composed a fund-raising letter in February 1984 sounding a familiar theme: "Without your support, conservatives like me wouldn't even be in the Senate fighting for President Reagan, wrestling against Ted Kennedy or standing up against the budget busting legislation liberals like Jesse Jackson would love to pass each day—like the billion-dollar Martin Luther King holiday."

Along with the letter went two handbills. One showed an unflattering photograph of Jesse Jackson and selected quotes ("We want it all" and "From the outhouse, to the courthouse to the statehouse, to the White House, march on, march on.") The second showed a photograph of Governor Hunt and Jesse Jackson taken in March 1982 when the two met at the Governor's Mansion in Raleigh. Also included were reprints of newspaper clips about Jackson's voter registration drive in North Carolina.

Hunt recognized that black support might be his margin of victory in November. Black civic leaders organized a one-hundred-dollar-a-plate luncheon in Raleigh in December and raised fifty thousand dollars for Hunt. "You know why Governor Jim Hunt and nine out of eleven of our North Carolina members of the United States House support the Martin Luther King holiday for this country," one speaker declared. "We know North Carolina has climbed upward since we set aside the dead weight of discrimination in this state and country."

At the same time Jackson charged into areas that had an embarrassing potential for Hunt. In late December he called for changing the National Democratic Convention delegate selection rules shaped by the Hunt Commission. He charged that the commission's changes diluted the power of interests near the people and returned the nominating clout to the party's old-line moderates. In the liberal vernacular, it resurrected the "smoke-filled rooms." But most Democrats agreed that catering to single-interest groups had gone too far in 1980. They welcomed the reenfranchising of experienced officeholders who knew how to win elections and govern. Still, the Jackson insurgency raised a delicate question about how Hunt could maintain strong black support at home without alienating Jackson or stirring up the white backlash encouraged by Helms.

In a different realm the governor stood firm on his capital punishment views by refusing to commute the sentence of James W. Hutchins, fifty-four, slayer of three law enforcement officers and first prisoner to face the death chair in twenty-three years. During the exhaustive legal maneuvering by defense attorneys, Hunt never tipped his hand, but the governor was strongly on record as approving the death penalty for first-degree murder. "As a college student I was opposed to capital punishment," he said. "But in later years, after I read a lot of theology, I came to realize that human beings have an awesome responsibility to maximize love and to minimize hurt, and especially death. I believe that capital punishment is a deterrent in most cases. If the law is enforced fairly and people are made aware of that, I believe it will result in fewer murders and thus more lives will be saved."

Heavy pressure was brought to bear on the governor as the Hutchins case moved to a climax. Most of the hundreds of telephone calls and letters he received opposed the death penalty, but Hunt allowed the execution to proceed.

One of the governor's major chores involved preparing position papers on public issues he would discuss in the campaign. Hunt tapped resources at the university at Chapel Hill and Duke University. He obtained counsel from academic experts, especially in foreign policy.

The governor's first venture in this field came in late January when he voiced support for President Reagan's Central America policy. He favored the Grenada invasion, a strong military presence, and economic assistance. "I believe in the Monroe Doctrine," he told executives of the North Carolina Association of Chambers of Commerce. "I think other nations ought to stay out of this hemisphere. I think Russian attempts to subvert nations here and to assist in Communist take-over is something we absolutely have to prevent without any question whatsoever."

Hunt noted that such views were not out of line with his previous stands, such as opposition to the nuclear freeze. The governor mentioned his two years in Nepal and said: "I've been out there working with those peasants and farmers. I've been out there with people so poor they didn't have plates and cups and saucers to eat on. We have got to help those countries have a successful economy so those people will want to defend their country. . . . I think we've got to give the kind of foreign aid President Reagan has indicated he thinks is necessary."

Hunt's support of Reagan's foreign aid program put him at odds with Senator Helms's perennial opposition, but his endorsement of the Reagan program also brought grumbling from some of his supporters. The *Raleigh News and Observer* noted that Hunt could "hardly match the stridency of Helms' anti-communism. When the governor talks as he did last week of 'Russian attempts to subvert nations here and to assist in Communist takeovers' his views came across as a mere pale copy of the Helms-Reagan rhetoric. With too much 'me-tooism' from the governor, a lot of voters might decide just to stick with the genuine radical."

In late January Hunt encountered other grumblers in his camp. The North Carolina Association of Educators, representing fifty-two thousand members who had always been Hunt enthusiasts, refused to endorse his senatorial candidacy. Members of the educators' executive committee said they were upset over small salary increases for teachers. "The Hunt Administration is fast on rhetoric and slow on substance," said NCAE President Frances Cummings of Lumberton.

NCAE executives said they might reconsider their position after the May 8 primary, but they were dissatisfied with Hunt's recommendations for a salary freeze for two years during the recession. The NCAE pushed for a 25 percent increase in pay. Its executive committee said it was "looking for

[Hunt] to change in June" when the General Assembly convened. "The governor will do what he thinks is right for the schools," said Gary Pearce, Hunt's press secretary. "He will not change his approach just to get the endorsement of the NCAE."

Senator Helms lost no time getting into this controversy. In early February he launched a five thousand dollar radio advertising campaign criticizing Hunt's record on education. "North Carolina's public schools are in trouble," the ad charged. There had been no improvement between 1972 and 1982. A "Teachers for Helms" Committee, headed by Bill Metcalf, a principal at Granite Falls, noted that the state's SAT scores were "among the lowest in the nation" and the percentage of state money going to education had dropped from 45.6 percent to 40.4 percent during Hunt's term as governor. The North Carolina system, the ads charged, had fallen below that of the District of Columbia, which "has a reputation for a very weak school system. . . . Governor Hunt has attempted to use education to advance his political career at the expense of our children."

Hunt fought back. "I want you to know I'm not going to take that lying down," he said. Helms "may be trying to cover up the fact that he has never done anything at all for education." The governor noted that SAT scores were not a valid measurement of educational quality, since not enough students took them to make them an accurate yardstick. The best measurement, he continued, was annual testing of all children, and those tests showed North Carolina above the national average in all subjects for the first time ever. "So our schools are getting better."

But Helms's disparagement of Hunt's core achievements indicated how heated the campaign had become. In mid-February Hunt again sought the support of the NCAE. "I am the governor who put education first in North Carolina," he said. But President Cummings would not budge. "Two weeks ago we felt compelled to send an old friend a message," she said, adding that for the previous three years education had been "taken off the front burner."

Hunt was deeply annoyed by the senator's all-out attack on what he viewed as the center of his strength. "His attacks deserve an F for honesty and accuracy," Hunt said. But the NCAE's defection plus Helms's efforts to capitalize on it had been jarring. Asked how he could promote himself as an "education governor" when he had not received the NCAE's endorsement, Hunt replied: "You'll have to ask them that question. But everywhere I go, teachers and educators come and tell me that they are for me and they are working for me and I think the NCAE will look at that again perhaps."

As spring approached, the initiative had swung substantially in Helms's direction. Many of the senator's bitter confrontations in the Senate had been forgotten. His massive advertising campaign had borne fruit. Hunt's operators were torn between wanting to launch their own counterattacks immediately and holding off until later, when their efforts might prove more beneficial. Reporters encountered an upsurge of support for Helms all around the state. The messy controversy among leading candidates for the Democratic presidential nomination enhanced a pessimistic feeling among Tar Heel Democrats. As the North Carolina Democratic presidential primary approached on May 8, Hunt maintained a hands-off neutrality, although earlier he had privately supported Walter Mondale.

The same fractured situation existed in the gubernatorial contest. Three Democrats previously associated with Hunt—Eddie Knox, his chairman of the Advisory Budget Commission and North Carolina State University classmate; Tom Gilmore, a former associate member of his cabinet and also a college friend; and Lauch Faircloth, his secretary of commerce—were among six major contenders. Hunt refused to endorse any of the trio and requested members of his cabinet not to get involved. Hunt knew that since the time of the Gardner machine governors had not fared well in trying to handpick their successors. Besides, he had troubles enough without taking on additional burdens.

As it turned out, none of Hunt's friends won the nomination. It went instead to Attorney General Rufus Edmisten, who had never been closely allied with Hunt. Although he had a well-organized machine, he was not trusted by the business establishment and was considered vulnerable to Congressman Jim Martin, the ablest gubernatorial prospect the Republicans had fielded in more than a decade.

On every front, as summer approached, Hunt's fortunes seemed to diminish as Helms's improved. The senator's steady slugging at Hunt as an indecisive candidate was having its effect. Even as Hunt began to unveil his position papers on economics, the environment, foreign policy, and Social Security, Helms's withering media attacks continued. "I don't know where he stands on anything," Helms said. "I think he stands pretty much where the political popularity may be."

Besieged by Helms's persistent challenges for television debates, Hunt agreed to participate in several after the May 8 primary. But even then the governor's and the senator's seconds had trouble designing a format and ground rules that both sides could approve.

"You folks keep telling me it's the toughest campaign I've ever had," Helms had told reporters when he filed for reelection in February. "We'll see. I think Governor Hunt's going to be surprised and not pleasantly so."

20. The D'Aubuisson Connection

As the summer of 1984 arrived, the *Economist* of London, in a commentary entitled "Mud among the Tar Heels," suggested that the Helms-Hunt campaign had become a contest to see who had the funniest friends. Was it Hunt with his blacks and trade unionists? Or Helms with his Latin American dictators?

The comment contained a measure of truth. In May, after enduring Helms's barbs about his limousine liberal associations for a year, the governor began attacking the senator, in the media and elsewhere, for his dubious record of support for Social Security and his friendships with Argentina's former president Leopoldo F. Galtieri and El Salvador's Roberto D'Aubuisson. "When you look at the friends Jesse Helms has around the world," Hunt's television ads charged, "it's no wonder he's made enemies for North Carolina in Washington."

Helms responded scornfully: "I think [Jim Hunt] knows as much about foreign policy as a pig does about roller skating." But Hunt's comments about Helms's links with some of Latin America's "least liked and toughest men" focused attention on the senator's preference for authoritarian leaders. As chairman of the Senate Foreign Relations Subcommittee on the Western Hemisphere, Helms had established contacts all over the area, especially among right-wing leaders in Chile, Bolivia, Argentina, and El Salvador.

Helms first voiced public support for Roberto D'Aubuisson as early as 1980 in a Senate speech. In a major series of articles published in February 1984 the *Albuquerque Journal* reported that Helms's foreign policy aides had helped a rightist coalition headed by D'Aubuisson establish what became the National Republican Alliance (ARENA) in 1981. These aides, John E. Carbaugh, who left the senator's staff in 1983, and Christopher Manion, maintained close contact with D'Aubuisson, according to the newspaper. D'Aubuisson, a former army major, who became a candidate for the presidency of El Salvador in 1984, was widely accused of having ties with right-wing death squads involved in the slaying of Archbishop Oscar Romero and other government leaders.

Senator Helms said of the *Journal* articles: "I have never seen as much garbage in my life." As if to prove his point he continued lobbying for D'Aubuisson. The State Department had repeatedly denied the former

Salvadoran major visas to visit the United States. Helms insisted that D'Aubuisson was a "free enterprise man and deeply religious" and that his ARENA party was very much like the Grand Old Party in the United States. Manion, who was a Foreign Relations Committee staffer, admitted meeting with D'Aubuisson before ARENA was formed, but denied talking about its organization. D'Aubuisson said later of his relationship with Helms's aides: "With them I was able to have explained to me the ways of politics in the United States. . . . We had to get information to learn about the political ins and outs of the United States and in that they were most instrumental."

The Reagan administration supported José Napoleon Duarte, head of the Christian Democrats, in the important March 25 presidential election, which Duarte won after a runoff. Helms described Duarte as a socialist who favored land reform.

Helms's D'Aubuisson connection exploded anew in early May. Helms wrote President Reagan a letter accusing the United States ambassador to El Salvador, Thomas R. Pickering, of interfering in the Salvadoran presidential election and called for his removal. The letter was curiously released in El Salvador before it was revealed in Washington.

White House spokesman Lawrence Speakes said Reagan had "full confidence" in Pickering and had no intention of removing him. Governor Hunt accused Helms of "undercutting our policy in El Salvador." Whether citizens agreed with Reagan administration policy in Central America, the governor said, "the President of the United States, not Senator Helms, should be conducting foreign policy. . . . [Helms] has no business trying to be secretary of state."

Senator Charles Percy (R-Ill.), chairman of the Senate Foreign Relations Committee, also rebuked Helms by describing Pickering as "a superb professional diplomat who is carrying out the President's and Congress's policy in El Salvador. There is no substance to the charge that the ambassador has sought to 'rig the outcome' of the election or to 'manipulate the electoral process.'" Senate Majority Leader Howard Baker also defended Pickering and said of Helms: "Jesse does what Jesse feels he must do."

A third round in the highly charged battle between Helms and his critics unfolded that same month. The *New York Times* reported that the chairman and vice chairman of the Senate Intelligence Committee had rebuked Senator Helms for disclosing secret information in violation of Senate rules. The rebuke was made, the newspaper said, in an "Eyes Only" letter to the Senate majority and minority leaders. It was handwritten and delivered by Senator Barry Goldwater, chairman of the committee, and Senator Daniel

Moynihan, the vice chairman. The written criticism, the newspaper declared, was repeated in conversations between the committee and Senate leaders. The information revealed involved the United States role in the El Salvador elections, which formed the core of Helms's attack on Ambassador Pickering.

But the *Times* report, while accurate in part, turned out to be confused and not completely true. Helms angrily denied that he had disclosed secret information. "I reject it out of hand. . . . It is a canard, a falsehood and a political ploy." Helms, who was not a member of the Senate Intelligence Committee, said his information had come from news reports and from contacts in El Salvador. His only knowledge of the Goldwater-Moynihan letter, he insisted, had come from the *Times* story. "I don't know if this letter exists," he said. "Neither Goldwater nor Moynihan mentioned one word of this to me." In an hour-long press conference with North Carolina reporters, the senator downplayed the role of Goldwater and charged that Moynihan, who was a supporter of Hunt, was behind the allegation. "I can't believe that Barry Goldwater is accusing me of leaking classified material. My present predisposition is to challenge Mr. Moynihan, who is on Governor Hunt's campaign committee, to show one scintilla of evidence that I have leaked anything."

In a later interview Helms said he had encountered Goldwater on the Senate floor and asked whether he had "rebuked" Helms in a letter. According to Helms, Goldwater said: "I did not, and I'll go to North Carolina and say that." Goldwater told the *Charlotte Observer*: "I'm convinced now that Helms did not get his information from the committee or a leak from the committee." Other senators, including Baker, Robert Byrd, and Moynihan, declined to comment because the letter dealt with a classified matter. As more information became available, the political overtones grew stronger.

Helms never relinquished the offensive. He said he was being treated under a double standard. There had been no uproar earlier, he said, after leaks from Congress about covert CIA mining of harbors in Nicaragua. "I think an 'Eyes Only' letter, if it exists, will be as far as the matter goes," Helms said. "The [intelligence committee] had leaked like a sieve for years."

Helms turned out to be right. As he continued to castigate the committee for "classifying information relating to the improper meddling of the State Department and the CIA," both Republican and Democratic senators clammed up and backed away. Columnist Mary McGrory explained it this way: "Democrats, who find Helms obnoxious on many counts, have held their fire because they fear that if they haul him up before the Ethics Committee, North Carolina voters might see it as a blatantly partisan move intended to help Governor Hunt, who is in a neck-and-neck race with the ultra-conservative Helms. . . . Republicans, who are grinding their teeth over Helms's declaration that D'Aubuisson, Duarte's beaten right-wing rival, is 'someone who openly espoused the principles of the Republican Party of the U.S.' are nonetheless rallying to Helms for the larger good of re-electing him and keeping Republican control of the Senate."

Behind the partisan bickering lay the fact that the United States government apparently had dabbled in the El Salvador elections. The *Wall Street Journal* quoted unidentified intelligence sources as saying that the CIA funneled $2 million into the country to help parties competing with D'Aubuisson. The Reagan administration and the State Department did not label this pro-Duarte money because it was given to anti-D'Aubuisson groups, such as labor unions, which supposedly strengthened the democratic process. Officially the United States government favored neither Duarte nor D'Aubuisson, but most of the CIA funds wound up supporting Duarte. In his usual style Helms put it bluntly: "They had bought Mr. Duarte lock, stock and barrel, and they didn't want the invested capital to be wasted by the Salvadoran voters rejecting the merchandise. They wanted the trappings of democracy to enhance the product, but they did not want to risk a real commitment to freedom."

In late June a Reagan administration official and two sources in El Salvador announced that United States intelligence sources had uncovered a plot by right-wing Salvadoran extremists to kill Ambassador Pickering in May. The initial reports had Roberto D'Aubuisson involved, but later information cleared him of direct participation, although members of his ARENA party were implicated.

When the plot was uncovered, the Reagan administration sent its special envoy, General Vernon A. Walters, to El Salvador to warn D'Aubuisson and ARENA of "serious consequences" if the plan were carried out. Walters, according to administration sources, met D'Aubuisson on May 18 at the ambassador's residence with Pickering himself present. "Walters read the riot act," an administration official said. "The message was that we knew what was going on and it had better not happen."

General Walters allegedly told D'Aubuisson there was a place in Salvadoran politics for him as an opposition leader if he chose to take it. In a final move, he offered the former officer a visa to visit the United States, which the State Department had previously refused to grant.

These reports of Walters's visit with D'Aubuisson, however, were denied by another administration official. Later, toward the end of May, Senator Helms attended Duarte's inauguration in San Salvador as a member of the official delegation to the ceremonies. Senator Baker said he asked Helms to attend on behalf of President Reagan. While there, Helms had a two-and-one-half-hour meeting with D'Aubuisson. "I was the only one who has any credibility with the ARENA party," Helms said. "The main purpose was to get these two men [D'Aubuisson and Duarte] to work together because they have to if they are going to save their country." In a newspaper interview on June 5 Helms said D'Aubuisson expressed considerable bitterness toward Duarte.

Later in June, when the Reagan administration revealed the Pickering death threat, Senator Helms became somewhat less enthusiastic about his role as D'Aubuisson's mentor. But by that time he had already invited D'Aubuisson to visit the United States and the Salvadoran leader, by then in possession of a visa, had decided to make the trip. When a reporter called Helms in mid-June to inquire about a Washington reception his staff was planning for D'Aubuisson, Helms raised doubts that the gathering would take place. He said he was "too busy" to spend much time with that matter and if such a gathering occurred, it would be up to Senator Percy, chairman of the Foreign Relations Committee, to host it. "I'm not D'Aubuisson's agent," Helms said. "I'm being portrayed as D'Aubuisson's agent, and I decline the honor."

But D'Aubuisson came all the same. Invitations had been extended to a large number of senators to meet him. Only a few turned up at the Capitol. The next day D'Aubuisson held a press conference at which he said he would oppose Duarte in a "constructive, conscientious way" and denied involvement in the plot against Pickering. He said he knew nothing about it and bore no grudge against the ambassador, whom he described as a "most capable officer." D'Aubuisson also denied reports suggesting he believed Pickering had channeled CIA funds to Duarte's party during the election campaign.

The growing furor over Helms's D'Aubuisson connection had not failed to cause repercussions in North Carolina. If Helms had begun to feel that his relationship with D'Aubuisson was unprofitable in the senatorial race, Governor Hunt was sure of it. He attacked Helms strongly, declaring that North Carolinians deplored kidnapping and murder, whether done by Communists or anti-Communists. He said evidence linking D'Aubuisson with death squads that had left an estimated thirty thousand people dead was overwhelming. "It was strong enough to have concerned the President, the secretary of state, the Senate majority leader and minority leader and the Republican chairman of the Senate Foreign Relations Committee—all of whom declined to meet with D'Aubuisson."

In late June the *Raleigh News and Observer* reprinted a *New York Times*

Syndicate story about the plot to assassinate Ambassador Pickering. At the Republican Party state convention that same month in Raleigh Republican anger over the *Times* report boiled over. David Tyson, a worker for the Helms for Senate Committee, offered a resolution condemning the *News and Observer* for its "distortions and attempts to cover up the truth" and called the newspaper "the Jim Hunt hit squad." It asked that "all reporters and staff of the *News and Observer* be expelled from this building."

Tyson's remarks brought the crowd to its feet, cheering and yelling. Barry McCarthy of Elizabeth City, the convention chairman, said no further debate was needed. He instructed that *News and Observer* reporters Daniel C. Hoover and Rob Christensen be escorted from the hall. As they were being conducted out, McCarthy announced that "the cancer has been surgically removed." He added that the newspaper had abused the party and its members with inaccurate stories. "If they can't get it right, they won't get it at all."

Afterward, though, Congressman James G. Martin, the GOP nominee for governor, and Carter Wrenn, executive director of the National Congressional Club, had second thoughts. The Associated Press reported that Martin was overheard telling Wrenn that the expulsion was a "serious mistake." A short while later former congressman Eugene Johnston, of Greensboro, chairman of Reagan's state campaign, offered a motion to allow the *News and Observer* reporters to return. Martin, Johnston, and Congressman James T. Broyhill, as well as other GOP legislators, apologized to Hoover and Christensen. At a luncheon in his honor Martin said: "I believe in our action this morning we did make a mistake." The crowd applauded. "There was some red meat on the floor, and we went for it."

The Republicans were not the only group who thought they saw "red meat on the floor." The last week in June, Hunt and his advisers toughened their television advertisements on the D'Aubuisson connection. In an ad which opened with the crack of rifle shots in the background and still photographs of crumpled bodies, a voice intoned: "This is what they do—death squads in El Salvador. Innocent men, women and children murdered in cold blood. This is the man accused of directing those death squads, Roberto D'Aubuisson. And this [a photo of Helms] is the man whose aides helped D'Aubuisson set up his political party in El Salvador. This is Roberto D'Aubuisson's best friend in Washington, maybe his only friend. Now, Jesse Helms may be a crusader, but that's not what our senator should be crusading for."

When the *News and Observer* called Helms for a comment, the senator was ready: "It's one thing to attack me on Social Security and taxes and school prayer. But when Jim Hunt starts involving me with murder, well

. . . I'm just absolutely astonished he would stoop that low." Senator East said that D'Aubuisson had "been a victim of cheap left-wing McCarthyism." The governor's campaign spokesman, Will Marshall, called it a realistic appraisal. "It's disturbing because the reality it shows is disturbing. Senator Helms has tried to bury his head in the sand and say that reality doesn't exist."

Another source offered unexpected criticism of Helms. In an editorial entitled "A Tale of Two Jesses," *Business Week* magazine castigated both Senator Helms and the Reverend Jesse Jackson for meddling in foreign affairs. It hit Jackson for heaping criticism on his own country while standing beside Cuban President Fidel Castro in Havana and Nicaraguan leader Daniel Ortega Saavedra in Managua. It flayed Senator Helms for using his Senate Foreign Relations Committee post to "undercut American efforts to build a stable government in El Salvador." "U.S. foreign policy is conducted by the President and the people he appoints," the editorial concluded. "He has not appointed either Jesse."

21. The School of Hard Knox

"Frankly I'm getting a little tired of snap, crackle, pop and Jesse," Jim Hunt told a reporter in June. He was referring to the barrage of early-morning television commercials unleashed by the Helms people which had dramatically undermined his lead in the senatorial race. But in the Hunt camp this was no joking matter. For fourteen months the governor had been subjected to a blistering attack which portrayed him as indecisive and hypocritical and associated with Georgetown liberals, union bosses, and black activists. The polls showed that Hunt's commanding lead of a year earlier had fallen in all demographic classifications except that of "least well educated" (meaning mostly blacks). Helms's support was up among whites, the elderly, and independents. But his largest gain was among high school graduates. In a late May Gallup Poll Hunt's positive job performance rating was down from 68 percent to 55 percent and those who disapproved were up from 23 to 35 percent.

As the Helms-Hunt contest drew neck-and-neck, academicians agreed with politicians. "Hunt was seen as decisive, moving ahead, leading the state," said Thad L. Beyle, a political science professor at the University of North Carolina at Chapel Hill. "What the Helms advertising did was create an image that he was not a leader of that type. One of the things they created was the image that Hunt was wishy-washy and had an inability to take stands." Merle Black, another political scientist at the university, concurred: "The common theme [in the advertising] is that Hunt is two-faced, hypocritical, says two things that are contradictory." Black said the ads consisted of "half-truths, quarter-truths and gross distortions of the truth."

In the Hunt camp alarm over the governor's sag produced shifts in high-command strategy. In April Gary Pearce, the governor's press secretary, became codirector of the Hunt for Senate Committee along with Joe Grimsley. Those who had been reluctant about slugging hard (and perhaps getting too personal) were overruled by the more aggressive.

From the beginning Hunt had insisted he was a fighter and had no intention of waging a tepid campaign. When Hunt visited Washington in late May, he found the mood among Democrats glum. "You really ought to start the slugging," said Senator Alan Cranston (D-Calif.). "I'm slugging right now," replied Hunt. "People's hopes for Hunt have begun to fade up here," said one well-connected lobbyist.

Hunt insisted he would regain the momentum. "He [Helms] is going to have to defend that voting record, and he can't do it," Hunt said. "I've got fire in my eyes." Earlier in the year Hunt had defined the main issue as "the future of this country." Following the Democratic primaries in May and June (in which Hunt's allies were defeated by Attorney General Rufus Edmisten), the governor's campaigners initiated a series of television commercials attacking Senator Helms's votes on taxes, farm policy, Social Security, and foreign affairs. "Now that the primaries are behind us," Hunt declared, "it's time to focus on the real issues of this race."

Gallup Poll evidence of strong support for Helms among the elderly led the Hunt campaign to focus attention on Helms's Social Security record. All during his career the senator had waged war on government entitlements, with Social Security a prime target. Helms had earlier voted repeatedly for Social Security and disability cuts, but in the 1980s he had taken a different tack. In 1983 he had launched his quickly aborted attempt gradually to "privatize" Social Security. Hunt ads charged that Helms had displayed a "mean-spirited attitude" toward the elderly by voting constantly to weaken Social Security and Medicare. Helms responded that "the senior citizens, the people on Social Security, they know that Jesse Helms is going to look after the Social Security program. . . . If we have a society that turns its back on the senior citizens, then we have a heartless society."

But Hunt was not deterred. Elderly voters, he said, "simply don't know what he [Helms] has been doing. . . . The thing he's most afraid of is . . . that [they] will find out. . . . I think he's absolutely terrified." Helms had been one of nine senators who opposed recommendations of President Reagan's bipartisan commission on Social Security, which were enacted in 1983.

As Hunt broadened his offensive, the Helms group responded. They produced television ads defending Helms's record on Social Security and quoting from a portion of a 1983 speech in which he promised that those who have contributed to the system would receive Social Security benefits. Similarly defensive ads appeared after Hunt's dramatic television commercial displaying dead bodies in Central America and linking Helms with right-wing dictators. Helms went on television to deplore the ads. "I thought better of the governor than that," he said solemnly. "One of my daughters said, 'Daddy, does the governor have no shame?'" Gary Pearce replied: "When you're running against Helms, it's hard to be accused of being too negative. It's like being called ugly by a frog."

In late May Hunt called for the resignation of Dr. C. Everett Koop, the nation's surgeon general, whom Helms had persuaded President Reagan to appoint. Helms shared Koop's strong anti-abortion views, but Hunt was worried about his animosity toward tobacco. Dr. Koop, like surgeons general before him, had called smoking a major cause of chronic obstructive lung disease and encouraged an anti-tobacco movement which had as its goal a "smokeless society" by the year 2000. Hunt said Koop's objective was "tantamount to a prohibition on the use of our tobacco products. . . . We've taken some hard knocks before but nothing like that. . . . It is outrageous and irresponsible to suggest that the tobacco industry just disappear in the next 16 years."

Hunt also referred to the similarity of Koop's and Helms's views on abortion and added: "We see what Senator Helms's priorities are. To him abortion is more important than tobacco." This produced a storm of adverse comment from anti-abortionists across the state.

Helms labeled Hunt's criticism "sheer demagoguery" and declared: "I don't know of any physician in the country who will recommend that you get up in the morning and smoke a cigarette." This led Hunt, whose family had been in tobacco farming for three generations, to step up his offensive. "Tobacco is not necessarily unhealthy when used in modest amounts," he said. "Tobacco can be something that relaxes people. It can have very beneficial psychological effects. . . . [But] it ought to be used in modest amounts."

Hunt recommended a government program of financial aid to help the support program unload some 757 million pounds of tobacco in storage. He proposed a plan similar to the payment-in-kind program (PIK) launched by President Reagan on behalf of farmers of other crops. He also supported increased tobacco exports.

Even the *Raleigh News and Observer*, a staunch Helms critic, thought Hunt had gone too far. "It does neither the state's image nor its tobacco farmers any good to have North Carolina's two most prominent politicians railing against federal officials who warn people against smoking," the newspaper said in an editorial. "A credible case can be made for an agricultural program to assist tobacco farmers. No such credibility exists for assertions that cigarette smoking is beneficial."

As the level of the argument soared in both camps, no subject was too small or bizarre to be ignored. The give-and-take on one issue—support for Israel—momentarily flared, despite the fact that North Carolina's Jewish population is minuscule. In April, Arthur Cassell, a High Point furniture manufacturer, wrote a three-page letter, part of a nationwide fund-raising mailer, which charged that "by any measure Jesse Helms had, by far, the worst anti-Israel record of any member of the U.S. Senate." Cassell noted that Helms had voted wrong in twenty-five votes over the past five years on matters of "vital concern to Israel." He opposed the Camp David agreements, Cassell said, and voted against funds to carry out the treaty. In 1982 Helms demanded a break in diplomatic relations between the United States and Israel. Included in the mailer was a note from Hunt warning that Helms was "rallying his supporters on the radical right against things you and I care deeply about."

In early June the Hunt organization discovered that Senator Helms had made a speech and written a letter to President Reagan the previous month suggesting that under certain circumstances he favored moving the United States embassy in Israel from Tel Aviv to Jerusalem. Helms also declared that the "United States should never pursue any plans that envision a separation of the West Bank from Israel."

These comments brought charges from the Hunt campaign that Senator Helms had "flip-flopped." Helms's latest statements, Hunt supporters said, contrasted with a position he had taken in 1979 when he criticized the Camp David accords. In a Senate speech at that time he warned that the peace treaties didn't go far enough in settling disputes in the Middle East. Among other things, Helms said Israel's refusal to relinquish the West Bank, captured in 1967 from Jordan, was a block to a "comprehensive peace with the Arabs." In 1983 Senator Helms suggested "breaking U.S. relations with Israel because of the Lebanese invasion."

Will Marshall, a Hunt aide, declared that "Helms is guilty of an astonishing flip-flop on a major foreign policy issue." His letter and speech, Marshall said, "were a cynical and calculated move to improve his standing in the American Jewish community." Helms's foreign policy aide, James Lucier, acknowledged that Helms was taking a different stand on the West Bank, but he attributed it to "different circumstances" in the Middle East and the threat of Soviet influence.

By July the Hunt campaign had received $118,000 from Jewish-related political action groups. In Greensboro Senator Helms said: "The only Jewish citizens who are not supporting me are left-wingers who wouldn't be supporting me anyway."

In mid-June the candidates became embroiled in a hassle over a Helms television commercial depicting North Carolina as a high tax state and blaming it on Hunt. The commercial claimed that North Carolinians "pay the highest state taxes in the South" and that under Hunt "state taxes [had] soared to an all-time record high." Hunt supporters and top budget officers replied that the Helms ad painted "a totally misleading picture of the tax situation in North Carolina." Revenue Secretary Mark G. Lynch said North Carolinians were paying 11 percent of their personal income for state and local taxes when Hunt took office but that since that time the amount had decreased to 10 percent. Lynch's figures compared state and local tax burdens combined because in North Carolina the state is responsible under the law for a wide range of services, including the financing of roads and schools, that are primarily the responsibility of local government in other states. When informed of Lynch's remarks, Claude A. Allen, Helms's press secretary, said: "I've never heard a tax collector say taxes are too high." Gary Pearce replied: "Senator Helms and his staff are guilty either of some very shoddy research or of knowingly broadcasting a lie from one end of North Carolina to the other."

In the meantime bitterness from the lately concluded Democratic gubernatorial primaries had overflowed into the Helms-Hunt contest. Hunt's old North Carolina State University friend, Eddie Knox, defeated in the runoff by Attorney General Rufus Edmisten, attacked Hunt, charging that his failure to allow his organization to help Knox had been a "critical factor" in Knox's defeat. Hunt, he said, had refused to let some of his lieutenants work for Knox, but had permitted others to work for Edmisten.

"I ran [Hunt's] gubernatorial campaign against a Mecklenburg candidate [in 1976 against Ed O'Herron]," Knox said in explaining his criticism. "I raised him money both times he ran. I've done everything he asked me to do, including bending over and supporting [gubernatorial] succession when I personally opposed it. Friendship is supposed to go two ways." Knox reiterated his support for Democratic candidates, saying he intended to vote for the Democratic ticket in November, but he said he would not campaign for Hunt or Edmisten. "I think I've been pretty gracious to say that I'm going to vote for the Democratic ticket when I know that my friends not only did not help me but in instances worked against me."

Knox's anger spilled over into the senatorial contest in another way: both his wife, Frances, and his brother, Charles, announced they had switched their allegiance and would work for Jesse Helms. An elated Helms invited the two to accompany him in a flying trip across the state to publicize their defection. (The new alliance had been worked out by Steve Walsh, Helms's finance chairman in Mecklenburg County and also a Knox supporter. He arranged a meeting between Helms and the Knoxes in Washington on June 26 and the public announcement came the following week.)

Frances Knox said Hunt had not been true to his word: "He made a lot of promises to Eddie which he didn't keep," she said. "Over the past 11 years I have watched Jim Hunt. I've seen him go from a very caring and sincere person to a masterful politician. North Carolina can no longer afford politics for a politician's sake."

Charles Knox, who noted that Helms's daughter had married his first cousin, said he didn't agree with Helms on every issue, "but we do agree on almost all the issues. . . . I'm proud to know that Senator Helms will take a position on every issue. His opponent, Jim Hunt, is not that courageous and decisive. . . . I think it will be a mistake to waste Senator Helms's seniority just for the sake of change. That's especially so when change will bring uncertainty in position and performance."

The Knox defection in early July fell like a bombshell on the Hunt camp. The governor shook his head over the news and said he was "deeply disappointed, absolutely baffled by why they would do that." Months before it had been evident that the governor would face troublesome decisions in the gubernatorial race. Three of his political allies, two old friends from his college days, were among six major contenders to succeed him. Initially he had decided not to get involved for two reasons: in North Carolina governors have been notoriously unsuccessful in anointing their successors, and politicians actively seeking office have generally found it counterproductive to dabble simultaneously in other campaigns. (Hunt, however, made an exception in May by endorsing former state senator Henry Frye, a black legislator, whom he had appointed for election to the North Carolina Supreme Court.)

Hunt requested his cabinet officers to remain neutral in the governor's race, but pressures to signal his quiet support one way or another came nevertheless. One episode involved Knox's wife, who after the first primary called and invited Hunt's campaign director, Joe Grimsley, to meet with Knox in a downtown Raleigh hotel. When Grimsley arrived, he said later, he was surprised to find about a dozen Knox aides also in the room. Some of the questions asked during his thirty minutes with the group involved Hunt's campaign plans during the next thirty days.

Neither side was willing to talk about other details of the meeting. Knox himself was, as a reporter termed it, "unusually tight-lipped" about it. When asked whether Hunt's campaign would swing behind him, Knox replied: "I don't know. I can only tell you I have been disappointed that some have been permitted to participate and some haven't." Knox referred to the active campaigning of Hunt's chairman of the State Beverage Control Commission, Marvin L. Speight, on behalf of Edmisten. Speight, whose appointment was not cabinet level, said he talked to Hunt a year earlier about the matter. "I said to him, I'm with you [in the Senate race], but Rufus is my friend, and I'm going to support him." Speight said Hunt replied: "You're not in the cabinet, so go ahead."

Knox cited Transportation Secretary William R. Roberson, Jr., and Administration Secretary Jane Patterson as two Hunt officials advised not to get involved in his campaign. "Give me a Jane Patterson and a Bill Roberson against a Marvin Speight and I'll win 2-to-1," Knox said. But while they favored Knox in the runoff, Patterson had initially favored Tom Gilmore and Roberson, Lauch Faircloth.

Knox associates said that his bitterness was based not only on Hunt's neutrality but on the failure of his organization to offer immediate help with Knox's six-hundred-thousand-dollar campaign debts. Hunt's camp said the governor had twice offered help, but mostly after the November elections. "The governor would have liked to be more helpful," said his aide Will Marshall, "but he's locked in a tough race with a 3-to-1 spending disadvantage, so he offered to do what he could." Hunt gave the Knox campaign a personal check for one thousand dollars. Late in July, Hunt's check was returned in a plain envelope with no message.

Knox also indicated that his grievances included a lack of assurance from the Edmisten camp that state workers who had supported Knox would not lose their jobs if Edmisten won. "Eddie is so bitter you can't talk to him," said one Democrat with ties to Hunt. "In my view, this is a politically disastrous situation if it is not handled quickly. It will not only hurt Rufus —it will help bring Hunt down." Another Hunt supporter said: "Eddie kept cussing Hunt and saying the [Democratic] Party was Hunt's party."

The Knox defection brought vigorous reactions from all directions. Senator Helms himself said the Knoxes' endorsement would "have enormous impact" on his campaign. His supporters generally praised the Knoxes for their independence and welcomed them into the fold. "We'd be delighted to have him [in the Republican Party]," said Representative Roy Spoon (R-Mecklenburg). "He's dead as far as being a Democrat, but he'd be a good asset for us." One registered Democrat said the Knox switch was "a real show of strength and courage."

Hunt associates near the campaign were cautious about commenting on Knox's future, but other supporters were not. "He can hang it up politically," said Senator A. D. Guy (D-Onslow). Other Hunt partisans called Knox a "turncoat." One declared that "only John McEnroe keeps H. Edward Knox from being the poorest loser in the English-speaking world."

In an editorial entitled "Crybaby Eddie," the *Greensboro News and Record* said Knox had "fallen off the deep end of state politics. With a few whiny words he has cut off his nose, shot off his toes, and blown away any chance that he had of making a statewide political comeback." The *Raleigh News and Observer* noted that "even the slightest suggestion by Hunt that he wanted to crown Knox would have aided Helms's charges that Hunt sought to perpetuate a political dynasty in the state."

Some Knox supporters, particularly in the Charlotte area, joined the Knoxes in moving to the Helms camp. Immediately afterward Knox said he had received more than 150 calls. An aide said about half were supportive. One said, "We're sick of Hunt too," and another, "I understand, don't blame you." But Harvey Gantt, the black mayor who had succeeded Knox and had been his ally, denounced the move and said: "Senator Helms' record on issues related to equality and justice is diametrically opposed to the ideals for which the Democratic Party traditionally has stood." J. Neil Pharr, mayor of Carolina Beach, put it another way: "The party is bigger than any one candidate. I don't believe the Democrats who supported Knox are going to desert and vote for Helms. Our votes aren't for sale."

But several press comments noted the similarity between this split and the one that followed the Democratic runoff primary for governor in 1972. Then many supporters of Lieutenant Governor H. Pat Taylor refused to support the winner, Hargrove "Skipper" Bowles. That helped elect North Carolina's only Republican governor in this century, James E. Holshouser. It also helped a novice Republican challenger named Jesse Helms win his Senate seat.

22. The Windsor Story

Even those observers who in the spring had termed the Helms-Hunt campaign "mud-wrestling" and a "back-alley brawl" were startled to see it sink to even greater depths by mid-summer. In early July a Chapel Hill weekly newspaper editor, an avid Helms supporter, published a detailed story based on an alleged rumor that Governor Hunt had had "a lover who was a pretty young boy" in college and "a girl friend in his office." The front-page article was headlined "Jim Hunt is Sissy, Prissy, Girlish and Effeminate." The story appeared in a tabloid called the *Landmark* edited by Bob Windsor, a rotund, self-labeled "redneck" who wears bib-overalls. It specified that the student "lover" was "presently employed by the U.S. State Department" and the girl friend was "a former high-priced call girl used by the banks and big companies in Winston-Salem to entertain their guests."

Even though Windsor said he'd made "no efforts to check out [the facts]" and did not "claim they are truth or factual in any way," the story made the front page of *Raleigh News and Observer* on July 6 and other state newspapers the following day. Accompanying the first story was a statement from Hunt headquarters saying the governor had "instructed his special [campaign] counsel, former State Supreme Court Justice J. Phil Carlton, to determine appropriate legal action."

Within twenty-four hours the governor mailed Windsor a registered letter demanding a retraction. Hunt also asked Carlton to "determine the relationship between Senator Helms, his campaign and the *Landmark*." The same issue of the newspaper contained seven photographs of Helms, including one showing Helms with his arm around Windsor, captioned "Jesse Helms Is Mighty Good Hugging." It also included one and one-half pages of advertising by Helms's campaign committee, a center spread of photographs from the recent state GOP convention, and articles headlined "Republicans United" and "Frances Knox Endorses Helms."

Windsor's tabloid had been publishing a steady stream of anti-Hunt stories for months. But the gay issue had been brought into the campaign even earlier in fund-raising letters written by the Helms Campaign Committee. In August 1983 a five-page letter signed by Senator Helms was devoted almost exclusively to the theme that homosexuals "have drawn a bulls-eye on my campaign. . . . Make no mistake: The so-called gay-rights crowd has the cash to bankroll my opponent."

In January 1984 Windsor's newspaper had accused Hunt of making "a deal with the faggots, perverts, sexual deviates of this nation." Early in June a Helms supporter, J. C. D. Bailey of Rocky Mount, used the article in a quarter-page advertisement in the *News and Observer*, captioned: "Governor Hunt, did you, or did you not, accept a $79,000 contribution from gay activists?" The same question was echoed by State GOP Chairman David T. Flaherty, who said the Hunt campaign had "waffled" on the question of receiving homosexual support and had tried to "obscure" the issue. Flaherty maintained that Senator Paul Tsongas (D-Mass.), who had helped sponsor a Hunt fund-raising dinner in Boston, had also cosponsored legislation in Congress prohibiting discrimination in employment on the basis of sexual orientation. He also said New York gays purchased at least one hundred to seven hundred tickets sold for a Hunt fund-raiser in New York City.

David Price, chairman of the state Democratic Party, responded by asking the Federal Elections Commission to investigate the Helms re-election committee and its supporter Jack C. D. Bailey. Price said the ad was false and unfounded. He said Bailey was a member of Helms's state finance committee and, "as such, he is expressly forbidden by federal law" from advertising under the guise of "independent" political activity. Responding to a Flaherty question about whether Hunt favored giving homosexuals equal employment opportunities, Gary Pearce, campaign codirector, said: "[Hunt] believes everybody ought to be treated fairly."

Windsor's July article, however, jolted even the Helms camp. Claude Allen, Helms's campaign spokesman, immediately announced: "We think the story is preposterous and not based on any reputable sources." Senator Helms ordered all advertising canceled in the *Landmark* and declared in a statement: "Let me say as emphatically and unequivocally as I know how that I believe Governor Hunt to be, personally, a moral family man. Any suggestion to the contrary is repugnant and unfair, and has no place in a political campaign." Helms added that while "this type of rhetoric is not uncommon in American politics, I nevertheless regard it as destructive and demeaning to the political process."

Hunt himself blasted the reports as "scurrilous lies and slander" and said, "I'm not going to take it. . . . You know, when I got into this campaign, I knew it was going to be tough, but I really never had an idea it would get this mean and this vicious. I'm going to file a suit unless these people fully retract and apologize for what they have done. But more than that, this kind of thing happening makes me more determined than ever to win this campaign and to defeat the kind of forces that engage in that kind of thing in this state." Hunt also said he believed the Helms campaign was involved with the *Landmark*. "I think they're tied in without any question whatsoever. They've been the main sponsor of that newspaper. Every article in there is either against Jim Hunt or for Jesse Helms."

The normally garrulous Windsor had delivered hundreds of additional copies of the *Landmark* to the State Legislative Building on the day the *News and Observer* put his charges on the front page. He told one reporter he was "loving" the furor it had created and was considering printing another twenty thousand copies. He was less effusive later that day, saying he would hold a press conference the next morning in Chapel Hill.

At his press conference, held outside his newspaper office, Windsor read a prepared statement saying he was "dead wrong to publish" and "humbly and sincerely" apologizing to the governor. "I have discussed this with people whose judgment I respect," he said. "I have prayed about it. I have asked God to forgive me this transgression and believe He will. . . . If I had to do it over, I would not have published it. If I could undo it, I would. . . . I can't put up a fight when I feel I'm morally wrong. If I thought I was right . . . I'd fight you and anybody else tooth and toenail."

Windsor pointed to several hundred copies of his paper stacked behind him and said he would destroy them. Several days later, however, a number of copies were mailed from the paper's publishing house near Raleigh.

The Windsor affair reverberated across the state for several days. Senator Helms denied that his campaign and the *Landmark* were connected. "The next thing the governor is going to blame me for is the bubonic plague, and I didn't have anything to do with that either." He also sharply criticized the *News and Observer* for giving so much prominence to news stories about the *Landmark* article. "They are the ones who are maximizing this thing for the governor," he said. "It could've been handled far differently and far better." Finally, he chided the newspaper for reprinting a photograph from the *Landmark* showing Helms and Windsor arm-in-arm. He said the photograph was one of some thirty-five taken at a recent campaign event in which supporters lined up to have their pictures taken with the senator.

Saturation coverage of the *Landmark* controversy, especially by the *News and Observer*, differed somewhat from coverage of similarly smutty political dogfights in North Carolina. As former governor Bob Scott observed, such rumors in the past had usually appeared in anonymous leaflets. This was the case in the Frank Graham–Willis Smith senatorial contest of 1950, when racially derogatory material, such as doctored photos and unsigned handbills, appeared at mill gates.

The Windsor story was different. It not only contained unsubstantiated barnyard gossip but its publisher initially took responsibility for it and bragged about it. Former senator Robert Morgan, defeated by Helms's colleague John East in 1980, thought full coverage might "serve a purpose to let people know what has been going on. . . . This kind of demagoguery is very successful until it gets out of hand. This recent article may have reversed the trend. It was so scurrilous, I think the people of this state may wake up."

Politicians of all stripes were astounded. "There's been a lot of things said and done, but nothing like that," said North Carolina's eighty-four-year-old secretary of state Thad Eure whose political memory went back some sixty-five years. "I don't recall anything that scurrilous in North Carolina politics, ever," said former governor Terry Sanford. When asked to comment, State GOP Chairman David Flaherty declined, but then said: "I like [the *Landmark*] better than I do the *News and Observer*."

23. When Helms Wasn't Helms

"I've been ready for 18 months," Jesse Helms said of the first state-wide television debate with Jim Hunt on Sunday, July 29, 1984, in prime time. His only preparation, Helms told a reporter, was to get a haircut, as suggested by his wife. As it turned out, the senator had made more preparation than that, but he underestimated the forensic ability and tenacity of Hunt. Neither candidate stumbled badly, but Helms got not only a haircut but also a close shave.

Fifteen months earlier, when Helms launched his media blitz, his initial theme—"Where does Jim Hunt stand?"—had emphasized allegations that the governor was fuzzy on issues and constantly changed his position. Helms hammered on the idea that the two candidates needed face-to-face confrontations. Hunt, the senator declared, was afraid to debate because he was uninformed and inexperienced.

The Helms forces had raised the same theme time after time as they tried to portray Hunt as a youthful novice, not a mature leader capable of serving in the Senate. Helms's senior aide, Tom Ellis, liked to sound off on the subject. Hunt, he said, was a "pretty good governor if you want a nice guy and a ribbon-cutter," but what we needed was a real leader.

The governor had refused to accept the senator's challenge to debate then for several reasons. First, he thought it was too early; it would interfere with his gubernatorial duties. More important, though, it jarred his sense of political timing. Hunt's popularity remained high in 1983. He led Helms in all the polls. Hunt concluded it would be best to wait until the campaign had been formally joined. "I'm not yet a candidate for the Senate," he said. "I'll make that decision after the May primary."

For a while then, as the television assaults continued, Hunt became the quarry and Helms the pursuer. As Helms's media campaign melted Hunt's lead, however, those roles changed. By spring 1984 Helms had taken the lead in some polls (Helms scored 50 percent to Hunt's 46 percent in a May Gallup Poll). In early June the lead seemed to change again, as another poll gave Hunt a 47 to 42 percent edge. "Governor Hunt was way out in front," said Senator Lloyd Bentsen (D-Tex.), chairman of the Democratic Campaign Committee. "Senator Helms spent $50,000 a week and burned up a lot of rubber in the process."

The money-raising contest also became frenzied. By mid-summer Helms's organization had raised $8.42 million, eclipsing the senator's own 1978 record. It was by far the most expensive nonpresidential campaign in history. Hunt's effort to counter his opponent's money machine was barely cranked up at the start of the election year. Counting $1.04 million raised during 1983 by the defunct North Carolina Campaign Committee, the Hunt total stood at about $6.21 million by mid-1984. He had begun running television ads on a regular basis as the year opened, but they were not nearly as profuse as Helms's, which appeared at all hours on television—during the morning shows, the soaps and children's programs, and evening prime time. One native North Carolinian now living out of the state who was vacationing at home in mid-summer said her small children had been noticing it. "Who is that bad man named Hunt?" one of them asked.

Both sides generated money from the wealthy and famous. Charlton Heston and Bob Hope supported Helms. Gore Vidal and Dean Rusk contributed to Hunt. Both candidates became sensitive about out-of-state contributions and refused to publicize their trips to raise money. Hunt attended a lavish oceanside fund-raiser on a yacht during the San Francisco Democratic National Convention. Helms flew around the country, from Illinois to Texas, meeting his supporters at equally lavish parties.

As the date arrived for the first debate, both camps sought to do what every skillful politician knows he must do: Take the offensive and control the agenda. That had included negotiating the best possible rules and format for the debates. Those sensitive negotiations consumed several months, out of which came a seven-page "memo of understanding." The Hunt group wanted a live television audience. Helms's seconds favored a minimum of formal rules and a more open format that would allow for give-and-take between the candidates.

The president-elect of the North Carolina Broadcasters' Association, George Diab, was designated as moderator for the first debate, scheduled for the Raleigh studios of the UNC Center for Public Broadcasting. Fifteen members of the press were permitted in the studios to watch the proceedings (almost like being a witness at an execution, someone observed), along with three representatives from each candidate's staff. Some fifteen commercial television stations across the state, plus the public broadcasting system, aired the debate at seven o'clock in the evening, preempting "Sixty Minutes" and other prime-time fare. An estimated one million people tuned in.

The format produced a lively exchange. Each candidate had a two-minute opening statement and a one-minute closing statement. The first speaker was chosen by a coin toss. The moderator first asked questions directed by the candidates to each other. Then he asked questions submitted by radio-television news directors. Finally the candidates asked each other direct questions. Rebuttal times were allowed during each series of questions.

From the start Helms sought to present himself as a kindly, fatherly figure, not the smarmy, heckling alley fighter his critics proclaimed him to be. He kept snapshots of his grandchildren before him during the debate, a reminder, as one commentator later put it, "to say nothing that would frighten them." The senator had planned an informal approach and thought he could deal with Hunt in an ad hoc manner.

The governor had prepared carefully. He canceled practically all his traveling engagements during the week before the debate. He used, among other associates, his chief legal counsel and old friend J. Phil Carlton, as a stand-in for Helms and videotaped several practice debates, then studied and discussed them. The governor's chief planning director was David Sawyer, his media consultant, who was given credit afterward for several skillful touches. Hunt visited the studio in advance and got briefings on camera angles.

Senator Helms won the coin toss and chose, some thought curiously, to let Hunt make the opening statement. Both men appeared tense at first. This was evident in Hunt's two-minute opener, which outlined the kind of senator he thought North Carolina should have. It was concise and forceful, but a bit stiff. Helms's reply was more informal, almost jovial and avuncular. He apologized for canceling some viewers' favorite prime-time programs and thanked the governor for his willingness to debate. "Now Jim and I have not always agreed on the role of government, on what role it should take in the lives of people," he said good-humoredly. He went on to acknowledge, in almost mock self-abasement, that he didn't possess "unusual wisdom" and that not all people agreed with his views. He ended by saying he'd "always leveled" with the voters and had stood with Ronald Reagan in his program to "turn the economy around." Clearly the senator had adopted the tone of a gentlemanly public servant not intent on starting a fight.

But Helms's first question to Hunt—one charging him with changing his position on several issues—was firm. Hunt's answer showed he had come prepared for vigorous combat. He contradicted Helms's judgments about his stands on the school prayer amendment, tax increases, and out-of-state fund-raising. "The difference between us is this," Hunt concluded on the subject of the deficit. "I would get that money by closing loopholes and having the wealthy pay, and you would do it by cutting across the board and making the average working man and woman pay more."

Hunt's first question to Helms focused on the senator's opposition to "every nuclear arms control proposal advanced by every President—Nixon, Ford, Carter and even Reagan." "Don't you believe we have a moral responsibility to our children and grandchildren to negotiate with the Soviet Union and try to prevent a nuclear holocaust from destroying our nation and the world?" he asked.

Helms replied that he believed in negotiations "if they could be meaningful." He said he supported arms reductions, not just arms control, but then he added: "We learned a sad lesson with SALT I and that was not a limitation treaty; that was an escalation treaty that obviously favored the Soviet Union." Helms said his position was to reduce arms but "stop fooling ourselves that we can sit down with the Soviets, who have out-negotiated us every time."

The debate moved into a series of tough questions, as Hunt became the challenger and Helms answered quietly and occasionally sardonically. The encounters remained good-humored, but there was a coolness and wariness underneath. Hunt criticized Helms on Social Security and tobacco and for opposing President Reagan's policies in Central America. The senator sought to turn the subject of his differences with Reagan into a commentary on anti-Communism. After Helms sidestepped a question about tax-exempt foundations financing his foreign trips, Hunt protested. "Jesse," he said, "that was an interesting answer. The only thing is, you forgot to answer the question."

When Helms sought to deprecate Hunt's support of establishing most-favored-nation status for China and criticized the governor's trip to Peking, Hunt defended opening relations with China and justified his trip as a chance to promote new markets for American tobacco. When Helms answered that the Chinese government was a "murderous regime," Hunt answered: "Is that the same regime that Ronald Reagan just visited . . . that Richard Nixon visited and virtually every President did? What's wrong with them? Don't they know who they're visiting? You know, it seems like you have all the knowledge about foreign affairs and nobody else has any. I think those presidents knew what they were doing."

On Social Security Hunt castigated Helms for opposing the recommendations of President Reagan's bipartisan commission for solving the funding crisis of 1983. He also criticized Helms for casting the deciding vote in the Senate Foreign Relations Committee that killed President Reagan's economic aid package for Central America and for backing Roberto D'Aubuisson and his right-wing party over moderate José Duarte's Christian Democrats, who were supported by the Reagan administration.

Helms appeared taken aback and answered vaguely, even apologetically. "As I said earlier," he replied, "the Lord did not make me impossible of error, nor did he make Ronald Reagan . . . or Jim Hunt." Helms returned to the subject of Communist terrorism and said Congress had a reluctance to take strong stands that would help countries like El Salvador protect themselves. "But, yes sir, I plead guilty to doing everything I can to stop [Communism] in Central America."

Helms defended his work on the Senate Agriculture Committee. He said that if North Carolina lost the chairmanship, the first in 149 years, "the tobacco program can be kissed goodbye." Helms also pledged to stay at the helm of the Agriculture Committee, rather than shift to the chairmanship of the Senate Foreign Relations Committee if it became vacant.

Hunt tried to get at Helms for voting to double the tobacco tax and turning his back on tobacco farmers. But the senator vigorously defended changing his vote and supporting President Reagan's tax increase, which would, he said, save an estimated $30 to $40 billion in combined taxes and spending. "Would you have just sat back and played the political side?" he asked Hunt. Hunt's reply was parochial and politically biting: "Jesse, you may have done one for your country, but you sure didn't do one for North Carolina and the tobacco farmers."

The senator seldom managed to get the governor on the defensive, although he frequently accused him of misstatements. At one point Helms asked: "What is it about these two figures [Walter Mondale and Ted Kennedy] that you admire so much?" Hunt replied that he had a "lot of differences" with them and that if he went to the Senate he intended to "get them to understand why they ought to be more moderate, and maybe more conservative like us Southern Democrats are."

Near the end of the hour Hunt made his most interesting ploy. He asked Helms to join him in a pledge to accept no more campaign money from outside the state. Let the people of North Carolina finance this campaign, he said. Helms waffled. First he asked if Hunt were having money-raising problems. Then he said the First Amendment might be involved. When Hunt pressed further, the senator charged that through gubernatorial emoluments—a state airplane, chauffeurs, limousines, bodyguards, and favorable press publicity—Hunt had built-in advantages. Hunt replied that he'd be willing to give up those extras if Helms would agree to cut off out-of-state contributions.

At that point time ran out. In his closing statement Helms asked viewers to support him in November, but then, in a continuation of his mild-mannered approach, said he would accept the voters' decision in good faith if they chose to elect a "new senator." He would then, he said, understand and be grateful for these past twelve years and "go home and watch my grandchildren grow up, which is no bad deal."

In his closing statement Hunt said he hoped the debate had given viewers "real insight into the differences between Mr. Helms and myself." He said the election involved more than "Jesse Helms and Jim Hunt." He thanked the voters for allowing him to serve as governor and hoped he had done so "in a way that God would approve of and that you would think is worthy. . . . And now let's look ahead."

The debate revealed a remarkable shift in campaign roles. Helms, who had been the challenger for fifteen months, went on the defensive. Hunt took charge and laid Helms's record on the table. In the process he appeared the stronger, better-informed candidate. It was apparent that Helms had expected a less formidable, less agile contender. Playing the grandfatherly role, he was not prepared for Hunt's aggressiveness and nimble rebuttals. If the senator had anticipated using a Ronald Reagan "there you go again" routine on Hunt, he failed. This was clear after the debate when a smiling governor walked over to shake hands with a glum, rather subdued senator. Hunt told reporters: "I think we had an opportunity to make all our positions. I think it will give us a boost." Later he claimed he had "won." In contrast, Helms said: "I don't think either side won. It was not the kind of debate format where you can really get down to brass tacks." It would have "little influence on the campaign."

Nobody, of course, could precisely measure the debate's influence. That depended on how strongly committed viewers were to each candidate and how many undecided voters were watching. But parties of all persuasions had strong views afterward.

Most academic observers gave Hunt the edge. "I thought Hunt really whipped him," said Merle Black, associate professor of political science at the university in Chapel Hill. "I didn't think it was even close. Helms was so non-specific, really unprepared. He apparently underestimated Hunt. Hunt looked credible, reasonable, on top of things."

Helms's defenders observed that the senator had been trying to reassure undecided moderates. He had intended to come over as a mannerly, gentlemanly debater, not some sort of monster trying to unleash a "kicking fight." "He certainly smashed that 'prince of darkness' image," said one. "He didn't make it an alley brawl." Some thought Hunt appeared "sarcastic and mean-spirited." A Helms insider confessed that the state's most formidable politician of his generation [Helms] had been turned into a "mushball" by over-coaching. Others wondered why Helms failed to attack Hunt more specifically on "liberal" issues, for example, the Martin Luther King holiday and Jesse Jackson's program.

Donald N. Schroeder, associate professor of government at Campbell University in Buies Creek, and a Helms supporter, concluded: "I'd have to say, over-all, in terms of what you want to get out of a debate, Hunt probably did what he wanted to do and Helms did not. In terms of more specific things, I'd have to call it a draw."

Behind the closed doors of the two campaigns, the view was that Hunt had carried the day. David Sawyer, Hunt's media consultant, reported that the governor's knowledgeable demeanor had more than established his credibility as a Senate candidate. Beyond that, the debate had recharged the batteries of his field troops. The contest disrupted the strategy of the Helms people and forced them to revise the direction of their media campaign to check inroads Hunt might be making. Hunt's advisers had not expected the governor to do so well in the first debate. They viewed Helms as a masterful debater and were surprised when he was unable to readjust his strategy and gain the offensive. Hunt's goal had been to expose the vulnerabilities of Helms's record. His people thought he had succeeded.

From the Helms camp came reports that Tom Ellis was furious and thought the debate had been disastrous. Those rumors were corroborated by a series of television ads aired the following week, charging again that Hunt had "flip-flopped" and misrepresented the issues. There were rumors that Helms would try to change the debate format, even that he would cancel the remaining debates. It seemed certain that he would listen more closely to those advisers who, as columnist Bob Novak reported, said, "Let Helms be Helms" and leave those family snapshots at home.

24. Time Out for Party Time

"Tom Sawyer found someone else to paint the fence, and so did I," said Jesse Helms at Ronald Reagan's coronation at the Republican National Convention in Dallas. At Kansas City eight years earlier, and even at Detroit in 1980, the Tar Heel senator had been a belligerent outsider waving a fistful of right-wing amendments, never sure his voice would be heard. By contrast, in the steaming Dallas of August 1984 Helms showed up at the platform committee meetings more as guardian than insurgent. Only once, when Senator Lowell Weicker objected to strongly worded language for a space-based defense system, did Helms enter the fray. "I am pro-Reagan and anti-Weicker," he said. "I will do anything I can to prevent Weicker from possibly undermining one of the finest presidents we ever had."

But the senator had little need to worry. No Republican moderates (or "liberals," as Helms insisted on calling them) had much say on the militantly conservative platform that emerged from the convention. Senator Helms *had*, like Tom Sawyer, found "someone else" to paint his fence. His helpers, banded together informally as the "Conservative Opportunity Society," were an energetic group of young congressmen, including Senator Robert Kasten of Wisconsin, Congressman Jack Kemp of New York, Congressman Newt Gingrich of Georgia, and Congressman Vin Weber of Minnesota. One platform drafter told a reporter: "They are the Jesse Helmses of this convention."

Like most of the delegates who came to honor the Great Communicator and certify him for another four years in the White House, neither the Old Guard nor the Young Turk conservatives sought to mar Reagan's celebration with a platform-kicking contest. From the start the draft platform reflected the President's stamp. The final platform touched all the conservative bases, from a reiterated stand against tax increases in 1985 and support for school prayer to demands that the President appoint Supreme Court justices opposed to abortion. No mention of the Equal Rights Amendment appeared, but there was support for a constitutional amendment to adopt a balanced budget.

Senator Helms found the convention in Dallas thoroughly satisfying. He was again cochairman of the North Carolina delegation, but unlike the Detroit convention, where the Tar Heels were split over the vice presidency, Dallas was devoid of major controversy. The senator, now among the best-known GOP personalities, found it difficult to move about the convention floor without encountering swarms of admirers eager to pose with him for photographs and get his autograph. "This is the man we get all the mail from," shouted a delegate from Minnesota who introduced herself and called her husband. In a convention that was short on news, the national media again pressed Helms for interviews, and the senator demonstrated that his tongue had lost none of its tartness, especially for the "liberal press." "I feel like I'm on a yo-yo," he told a reporter.

But Helms and his large Helms for Senate Committee, occupying some seventy-five rooms at the North Carolina delegation's swank downtown headquarters, the Plaza of the Americas hotel, had plenty to keep them busy. They applied themselves diligently to the never-ending chores of fund-raising. The senator himself spent two weeks traveling back and forth across the Lone Star State in search of reelection money. Besides Dallas he was in Abilene, Lubbock, and Houston. These functions were larger-than-life Texas bashes, mostly keyed at five hundred dollars a couple, with prominent GOP congressional celebrities thrown in to attract the crowds. The Texas money rolled in.

As it was at the receptions held for Governor Hunt at San Francisco, the press was excluded from these functions and had to be content with catching occasional interviews at the gates. At one fund-raiser Helms said he didn't like the business. "Fund-raising is a psychological phenomenon," he said. "I despise it. But it's necessary to run a campaign. You can't do without those folks."

The senior senator appeared more at home on the Sunday before the convention when he joined three thousand worshipers at Dallas's First Baptist Church, the largest in the South (twenty-five thousand members and a physical plant that covers five blocks). The guest preacher that morning, the Reverend Jerry Falwell, lost no opportunity to put Helms in the religious spotlight. "This senator," said the leader of the Moral Majority, "almost didn't run for the Senate because he had grandchildren down in North Carolina. I said, 'Senator, you are a national treasure. We can't do without you.' He said, 'My grandchildren can't do without me.' . . . There came a day when he felt in his heart that God wanted him to run again." Helms explained later, though, that it was his wife, not the Lord, who made him change his mind. "Various pressures were put on my wife and on members of my family," he said.

Falwell didn't confine his remarks about Helms to this single aside. Although he declared that he tried to soft-pedal politics in church, he interrupted his sermon three times with references to Helms. At the conclusion of the sermon the Reverend W. A. Criswell, church pastor, called on Helms for the benediction. The senator gave thanks for "the opportunity to be cleansed and renewed and reminded." Earlier he had listened carefully as Falwell offered personal testimony and biblical authority about the strength that losing can bring. "He's talking about all of us, maybe especially me," Helms said afterward. "Jerry's right. The things that make you strongest are your losses and defeats and disappointments."

A reporter noted that Helms seemed to enjoy the service. He hummed along to a lively rendition of "The Battle Hymn of the Republic" by the church's 250-member choir and put a fifty-dollar bill in the collection plate.

Voter registration booths had been set up at three locations around the church, and a notice in the church bulletin advised that voting was "every Christian's responsibility."

Jim Hunt's church activities had not been so widely publicized, if at all, at the Democratic Convention in San Francisco a month earlier. But the governor's fund-raising initiatives had been equally strenuous and widespread. As one reporter wrote, early every morning Hunt's campaign troops fanned out across the city to "prospect for money." They showed up at caucus meetings for various state delegations and dozens of headquarters hotels. At the caucuses Hunt aides made brief presentations to the delegates, urging them to take a "Dollars for Hunt" booklet, which included a series of four-dollar tickets totaling $250, to be sold to friends. Among those making appearances around San Francisco were two of the governor's children, Baxter and Rachel.

Hunt himself took five days returning to Raleigh from San Francisco, stopping along the way to attend to fund-raising. Stops included Portland, Denver, St. Louis, and Chicago. Later he flew back to Minneapolis, where he reportedly reeled in fifteen to twenty thousand dollars.

Hunt, like Helms, remained sensitive about revealing details of these fund-raising enterprises. His most publicized venture in San Francisco took place aboard a yacht, the *Lisa Marie*, cruising in San Francisco Bay. Fifty guests paid five hundred dollars apiece and dined on poached salmon, filet of beef, California shrimp, wine, and cheese. According to one reporter, Hunt, dressed in a blue-checked sports coat, seemed "like a fish out of water" among the high-fashion guests. The Democrats, too, had stocked the fund-raiser with as many big names as possible—movie and television stars along with political luminaries from the convention.

The governor found the goings-on at San Francisco considerably less comfortable and relaxing than Helms did his activities among the GOP millionaires and fundamentalists at Dallas. While he was personally at ease with the varied constituencies of the Democratic Party—feminists, blacks, unionists, and urban bosses—he knew that these groups did not rank high back home. Thus he kept his activities low key, in marked contrast to the prominent position he had taken at the 1980 Democratic convention in New York City. There he campaigned behind the scenes for Jimmy Carter, clashed with Senator Kennedy over the platform, addressed the convention, and emerged afterward as chairman of a national commission on party primaries.

At San Francisco, however, mindful of the Reagan popularity and rightward shift of American politics, Hunt maintained a low profile. None of the Democratic candidates, from Jackson to Mondale to Hart, had scored highly in North Carolina. As he had in 1980, Hunt was bucking a national trend. This time, though, he had a formidable opponent, an incumbent and a national political figure running in tandem with the Great Communicator. When asked about his support for the national ticket, the governor carefully said that he thought Mondale had "learned the importance of fiscal responsibility" and would "work hard to bring down the deficit." Gary Pearce took the same cautious line: "We're not trying to have a real strong role in the convention. He [Hunt] didn't think and I didn't think he needed the distractions." Asked about his goals for the convention when he arrived, Hunt said he wanted to "collect money and prayers." Both the governor and the senator collected plenty of both at San Francisco and Dallas.

Helms returned to North Carolina considerably encouraged by what had happened in Texas. "The majority of the American people agree with Reagan's policies as they understand them to be," he said. "I will not let go unchallenged any effort to go contradictory to the philosophies of Ronald Reagan." Helms saw his own reelection chances enhanced in the President's soaring national popularity. Immediately after the convention the Helms camp produced a new series of television ads featuring Reagan's endorsement of Helms.

Hunt, on the other hand, had no illusions about the nature of his uphill battle. Tar Heel Democrats had arrived at San Francisco thoroughly worried about Mondale's impending victory. While they were initially encouraged by the selection of Geraldine Ferraro as his running mate, they differed over how she would fare in North Carolina. "She came across as tough, but not hard," said delegate James VanCamp of Southern Pines and a Mondale supporter. "I think generally she has a start at talking to some of the people who are more conservative than the Democratic Party and see a woman [on the ticket] as an impediment."

In his usual style, the governor put the best face on everything. "We can elect our local ticket and our state ticket and we can carry North Carolina for Fritz Mondale and Gerry Ferraro. We can really do that," he told the eighty-eight delegates at their final convention caucus. Privately, though, the Hunt forces admitted that their task would be more a matter of withstanding the strong Reagan surge, even of preventing a landslide like that in 1972, which buried all the Democratic candidates and installed Republicans in the Senate and the governor's office.

25. The Big Guns of August

As summer wound down, both Governor Hunt and Senator Helms slipped away for brief vacations. The governor spent a week on the South Carolina coast with his family after the Democratic National Convention. The senator retreated to his Lake Gaston home in northeastern North Carolina after returning from Dallas in late August.

Although Labor Day ordinarily marks the start of the election season in North Carolina, the senator and the governor were by that time several months into the race and running hard. Early in the year Gary Pearce, the governor's campaign manager, commented on the grueling pace Hunt set. "He's a driven man," Pearce said, after returning with the governor from a Washington trip. "He's never still. He's always making notes, talking or planning. Coming back on the plane Wednesday night, both of us were dead tired. All I wanted to do was go to sleep. But there sat the governor signing letters, making notes and working as hard as ever. He's got some hidden energy that never lets him stop."

Helms's associates had observed this same hard-driving quality in the senator. A friend recalled that in his college years, when Helms washed dishes for thirty cents an hour to pay his tuition at Wake Forest College, he was always on the go. "Jesse worked all the time," he said. "He stayed up working late at night. He never stopped." And so it had been during the strenuous summer. In addition to the conventions, fund-raisers, and the first television debate, both men oversaw strategy and moved around the state touching campaign bases and sampling the political winds.

In June, Hunt launched his final gubernatorial initiative for education at a special session of the General Assembly. He requested a $299.6 million enrichment program, including 15 percent salary increases for teachers, extra millions for the new science and math school, and other equipment and services. The legislature responded by allocating education $255 million in surplus funds accumulated from the improving economy. It was Hunt's last session of the General Assembly, and he won most of his requests.

In early August the State Board of Education released figures showing that the scores of Tar Heel youths on statewide achievement tests continued to rise in 1983–84, with students outscoring their counterparts nationally in all subject areas and at all grade levels. Almost simultaneously Hunt received two other boosts. The Educational Commission of the States gave him the 1984 James Bryant Conant Award for educational and political leadership, and the North Carolina Association of Educators belatedly endorsed him in his senatorial campaign against Senator Helms.

In July Governor and Mrs. Hunt played hosts to Britain's Princess Anne, who visited Chapel Hill and Dare County to celebrate the four hundredth anniversary of the first English settlement of America. In Chapel Hill the Hunts entertained forty-five guests at a formal dinner for the princess, featuring chilled strawberry soup, smoked mountain brook trout, filet of roast duckling, and mocha meringue parfaits. Earlier, in the spring, the governor and Mrs. Hunt had flown to Plymouth, England, to unveil a plaque honoring the first English settlers.

The ongoing drive to woo the tobacco vote continued through the summer. Senator Helms won a victory when Congress voted not to extend the eight-cents-per-pack increase in the excise tax on cigarettes passed, with Helms and East casting the critical votes, in 1982. The legislation had a "sunset" provision, included at Helms's behest, which would return the tax to eight cents on October 1, 1985. The Helms camp was elated. "I feel sort of vindicated because my sunset amendment was upheld," Helms said. "I am deeply grateful to Bob Dole and the Senate conference committee for standing by me. Bob Dole doesn't grow a stalk of tobacco in Kansas." Congressman Charles Rose hailed the action as "great news for North Carolina," but then downplayed the political benefits to Helms. "With the help of the Democrats," he said, "Senator Helms and Bob Dole have put out a tax fire [for this year] that they started two years ago."

When the Flue Cured Tobacco Cooperative Stabilization Corporation estimated that the federal government stood to lose $250 million on the proposed sale of surplus tobacco from 1974 to 1981, Governor Hunt laid some of the blame on Senator Helms. "We would not have this surplus of tobacco stocks had it not been for the doubling of the federal cigarette tax coupled with huge federal deficits that have made it more difficult to sell our tobacco abroad," Hunt said in July. Helms replied that how large the loss would be "remains to be seen" and declared that the tobacco price-support program would continue to benefit the nation's economy even if the government sustained losses of that amount. "I hope critics of the tobacco program will be willing to give fair consideration to the economic benefits to the nation provided by our tobacco farmers," he said.

In the meantime Senator Helms's nomination of one of his former aides, Samuel T. Currin, thirty-five, for a federal judgeship stirred spirited opposition. Two dozen lawyers in Raleigh organized a campaign to block President Reagan's appointment of Currin, United States attorney for the Eastern North Carolina District, to the federal judiciary. In a letter to the Senate Judiciary Committee the attorneys accused Currin of making a false statement under oath in a personnel dispute involving the North Carolina Attorney General's Office. Among Currin's opponents was Helms's old friend Superior Court Judge Pou Bailey, who came down hard against the young lawyer. "I can conceive of no more dangerous a person than a fanatic with power," Bailey wrote in a letter. "If he [Currin] is appointed a judge, that's what we would have."

Helms responded that partisan politics lay behind the opposition. "It's politics, and I don't care to engage in any speculation about it," Helms said. But his friend Judge Bailey was not moved. "I didn't want to hurt Jesse in any way," he explained. But he reiterated that Currin's actions as United States attorney had convinced him that he should not be promoted. Bailey explained that some of Currin's assistants, working under his supervision, had attempted to "compromise" lawyers, but he declined to elaborate.

Senator Helms also felt more reverberations from the first debate. In a letter to the secretary of the Senate he admitted he had made "a technical error of omission" by failing to report four overseas trips, as required by law. In the debate Hunt had suggested that some of the tax-exempt organizations sponsoring Helms's trips were indirectly subsidized by the government. Hunt asked whether the trips had been disclosed, but stopped short of accusing Helms of violating the ethics law. After the debate Helms took a second look and decided to put out another potential fire. (One of the trips, paid for by a tax-exempt foundation Helms himself had helped establish, was the visit to South Korea in 1983 when he narrowly missed being on KAL 007, the plane shot down when it violated Soviet airspace.) "I wasn't hiding anything," Helms told reporters. He conceded he should have reported the trips, but said he was a victim of a "screwball" interpretation of the federal act requiring disclosures.

In mid-August a prominent conservative religious activist, the Reverend Coy Privette, revealed he had sold the North Carolina Baptist State Convention's computerized mailing list to the Helms Reelection Committee for $450. Privette, executive director of the Christian Action League, used the list, which contained 18,852 names of Baptist pastors and church leaders, for distributing a three-page Helms promotional letter signed by four leading Baptists. It urged church leaders to support the senator and conduct voter registration drives following Sunday services. It also requested campaign contributions and mentioned Helms's support for housing legislation favorable to ministers.

Privette's action provoked heated comment among Baptists. Many felt strongly about the separation of church and state and opposed Baptist organizations engaging in partisan politics. "It would not be an overstatement to say they [Baptist leaders] are incensed," commented R. G. Puckett, editor of the *Biblical Recorder*, the convention's newspaper. "It is an abuse of the Baptist denomination. . . . That list should not have been made available to anybody for political purposes."

Privette acknowledged he hadn't obtained permission to sell the list, apologized to the convention, and admitted he had made an "error of judgment." The chairman of the convention's governing body, the Reverend James I. Murphy of Durham, called the use of the list "an embarrassment to Baptists" and said the convention's executive committee had reaffirmed a ban on the use of the list by outsiders.

The controversy over the mailing list was only one of several developments as the Hunt-Helms campaign approached its final two months. After the first television debate in late July the Helms camp launched a two hundred thousand dollar television advertising blitz. It praised Helms's debate performance and accused Hunt of playing loose with the truth. Specifically, it charged Hunt with talking out of both sides of his mouth about raising taxes. The Hunt people came back with a television ad featuring former congressman Richardson Preyer, cochairman of Hunt's campaign. "It's one thing to talk about differences on the issues," Preyer said. "But to tell the big lie, that's wrong, flat wrong." Preyer declared that Hunt "is clearly on record opposing any higher taxes. He's a fiscal conservative who has balanced this state's budget eight straight years as governor. . . . It's been a campaign of lies and distortions and negative ads by the Helms campaign machine. The same kind of campaign they've run again and again in this state for years."

Claude Allen, Helms's spokesman, called the Preyer commercial "the second-most low, gutter ad in the campaign." (The first, he said, was an ad linking Helms with conservative leader Roberto D'Aubuisson and the Salvadoran death squads.) Allen said Hunt was "trotting out Richardson Preyer to try to create a smokescreen. Hunt again is trying to evade the fact that . . . he indeed voted for a $217 billion tax increase" at a National Governors Association conference in February. At that time Hunt voted for a tax hike resolution, but hedged by saying he opposed "some of the specific steps called for in the resolution. . . . We need to close non-productive tax loopholes, but generally I oppose any general increase in taxes which might choke off the current economic recovery."

Meanwhile, State GOP Chairman Dave Flaherty mailed forty-five thousand letters seeking funds for Republican voter registration drives. In the letter he mentioned 77,020 new black registrations signed up through efforts of the Reverend Jesse Jackson and called them "frightening" and "potentially disastrous" to GOP candidates. The letter was accompanied by a bumper sticker displaying campaign buttons for President Reagan, Senator Helms, and gubernatorial candidate James G. Martin. The president of the North Carolina Association of Black Lawyers decried the letter and called it an "exercise in hate-mongering that is really offensive to black people."

On August 22 a newspaper reported that the Helms committee had sent out a fund-raising letter that Senator Helms purportedly wrote while at the Republican National Convention in Dallas. The letter made it seem as though Helms had received news of campaign financing problems while at the convention and had immediately written an urgent appeal. In reality the letter had been written in Raleigh before the convention. "It's consistent with the campaigning under false pretenses they do," said Gary Pearce of the letter. "It shows you the level of integrity of their campaign, a manufactured telegram from back home, all of which was written before they ever left Raleigh."

At the end of August Democrats spearheaded by Congressman Charles Rose pushed efforts to prove that the Helms forces had violated federal election laws in buying thousands of dollars of campaign services from Jefferson Marketing, an arm of the National Congressional Club. Federal Election Commission regulations prohibit corporate contributions of more than five thousand dollars a year to a political action committee. Democratic lawyers charged that the Helms for Senate Committee had paid Jefferson Marketing about $190,000 during the preceding year. A spokesman for the FEC said that in past advisory opinions the commission had proscribed committees from acting as "vendors of services" and thus meriting exemption from contribution ceilings.

A Helms spokesman said that the Washington law firm of Covington and Burling had advised that the transactions were aboveboard. "The Hunt people are just trying to be devious," said Carter Wrenn, executive director of the Congressional Club. "They're twisting the law . . . and are trying to mislead people for political purposes. What they ought really to be doing is charging the fair rate for Hunt to use the state airplane."

As Labor Day approached, Senator Alan Simpson (R-Wyo.) visited Raleigh and held a press conference to apologize for ugly remarks he'd made about Senator Helms in 1982 during the bitter Christmas filibuster against a bill to raise federal gas taxes. At that time Simpson had said that seldom in his legislative experience of seventeen years or more had he seen "a more obdurate and obnoxious performance." He had predicted then that angry senators would seek revenge against the federal tobacco and peanut programs. "At the time I made those remarks," Senator Simpson said in Raleigh, "it would be generous to say that I was testy, tired and sure I wanted to get back to Wyoming because I could quickly see we would be there until New Year's Eve. . . . I was feeling puny. That is a phrase we use out West when you are off your feed."

Immediately after the 1982 encounter, Simpson said, he had promised Helms to come to North Carolina to help him campaign and that was the reason for his visit. "It was my idea," he said, "all mine." Helms's bitter foe, the *Raleigh News and Observer*, mused that the possibility of losing a Republican majority in the Senate must have struck Simpson as "more obnoxious" than Helms's filibuster. "This . . . was the first time in the history of U.S. elections," the newspaper concluded, "that a senator from Wyoming had traveled all the way to North Carolina to debate himself."

But Senator Helms obviously had plenty of big guns for the crucial moments of the 1984 campaign. Among them was President Reagan himself, whose thirty-second television commercials began airing across North Carolina immediately after the Republican National Convention. "I cherish my friendship with Jesse," the President said, "and I need his honesty and his outspoken patriotism back in the United States Senate. . . . Jesse's courage on the tough issues is an inspiration to all Americans."

The Helmsmen Ride High

26. A Severe Identity Crisis

"Okay, here's a little pop quiz to see if you've really done your homework in this busy political season," said a squib in the *North Carolina Independent*, a liberal biweekly Tar Heel newspaper. "This U.S. congressional candidate from North Carolina is for major increases in defense spending including development and deployment of the MX missile, the B-1 and stealth bombers and the Trident submarine and against the nuclear freeze. He advocates voluntary school prayer, balancing the federal budget and law and order. And by his own admission, a list of his financial backers reads like a Who's Who of business and industry in North Carolina. Give up? Here's a hint: He is running for the U.S. Senate, his initials are J. H. and . . . he's a Democrat."

The squib appeared in April, long before the American electorate had begun to coalesce in landslide proportions behind President Reagan. By September the issues separating Jim Hunt and Ronald Reagan had dwindled to a precious few. "Wary Democrats shy from Mondale while GOP candidates cling to Reagan," observed the *Wall Street Journal.* Hunt continued to support the Mondale-Ferraro ticket, but he didn't make it a campaign theme.

As Labor Day passed and the Democratic campaign showed no signs of catching on, Hunt backed spending cuts and tight tax laws more zealously than ever. He opposed Mondale's tax-increase program, but deplored the federal deficit. "We can care for our people without raising taxes on the hard-working middle class," he said. The governor strengthened his attacks on Helms's tax breaks for big corporations and the wealthy, for failing to support education and the elderly. But nowhere, except on the deficit and in an occasional reference to Reagan's foreign policy, did he buck the President.

Meanwhile Senator Helms had readjusted his strategy following his tepid performance in the first television debate. As the Mondale campaign floundered, he added new elements to his theme of "Where Do You Stand, Jim?" He answered the question by repeatedly labeling the governor a "Mondale liberal."

This issue became part of the senator's offensive in the second television debate on September 9 in Wilmington, in which Helms stopped being nice and forgot his grandchildren. Hunt had lost none of his assertiveness, but the senator had shifted his tactics and become his familiar pugnacious self.

This time both candidates stood behind lecterns instead of sitting. Helms seemed more comfortable standing. He used gestures and body language that had marked his debating stance in the Senate. "The turn to the side, the stern look with pointed finger, even the little prayerful bow are all Helms techniques on the Senate floor," wrote A. L. May of the *News and Observer*. "During the debate Helms could be heard off-camera making grumbling noises as Hunt talked, harrumphs that have echoed in the Senate chamber."

When the senator launched the debate with a question about the Martin Luther King holiday, Hunt replied forcefully: "I support [it] not just in [King's] honor but in honor of all citizens, black and white, who have worked for equal opportunity, have worked for the future of this state and this country, where people can work together. . . . Now, Jesse, North Carolina's been making a lot of progress. I know you've been up there in Washington these 12 years and maybe you really don't know what's been going on here. The people have been working together . . . black and white. . . . Jesse, this is 1984. . . . This is a progressive state. We're not going to go back now and open those old wounds. That's what you want to do."

Helms replied rather sardonically: "Governor, I want to congratulate you on a fine political speech. That's typical of you. . . . You're proud, you say, of your support of a national holiday for Martin Luther King, notwithstanding all of the aspects against it. Now you're doing the same thing about the so-called voting rights act extension. . . . Let's bear in mind that Senator Sam Ervin described that legislation as the most atrocious, and I'm quoting him, the most atrocious assault on constitutional principles ever committed by Congress. . . . Now which is more important to you, governor, getting yourself elected with the enormous black vote, or protecting the Constitution and the people of North Carolina?"

Hunt replied: "Jesse, which is most important to you, getting re-elected or having the people of this state upset and fighting and set at odds against each other?. . . My gracious, how far back do you want to take us? Hey, this is a state that is making progress, Jesse. . . . You're just out of touch with it. And the reason we've had so many new industries come in, the reason we're growing and making progress the way we are is because people are working together; they care about each other; and they're not following the kind of negative, divisive leadership that you've been giving."

Hunt's first question charged Helms with accepting more than $150,000 in contributions from oil and chemical industry interests and giving billions in tax breaks to big oil companies. Helms replied that the statements were not accurate; he noted that Hunt was the beneficiary of a contribution from the largest oil company in the world, Exxon. Helms said Hunt was "demagoguing this issue." Then he dismissed the subject and asserted that Hunt wanted to close tax deduction loopholes on mortgage loans and medical care payments. Helms appeared ruffled as he accused Hunt of "talking through his hat."

Hunt replied: "Jesse, I'm not talking through my hat. Now you're getting all hot and bothered, and we've just started the debate." Helms replied laughing: "Oh, yeah." Hunt: "Calm down now, let's go on through with all these questions, even though they may be tough. First, I'm in favor of keeping the deductions for mortgage interest we have on our homes. I'm in favor of keeping that deduction for charitable contributions. . . . You're the one who has come forward with the tax plan that would knock out that deduction. . . . The real question is fairness. You voted for $227 billion of tax cuts for the oil companies in 1979. You voted for $60 billion in 1981. . . . You had a choice between the working people, the average taxpayers, and the big oil companies and . . . you chose to stand with the big oil companies again."

Helms replied: "There you go again, Jim, distorting the whole record. Now [that] was a question of whether we were going to try to become energy independent in this country or whether we were going to continue to rely on Middle East oil. . . . But I want to get back to this question." He then restated his charge that Hunt had used only black-owned newspapers for publishing ads supporting the Martin Luther King holiday.

Hunt shifted the subject back to the senator's votes for the oil companies, but then he declared: "With regard to the little question you just put, I'll put ads wherever I choose to put them. You've got so many ads running everywhere, Jesse, in this campaign, surely you'll let me decide where to put the little bit of money I have."

The debaters then turned to a complicated set of questions about the SALT II treaty. Helms charged that Hunt had continued to support the treaty even after President Carter had withdrawn it following the Soviet invasion of Afghanistan. Hunt said Helms opposed sitting down to negotiate with the Soviets. Helms emphasized the Senate Armed Services Committee's strong disapproval of SALT II treaty ratification.

In the next question Hunt assailed Helms for voting against public education—against math and reading programs, vocational education, and loans for deserving students. "If you are re-elected, will you keep voting against education?"

Helms replied he wasn't against education but did favor taking the federal government out of it and returning responsibility for its support to the states and local communities. "The decline, the deterioration of our schools began when people of your persuasion, governor, trotted to Washington with their hands out saying 'Give us money, give us money,' and not realizing, or not caring, whether the federal government would send controls along with the money."

Then Helms criticized Hunt's education record in North Carolina, charging that he had favored teacher salary increases only when he was running for office and saying SAT scores hadn't improved during Hunt's regime. Hunt replied that SAT scores in math had gone up "since Jim Hunt became governor" and that reading scores were not down. He supported federal aid for education as vital, citing his own need for a loan when he took vocational agriculture as a youth. "We need to have children who are learning more in these early grades and all the way through. You have voted against those programs. . . . We're not going to ever become a great country unless you support those things."

Helms replied, again sardonically, that he noticed Hunt supported legislation that would have brought teacher unions to North Carolina. He added he was voting to get "federal bureaucracy" out of the schools and that he thought the quicker that was done "the better chance we have of increasing the quality of education."

The hour's debate went on to touch the issue of industrial development. This gave Hunt a chance to recount what his administration had done in eight years. Helms quoted figures to show that Hunt's statistics were extravagant and inaccurate. "Now while Governor Hunt is claiming all of the credit for 200,000 new jobs, I would point out to him that the state of Georgia created over 400,000 new jobs. Furthermore it appears that many of the jobs the governor has been claiming credit for simply do not exist. . . . And Governor, even your good friend the *Raleigh News and Observer* admits that your industrial recruitment program is largely . . . a creation of . . . the 'Hunt public relations machine.'"

A question to Helms from the news media asked why he favored taking Social Security out of the hands of the federal government and putting it under private control. "I wanted to give the option," Helms replied, "primarily to the young and middle-aged because eventually we're going toward that. I wanted to give them an option of investing part of the taxes they pay into IRA savings-account-type accounts. And we had . . . something like 12,000 responses from the people of North Carolina and . . . precisely three who did not favor it."

Then Helms returned to an earlier subject. The best industrial development, the senator said, would stem from a balanced budget, cutting federal spending, and letting the private sector go to work. Helms opposed "costly programs, largely ineffectual, costing up to $100,000 to create one job. . . . As you say, governor, you can't have it both ways. You can't continually advocate jacking up spending and then contend seriously that you are going to balance the budget and reduce spending. It doesn't work that way."

Hunt replied that he had not "favored jobs programs. That's the wrong way to do it. The federal government ought not to try to put people to work. The Appalachian Regional Commission and the EDA provide some funds for water and sewer that go to the local communities, the counties and the cities to help them bring in industry. And private industries, they're interested in that and it helps them. That's the kind of thing I favor."

Helms, who had occasionally appeared rattled during the first half of the debate, strengthened his attack near the end. He fielded Hunt's question about opposing the Superfund for environmental improvement by saying it was too expensive even for the Carter administration. Hunt replied: "You've opposed clean air, clean water. You were the biggest friend of James Watt. You've got the worst environmental record in the United States Congress."

Helms accused Hunt of making "another political speech." Then he said: "This is the man who let the PCBs lie out on the side of the road for two and a half or three years. He didn't do a thing in the world about it. And then when you were forced to make a decision, what did you do? You scraped it up and you dumped it on the county least able to resist, Warren County. So before you present yourself as a great environmentalist, governor, I think you ought to explain to those people in Warren County why you did that to them. . . . And governor, while we are at it with your environmental record, the people of North Carolina know you're trying to conceal it, but they know that you made a secret deal with the state of Virginia to pump millions of gallons of Lake Gaston water to Virginia Beach."

Hunt replied that such charges were "absolutely untrue." But Helms objected that Hunt was speaking on his time (as the governor had done earlier when Helms interrupted him).

Helms then charged that Hunt had "paid Mather Slaughter [a state employee] to spy on North Carolina sheriffs and write political reports to you. And when this was uncovered the legislature abolished Mr. Slaughter's job. You put him right back on the payroll. One newspaper reported that Mr. Slaughter was being paid $25,068 to do nothing."

Hunt replied that Slaughter was now being paid to do safety work at North Carolina's ports. Then he said, "I knew that you'd jump on this, any little thing you can find, instead of discussing the real issues that affect the future of . . . North Carolina. I sent a message. I said I don't want anybody on the payroll of North Carolina who isn't doing their work and earning every cent of their salary."

Then the governor introduced a challenge similar to the one he had made during the first debate, to abolish all campaign expenditures from outside the state. He challenged Helms to join him in prohibiting "negative ads" on television. Helms replied: "We haven't put on any negative advertising. We just told the truth about you. It's sort of like Harry Truman said one time. He said the Republicans think I'm giving them hell. I'm not giving them hell. I'm telling the truth on you."

Helms tried to return to the Mather Slaughter question. But Hunt refused to respond and repeated his challenge about negative advertising. When Helms again balked, Hunt asked if he'd be willing to agree that "anytime either of us is going to say something critical about each other . . . that instead of putting on some faceless reporter that we can't see, that we would go on television and say that about each other ourselves."

At that point the moderator, George Diab, called time. Hunt moved on to challenge Helms's leadership in agriculture as chairman of the Senate Agriculture Committee. Helms admitted that the agricultural economy had problems, but noted that the Reagan administration's reduction of inflation and stimulation of employment were the best answers. He also supported balancing the federal budget. But then he mentioned the Slaughter case again, which led Hunt to respond: "I think agriculture is worthy of having our discussion about it tonight."

Helms's last question to Hunt—the final question of the evening—touched on what Helms called the "over-riding issue of this campaign—credibility." "During this campaign the governor has suddenly tried to lead a lot of folks to believe that he really supports Ronald Reagan's economic policy." Then the senator quoted a series of statements in which Hunt had opposed the Reagan program: "'I have opposed what the Reagan administration is doing to this country. I believe their economic policy is a failure.' . . . 'Every day that Ronald Reagan serves as President of the United States I think that Jimmy Carter looks better.'" Helms said one newspaper reported that "Governor Jim Hunt strongly denounced President Reagan's economic policies, delivering a tirade." "Now we all know that these things are bound to be the governor's positions because he has flat-out assured us in the first debate that he has not changed his position on any issue. Now I think it's fair to raise questions about the governor's credibility when he now proclaims all of a sudden his support for President Reagan's economic policies. I mentioned this to the President today when I was with him. He said, 'Well, with friends like that, I don't need any enemies.'"

As the program ended, Hunt appeared on the defensive. The governor sought to counter the question by hoping that Jesse's friend could "get some help for our farmers in North Carolina and . . . for our textile industry. . . .

You see, when it comes to the bread-and-butter issues, when it comes to the jobs and education and helping the elderly people, you're not there. But you are there having a picture with the President. All that kind of thing."

In his closing statement, Helms sounded his theme of the evening: "Ladies and gentlemen, Governor Hunt has declared that nowhere in this country do the voters have a clearer choice between candidates than they have in this state. I agree the choice is clear. Mr. Hunt doesn't want you to know it, but he's a Mondale liberal and ashamed of it. I'm a Reagan conservative and proud of it. Walter Mondale ran up the most liberal voting record in the Senate, and Governor Hunt said that Mondale served well in the Senate. . . . Governor Hunt's position by his own words is clear. He said 'I have opposed what the Reagan administration is doing to this country. I believe their economic policies are a failure.' Well, my position is exactly opposite. I supported Ronald Reagan's goals."

Hunt's closing remarks were less forceful. He said, "The campaign really boils down to one question: Which candidate has the right priorities for the future of this state and this nation?" He listed his priorities again—economic growth and jobs, education, fairness for working Americans, concerns for the elderly. He asked his viewers to "compare my priorities with those of Senator Helms and ask yourselves which candidate represents progress and a vision for a better future."

The candidates' comments after the debate indicated that the encounter had not been lop-sided. "I did what I wanted to do . . . show the people what Jim Hunt is about and what his priorities for the future are," the governor said. Helms said he thought his performance had improved over the last debate, that he had adopted new tactics and they paid off. "I was trying to be a gentleman in the first debate. I just let him lob the grenades . . . in my lap. Tonight I lobbed some of them back and got under his skin a time or two."

"I think Helms came out much more aggressively this time, and he was clearly better prepared to make the point he wanted to make," said Abraham Holtzman, a political science professor at North Carolina State University. "I think Jim Hunt did better than Jesse. . . . Through most of the debate Hunt carried the points he was trying to make and was able to press them home on Mr. Helms. Some of them Mr. Helms could not answer."

"What Helms had to do was to paint Hunt as a Mondale liberal," said Donald N. Schroeder, associate professor of government at Campbell University in Buies Creek. "He did precisely that, especially at the end. He made that point quite clear."

"I think Jesse was not at ease during the first 15 or 20 minutes," said Dean Mimix, associate professor of government at Campbell University. "His rhythmic and breathing patterns were getting in the way. In terms of image, I think the governor came off a little more polished and self-assured. But as the debate went on, Jesse gathered momentum and steam and came across as a Washington insider and poised."

Some observers thought Helms made Hunt uncomfortable on the Mather Slaughter issue. Hunt aides complained that off-camera Helms tried to distract Hunt by playing an imaginary violin, pointing at Hunt, and laughing as he answered questions. Helms's murmurs under his breath could be heard; but since no reporters were present and the cameras did not shift to the candidate not speaking, this was not apparent to the television audience.

Aides from both camps charged that their opponents had twisted and distorted the facts. Gary Pearce said that Helms rather than Hunt had supported elimination of the federal income tax deduction from interest in a 10 percent flat income tax proposal he introduced in 1982. But Helms replied he had considered that only a "starting point." Aides disputed the size of the environmental Superfund. Helms said it was $6 or $7 billion more than the Carter Administration had indicated could be wisely spent. Pearce countered that the original Senate bill authorized only $4.1 billion and "when Helms threatened to filibuster, the bill was cut back to $1.6 billion." Helms said he had favored the President's START talks for nuclear arms reduction, but Pearce asserted that Helms had opposed a Senate resolution in 1982 expressing Senate support for the talks.

Whether the second television debate had swayed "undecided" voters nobody could be sure. Some viewers said they were oversaturated with rhetoric and switched channels or pushed the button. Others felt the debates had become nagging contests and exercises in name-calling. Helms's decision to drop his gentlemanly role had made the second debate more combative and competitive.

One week later a special Gallup Poll reported that Helms had narrowly improved his lead. The figures were 49 to 44 percent, which represented a one-point gain for the senator since a poll conducted in May. But the undecided segment had jumped from 4 to 7 percent, and the poll's margin of error was 3 percent.

In mid-September Mark Russell, the stand-up comedian, appeared at the Stevens Center in Winston-Salem and commented on the rising tensions of the senatorial contest. "North Carolina is a wonderful state," he said. "You've produced Sam Ervin, Billy Graham, Jim Hunt and Jesse Helms. I'd say you've got a severe identity crisis."

27. The Reagan Tide

In a speech at Wake Forest University in early October Jim Hunt compared his campaign to unseat Jesse Helms with some of the basketball games he'd played in as a youth. "When they start to rough you up, you had to give it back," he said. "For 18 months . . . my opponent and his right-wing network have pounded into people's heads a series of distortions and outright lies about my record."

From the start the governor's managers had recognized that challenger Hunt had to take risks. One of them was playing rough. Exposing all the nooks and crannies of Helms's record over twelve years would require candid discussion of the issues, and would sometimes risk slipping over into personal muckraking or character assassination. One of Hunt's major strengths had been his "Mr. Clean" image, his refusal to engage in gutter politics. Yet the governor saw danger in letting his formidable adversary picture him as weak or vacillating.

From the beginning Hunt had decided not to turn the other cheek when Helms hit at him. But controlling his combativeness became more difficult as Senator Helms's candidacy surged with Reagan's popularity. Hunt's provocative "dead bodies" television ad in the spring, linking Helms with Salvadoran "death squads," had generated concern among some of the governor's supporters. Hunt considered the senator's support for Latin American dictators a legitimate and vital issue, but Helms called it a personal attack and used it to counter Hunt's contention that only the senator engaged in name-calling.

"I don't think Jim Hunt's organization can stay with Jesse Helms on negative advertising," one Hunt aide told a reporter in late summer. "I don't think Jim Hunt can out-Jesse Jesse." This represented the views of some Hunt advisers who were convinced that such ads could produce a deadly fallout. The aide went on to explain: "There is this notion that you're not a real man in this state unless you cut up your opponent. The voters . . . are a lot more educated and sophisticated than Jesse Helms gives them credit for, and Jim Hunt too."

Yet Hunt ultimately took a combative stance in the television debates. It was designed to expose Helms's record on such touchy subjects as Social Security, support for corporate tax breaks, slashes in veterans' benefits, and neglect of education. The governor mentioned these subjects repeatedly in the television debates, even as he tried to emphasize his positive vision for the future.

Helms's strategists, meanwhile, had perceived that Hunt was still remarkably popular after almost twelve years in office. They found few blemishes on his gubernatorial record, and trying to attack it directly seemed unpromising. Instead they planned a campaign to raise questions about Hunt's credibility and integrity. The television battle cry "Where Does Jim Hunt Stand?" was part of a grand strategy aimed at finally identifying Hunt as a "Mondale liberal." To do this the Helms campaign focused on inconsistencies between positions Hunt was taking in the campaign and things he had said and done in the past.

As the campaign approached its final six weeks, the shadow of Reagan's popularity loomed larger for the Democrats, and with it the possibility of a massive sweep which could transform the political landscape. The disarray of the ailing Mondale-Ferraro ticket reminded many Democrats of the Nixon coattails phenomenon twelve years earlier, when Helms first won office. A late September Gallup Poll had the President leading Mondale by 18 points in North Carolina. As Reagan's "Morning in America" crusade picked up momentum, the Hunt forces hunkered down and the Helms camp rejoiced.

Few Tar Heel voters had failed to join one camp or the other, and the division was close. Even those who over a dozen years had voted for both Hunt and Helms in different elections had made their choices. Only 7 to 10 percent largely nonideological, often moderate undecided voters remained to be fought over by the opposing camps. As the swing vote, they might easily determine the outcome.

Over the years Senator Helms had depended on the votes of many registered Democrats in a state where the margin against his party was three to one. He did it by soft-pedaling his criticism of the Democratic Party in general and zeroing in on his Democratic opponent. In 1984, however, Helms perceived the strong Republican trend and aimed his broadsides at the Democratic Party and tried to tie Hunt to its "liberal" leadership.

Pressures were especially evident in the business community, where many had remained registered Democrats in order to participate in primaries and local contests. As the GOP prospered, however, it became easier to take an openly Republican stance.

Hunt had courted this group assiduously. From the beginning of his administration the governor had put industrial recruitment and job expansion at the top of his political list. His allies in the corporate world extended from executive suites in the Piedmont to the tobacco baronies of the East.

Hunt had cultivated the friendship of business, sought its counsel, tried to serve its interests.

Some corporate executives cared little for Helms's personal style or his support for such issues as school prayer and abortion. Quite a few were occasionally embarrassed by the senator's stubborn pursuit of lost causes in Washington. But on the issues of most importance to them, economic issues, Helms was unwavering in his support for conservative positions. Many swallowed their reservations and went along.

As the autumn campaign unfolded, the Hunt camp found that running against a ticket which included both a powerful incumbent senator and a popular incumbent president produced problems he had not encountered in his earlier races. A strong governor who had won his previous elections riding with the national tide in 1976 and against it in 1980 began to find his own identity fractured. He struggled to maintain his own alliances in the Democratic Party, where an old-fashioned liberal was the standard-bearer, and simultaneously to avoid alienating moderates and conservatives whose views were often closer to his own.

An even more difficult assignment lay in getting the vital black vote to the polls without encouraging a white backlash. Earlier, during the heated presidential primaries, some Helms supporters down east had said, perhaps only half jokingly, that "you're going to have to choose between one Jesse or the other." Ever since Helms had tried to make political capital of a meeting between Hunt and the Reverend Jesse Jackson in the governor's office in 1982, the two had not been publicly associated.

Yet unless Hunt encouraged national black leaders to help him in North Carolina, an essential part of his support might not show up at the polls. "It's not a question of how the blacks will vote," said one Hunt supporter. "It's knowing how to get them to vote." When Jackson and Atlanta Mayor Andrew Young, Jr., visited North Carolina on voter registration missions in September, they carefully avoided open criticism of Senator Helms. At a Raleigh news conference Young repeatedly deflected questions involving the Hunt-Helms race. "I really don't know Mr. Helms," he said. Later he offered mild criticism, saying North Carolina needed to continue its tradition of brotherhood and justice and he wasn't sure that Helms saw things quite that way. Jackson's only reference to Helms came in an impromptu remark at North Carolina Central University at Durham. When a metallic object, probably a chair, crashed to the auditorium floor near the stage with a clang, Jackson remarked: "That was Jesse Helms's heartbeat."

Hunt ventured into another delicate area in September when he and Democratic gubernatorial nominee Rufus Edmisten addressed the North

Carolina AFL-CIO convention in Raleigh and won its backing. The Democrats promised to represent working people and said their Republican opponents were beholden to monied interests. Hunt also told the four hundred labor leaders that he was trying to build a broad-based campaign that included both management and labor. "It is because we have been fair and there has been progress that we have today working people like you and business leaders across North Carolina united in this campaign."

But then Hunt spoke of political risks in a state with large anti-union sentiment. Helms, he said, will "probably attack me" for this appearance. "I'm sure he is going to make something out of my visit today. He can say whatever he wants to. We'll answer that gentleman on November 6."

Bitter exchanges erupted during the third television debate on September 23 in Charlotte. During previous meetings Hunt and Helms had maintained a facade of studied civility even as they disagreed. During the third debate both candidates stepped up their caustic attacks. Helms, obviously bolstered by the Reagan momentum, exhibited some of the go-for-the-jugular skills that typified his debates in the Senate. Hunt scored decisively in only one of the dozen exchanges. Helms focused on Hunt's links with the "tax-and-spend" liberal policies of Mondale and mentioned his name forty times. The senator unleashed sizzling rhetoric and controlled outrage, which ultimately sparked Hunt's anger.

The climax came shortly after the debate's midpoint. Hunt had posed a question criticizing Helms's vote against veterans' pensions, which, he said, Helms called "welfare." "You have voted against funds for veterans' pensions and medical care for nine years running. You've tried to cut retirement and disability benefits for veterans. You've even voted for cuts that could force some VA hospitals and clinics to shut down entirely. How could you justify these votes against our veterans?"

Helms denied casting "votes against veterans" and cited his backing from veterans' groups. The exchange that followed was one of the sharpest of the whole series of debates.

Hunt: Now Jesse, I can see that you're really bothered by this question.

Helms: No.

Hunt: And by golly you ought to be because you have been calling it welfare. . . . Now I've got every single one of your votes right here, senator. You can't fool me, and I don't think you're going to fool the people of North Carolina . . .

Helms: Which war did you serve in?

Hunt: I did not serve in a war.
Helms: Okay.
Hunt: Senator Helms, now wait just a minute since you asked that question.
Helms: No, Mr. President, I was . . .
Hunt: I was in college, Mr. Moderator, during the time of the Korean War, and I was too old with two children when Vietnam came along. And I don't like you challenging my patriotism, senator.
Helms: I haven't challenged your patriotism.
Hunt: Yes you have. You know exactly what that question was, was calculated to do.
Helms: Well, I just wondered a . . .

Then the senator sought to explain his votes against transfer payments, which, he said, did not mean he was against veterans' benefits. "But I say again, governor, and I wish you'd look at me instead of looking down, I say again that the veterans of North Carolina, they don't want the federal government looking after them, they want a strong, stable government."

As it turned out, Hunt had misspoken about being in college during the Korean War. He was thirteen years old at the time. Afterward State GOP Chairman Dave Flaherty said Hunt's "blatant misstatement" called into question the rest of "his so-called military record." Hunt spokesman Will Marshall replied that "it's bad enough that Jesse Helms would take a cheap political shot like that. Now he's got Dave Flaherty out trying to continue this slur." Marshall said Hunt's error was due to his agitation over Helms's question. "Anytime someone impugns your patriotism, it would tend to make you angry."

After the heated exchange Hunt seemed unable to counter Helms's thrusts. The senator resumed his slashing attack on Hunt's "liberalism." He cited quotes from the governor's associates, Commerce Secretary Lauch Faircloth, and former governor Bob Scott. Hunt tried to change the subject, but Helms returned to it again and again. "I've heard you try to pretend to be a conservative. I've heard you say now tonight that you don't agree with Walter Mondale. Well, we've got to look back and see what the labor unions and Jim Hunt did to orchestrate the nomination of Walter Mondale. Governor, the problem I have with you, and I'm surprised about it, is that you're all over the lot. You're one thing today, you're another thing tomorrow. And the people know that. They know about the flip-flops, the windshield wiper."

The governor again defended his record. "The real truth is the people of this state know that Jim Hunt is a Democrat, and he's proud to be a Democrat," Hunt said. "Ours is the party of the people that has done so many good things for the people of this country. It's also made some mistakes. And it's made some mistakes of over-spending and of taxing too much. . . . I'm part of a new generation of Democrats who believe in three things: Number one, balanced budgets; number two, economic growth and providing jobs for people; and number three, racial justice."

Earlier in the debate Helms had adopted the Hunt strategy of challenging his opponent. The subject was embarrassing for Hunt: his repayment, under goading from the Republicans, of an additional $185,939 for use of state-owned aircraft and cars for political travel. "Would you agree to the appointment of a special prosecutor to investigate your admitted violations of state law, including the $185,000 you have confessed to, involving the misuse of state planes, helicopters, automobiles and state employees, for your political purposes?" Helms asked.

Hunt replied that he had "not misused any state property at all," that after calling in an outside auditor his campaign had paid "at the highest rate we could possibly pay," which was incidentally "more than President Reagan pays for his own use of Air Force One." The governor then added that "now that I've opened my books I would challenge you to do the same thing." He requested Helms to release the financial records of the National Congressional Club and its subsidiary, Jefferson Marketing Corporation, to ascertain whether payments to the latter had been used to disguise violations of campaign spending laws and provide cut-rate advertising costs.

Helms: I'm going to give you five seconds to answer my question, yes or no, about the special prosecutor. Yes or no. For once, answer a question, Governor.

Hunt: You don't have to answer a question.

Helms: No, Mr. Moderator, I don't.

Hunt: There's no reason for it. I told you, Jesse, that I had . . .

Helms: So your answer is no. Mr. Moderator, charge that time to him . . .

Hunt: Jesse, I told you that I had paid to use those aircraft.

Helms: Mr. Moderator . . .

Morris (Lee Morris, moderator): Gentlemen . . .

The bitter exchange went on without resolution until Morris said: "Gentlemen, I'll have to call time."

Senator Helms had dominated the third television debate. Its subject matter had ranged broadly, but the initiative had remained with Helms most of the time. He stuck doggedly to his principal theme, a simple one which he enunciated at the start and conclusion of the debate. In ending he put it this way: "Your choices will be clear in both the presidential race and the Senate race in North Carolina. And I say again, Mr. Hunt is a Mondale liberal and ashamed of it. And I'm a Reagan conservative and proud of it. Now Walter Mondale, as he has said tonight, is Mr. Hunt's man. Ronald Reagan is my man. Now that's the measurement of your choice in November."

Hunt, on the other hand, avoided linking his fortunes with Mondale. In his opening and closing statements he chided the senator's negativism and his bias toward the wealthy and privileged and reiterated his support for "people and progress" and programs like Social Security, protecting the environment, education, and economic opportunity for us all.

Six political scientists, polled by the *News and Observer*, agreed that Helms had scored strongest in the third debate by setting the agenda and keeping Hunt on the defensive. "I think this is the performance that Helms supporters have been waiting for throughout the campaign," said Donald N. Schroeder of Campbell University. "He came out every bit as aggressive as in the last debate, but he was much more polished and better prepared." "Hunt looked more apologetic and not on top of things and not really getting with it," said Professor Merle Black of the University of North Carolina at Chapel Hill. "I can see Jesse getting a little better from the first to the second and from the second to the third debate," said Professor Dean Mimix of Campbell University.

While the professors thought Helms grew stronger and Hunt weaker as the debates progressed, they also felt fewer people watched and fewer still were swayed. Increasingly criticism mounted about the name-calling and grandstanding. "In a lot of ways I think the debates are degrading," said one political observer. Another said: "It was sixty minutes of posturing. . . . I was bored. I'm sure it put some voters to sleep."

When questioned by reporters after the third debate, Helms and Hunt continued their sharp attacks on each other. "The last thing [Hunt] wanted, next to a case of leprosy, was a special prosecutor to look into the full extent of how he has milked the taxpayers of this state for four years or more," Helms declared. "[Hunt and Mondale] are inseparable. . . . They are the Siamese twins." "Senator Helms will not talk about the real issues because he doesn't want people to know how he's voted," charged Hunt. "He keeps trying to throw things off on me and run me down."

As the last month of campaigning arrived, the dramatic upswing in Reagan's support had nudged the Helms-Hunt contest. A mid-September poll showed that GOP gubernatorial candidate Jim Martin had even begun to chip into the commanding lead of Democratic candidate Rufus Edmisten. The combative debate stances of Helms and Hunt gave promise that the final weeks would be marked by more bitterness and invective.

28. "Macabre Wild Card"

The pouring rain at Marvin Speight's ninth annual fish fry on the Carolina coast on the last weekend of September, which drove some twenty-five hundred Democratic party faithful indoors, seemed symbolic of the problems that had overtaken Governor Hunt's campaign in recent weeks.

Ronald Reagan's burgeoning popularity was only one matter of concern for the Hunt camp. The governor had fared poorly in the television debates since the first round in late July. In the two September encounters Helms rediscovered his feistiness and centered his attack on excoriating Hunt as a "Mondale liberal." He even needled Hunt about not having served in his country's uniform, a subject not particularly germane to the campaign but one which attracted attention. It led the *News and Observer* to mention Helms's World War II wartime duties, which, it noted, "never took him across the state line. . . . [His] most dangerous combat involved changing the ribbon on the typewriter he used for cranking out [navy] press releases."

At the Speight fish fry, Hunt's legislative counsel, Zebulon Alley, recited a poem entitled "Ode to Jesse's Valor." Its opening stanza went: "What war were you in, Jesse? / Were there Nazis or Japanese or both? / Were the battles in icy cold waters / Or in deserts or deep jungle growth?" It concluded: "Now tell us your war record, Jesse / Your brave deeds should surely be known / When all your battles were verbal / And all your weekends in Raleigh at home."

The Hunt camp also tried to spoof one of Helms's television ads. The Helms ad showed the governor raising his hand in support of higher federal taxes at a governors' convention in Washington. The new Hunt commercial began: "They don't allow news cameras in the Senate and Jesse Helms must be glad of that. So this is an actual artist's drawing of Jesse Helms voting to . . . " The ad went on to depict Helms in six different sketches with his hand raised, supposedly voting to cut Social Security and veterans' benefits and favoring tax breaks for oil companies.

But the Hunt strategists could find little humor in one issue that confronted the governor in late summer. In August a superior court judge scheduled the execution of a fifty-one-year-old grandmother, Margie Velma Barfield, four days before the November 6 election, and it was expected that her attorneys would ask Governor Hunt to commute her sentence to life imprisonment. Mrs. Barfield, a private-duty nurse and cook, had been convicted in 1978 of the arsenic poisoning of her boyfriend. During the trial she also admitted poisoning her mother and two elderly residents who had employed her as housekeeper.

The Barfield sentence had been under appeal for years. The court had set the execution for August 31, but in July the United States Supreme Court issued a stay in order to consider additional evidence. When that court subsequently declined to hear the appeal, the case was remanded to Bladen County Superior Court, where Judge Giles R. Clark, a college roommate of Republican Governor Jim Holshouser, who appointed him to the bench in 1975, set the execution for November 2. Hunt's office immediately announced that the governor would "make a prompt decision" on a plea to commute the sentence, but, aside from any feelings they might have had for Mrs. Barfield, Hunt's strategists were worried about the timing of the death sentence and its potential impact on the senatorial election.

The North Carolina Association of Black Lawyers charged that Hunt's decision would inevitably be tainted with politics and asked Hunt to delay the execution in order to establish a citizens' panel to review the case. Hunt denied the request. Then in mid-September a group of five University of North Carolina professors asked Hunt to issue a reprieve until after the election on the grounds that his decision and politics had become irrevocably mingled. "This rush to a life-or-death clemency decision on the veritable eve of election puts undue pressure on you and is unfair to both Velma Barfield and to the people of North Carolina," said the letter. "We deserve a determination on this crucial issue in an atmosphere totally unclouded by any suspicion of political taint." The five also asked Hunt to appoint a commission to advise him on the case.

Hunt refused to act on these suggestions. He said his decision would be apolitical and based on information he received about the case. On September 16, immediately after Mrs. Barfield's lawyer submitted Hunt a petition requesting executive clemency, the governor set up meetings with supporters and opponents of the execution. Members of Mrs. Barfield's family asked him to spare her life on the grounds that drug addiction had led to her crime and that while in prison she had overcome her past and become a source of spiritual guidance for other inmates. "We have great compassion for the other families who have suffered," said Mrs. Barfield's son, Ronnie Burke. "We are victims ourselves. Our grandmother was one of the ones who was poisoned. We have forgiven our mom because we know that during that ten-year period when she was addicted to prescription drugs, her mind was not right. She lived from pill to pill. But unless you know her as well as we did, often it was impossible to tell that she was under the influence of drugs."

Evangelist Billy Graham's daughter, Ann Lotz, was among the petitioners for clemency along with friends, relatives, ministers, and former prison inmates. Mrs. Barfield's attorney, James D. Little, showed the governor a fifteen-minute video tape about a visit his client had with her family on Easter.

The following day the governor was visited by some forty supporters of the execution. They included families and friends of the two men poisoned by Mrs. Barfield, and they brought along two thousand letters supporting their position. "[Mrs. Barfield] is an outstanding liar," said Alice Taylor Storms, daughter of one of the poisoned men, as she stood with her two small children and other family members outside the State Capitol. She argued that Mrs. Barfield had not been under the influence of drugs, had not been rehabilitated, and would kill again if set free. "Up until my father's death, each time she had the opportunity to be rehabilitated. A serial killer does not want help. They enjoy killing and Velma Barfield enjoys killing. She enjoys watching people suffer and die and then watching the families as they suffer." The Reverend Raymond Ellis, pastor of Country Bible Baptist Church in Lumberton, the victims' hometown, said opponents of the death penalty had misinterpreted the Ten Commandments to suit their cause. "To kill by the state is not murder," he said. "It's fulfilling the law of God to take care of criminals. Those who disrespect your life and mine . . . people who deliberately disrespect the lives of people—capital punishment is appropriate for them."

After the hearings Hunt told reporters: "So often, the only side you hear are those people who favor clemency or oppose the death penalty. It's also important that you hear from victims—that you hear from their families. I'm making sure I get the information that will be helpful to me in making my decision."

Pressures on the governor increased as the Barfield case moved toward a denouement. Between June 1 and September 14 he received 1,203 letters about the case, 1,013 of which favored clemency. Some newspapers urged clemency. The *Raleigh News and Observer* quoted Mrs. Billy Graham in an editorial urging the governor not to approve an "unnecessary killing." "By putting Mrs. Barfield to death," it said, "the government of North Carolina would not deter anyone from committing a murder, would not protect the people from a dangerous person and, in general, would not make the state safer."

Traditionally Tar Heel governors have found clemency decisions among the toughest they have faced. On top of that Hunt knew that, whatever his decision, it would have political overtones, especially since, failing any further stays, the execution and the funeral would come in the last several days before the election. Joseph Grimsley, manager of Hunt's campaign, spoke to that point when the governor announced his decision. "Of course, it will impact the campaign," he said. "The question is how. Who knows?" Phil Carlton, Hunt's long-time friend, put it this way: "The timing is very unfortunate. It lends itself to the public perception that the decision would be a political one. That's at a minimum. It's beyond my comprehension why a judge would have set it the Friday before a Tuesday election."

On Thursday, September 27, Hunt spent much of the day at the Executive Mansion weighing his decision. Shortly before 4 o'clock he concluded his review of the case, gave Mrs. Barfield's attorney his decision and asked him to inform her, and called a news conference in his office, where he told reporters: "I do not believe that the end of justice or deterrence would be served by my intervention in this case. I cannot in good conscience justify making an exception to the law."

The governor's statement recounted arguments placed before him by supporters and opponents of the death penalty. He also said he had reviewed trial transcripts, issues raised in the appeals, and the formal clemency request. In addition he had had two members of his staff interview Mrs. Barfield. "My review of the case raises no question as to her guilt. She received a fair trial, presided over by one of the state's best judges. Her case has been reviewed in eight courts by 21 different judges."

The governor declared that "people on both sides are sincere in their convictions on this case" but "I cannot in good conscience justify making an exception to the law as enacted by our state legislature, or over-ruling these 12 jurors who, after hearing the evidence, concluded that Mrs. Barfield should pay the maximum penalty for her brutal actions. Death by arsenic poisoning is slow and agonizing. Victims are literally tortured to death. Mrs. Barfield was convicted of killing one person in this fashion; she admitted to three more, including her mother; and there was evidence of yet a fifth."

The Barfield case, linked as it was with an important senatorial contest, attracted worldwide media attention. The *New York Times* featured a photograph of Hunt on its front page. The *Miami Herald* headlined its story: "Death Row Granny Fights for Her Life." Coverage extended to the *London Daily Express* and *Libération* in Paris. Mrs. Barfield was interviewed by CBS News's "Sixty Minutes" and *Time* Magazine. The *Boston Globe* called her "a woman who has become a macabre wild card in the Deep South's hottest political race."

Both the governor and Senator Helms refused to speculate on the political implications of the decision. "North Carolina is a state that abides by the law," Hunt said. "As governor I have a responsibility to make the right decision in the interests of justice and protection of our people. I am satisfied I have made that decision."

Opponents of capital punishment were outspoken in their disappointment. "We will not stop the death penalty in this country until people get sick of the killing," said George H. Gardner, executive director of the North Carolina Civil Liberties Union. Daniel C. Pollitt, a law professor at the university in Chapel Hill, who had urged Hunt to delay the execution, declared, "We still have to vote for [Hunt]; it's just that it's much more difficult." The *News and Observer* castigated the insensitivity of the judge in adding to the governor's burdens, but concluded that the failure was the whole state's in becoming "a taker as opposed to a saver of lives." Judge Clark himself said the date of the execution was "in no way political."

Political or not, as one observer noted, the governor had set the stage for "an execution at a time when he would want his supporters to be marching toward the polls, not around Central Prison." Another, the Reverend Collins Kilburn, executive director of the North Carolina Council of Churches, declared: "I think there will be people for whom this will be a last straw. They won't go to Jesse Helms, but they just won't vote."

There was the possibility, of course, that Hunt's decision represented a net plus for his campaign, albeit an unwelcome one. Even though Mrs. Barfield would be the first woman executed in North Carolina in forty years, ardent opponents of the death penalty made up only a small portion of the electorate. A recent poll reported that 70 percent of North Carolinians favored capital punishment. The governor, whether he intended to or not, had quashed what could have become a sensitive issue between himself and Senator Helms if he had granted clemency. Throughout the campaign Helms had sought to portray Hunt as a "weak-willed liberal," one newspaper reporter commented, and even though earlier in the year Hunt had demonstrated support for capital punishment by refusing to grant clemency to another convicted murderer, intervention in the Barfield case would have guaranteed prolonged controversy.

Still, the Hunt camp remained nervous over the potential fallout. "Solomon himself can't tell you how that will affect people," said Phil Carlton.

29. The Punch-drunk Voters

In the first week of October pollsters sampling the North Carolina electorate discovered something unusual: the number of "undecided" voters in the senatorial race had begun rising. Could it be that excesses of the campaign —a too-early start, lavish expenditures, vitriolic exchanges, and overexposure—had generated a backlash against both candidates?

In a newspaper interview Helms acknowledged that in the television debates he and Hunt had behaved "like two long-tailed cats in a roomful of rocking chairs." He said he regretted appearing "harsh" and thought the sharp tone might have turned off voters. In Raleigh his press secretary, Claude Allen, carefully noted that the senator intended to emphasize the "positive" side of his record in the remaining weeks. Yet Helms's television ads continued to bombard Hunt as a "Mondale liberal" who supported tax increases, and his campaign once again reminded the voters that Hunt had accepted contributions from "radical homosexuals."

Attending the Vance-Aycock Dinner in Asheville on the eve of the first Reagan-Mondale debate, Hunt agreed that he and Helms had been perceived as harsh. "He [Helms] has come off far more strident than I have. I think it's primarily his doing; he's snapped at me."

The *London Economist*, which was following the campaign closely, surmised that "the voters are rather punch-drunk. Most of them knew where they stood when they started; they scarcely needed all this attention."

A leading Tar Heel educator got word to the Hunt camp that the governor ought to produce more television commercials showing Hunt "sitting under an oak tree with his father," explaining the good things he'd done and expected to do for North Carolina. Another top-level adviser questioned the new thirty-second commercials linking Helms with "a tight network of radical right-wing groups [Jerry Falwell, Nelson Bunker Hunt]" as "McCarthyism in reverse."

Hunt media adviser Peter Hart favored keeping up the pressure on Helms's negative record and his right-wing associations. The governor had hoarded much of his campaign money for a final push. He sought to keep the spotlight on Helms as "a mean little man," a holier-than-thou extremist posturing piety but grasping for power.

The same early October *Charlotte Observer* poll that revealed a rising mushiness index also indicated a slight shift that encouraged the Hunt camp: Hunt had taken a narrow 46 to 42 lead over Helms even as the "undecideds" jumped to 11 percent (with 1 percent choosing other candidates). A *Washington Post*-ABC News poll (September 23–October 2) showed Hunt leading Helms 51 percent to 42 percent with a 5.7 percent error margin. Helms's firm support had dropped from 54 percent three weeks earlier to 37 percent and Hunt's from 47 to 42 percent. While several questions showed that the voters had a poor opinion of both candidates, others revealed which issues had scored. Hunt's attack on Helms's vote for tax breaks for oil companies seemed effective. Helms's complaints about Hunt's use of state-owned aircraft for political purposes generated support.

But both candidates remained leery of polls. Hunt said he was pleased with the latest developments, but still considered the race "dead even." Helms said he didn't "place a lot of stock in polls, whether I'm ahead or behind." He added that the *Charlotte Observer* poll didn't have a good track record. In 1980, he said, it predicted that "Reagan would lose and John East would lose badly."

Just as the national pollsters were reporting that Reagan led Walter Mondale in forty-eight states and would win all but 11 of the 538 electoral votes, the Republican bandwagon hit an unexpected snag. In the first television debate on October 7 Walter Mondale came to life as a well-informed, articulate, and gracious critic of the President, while Reagan seemed hesitant, confused about his facts, and suddenly old.

After the debate the Democrats were euphoric: Mondale had kept his faltering campaign afloat. Among the Republicans there was consternation and recrimination. Senator Paul Laxalt (R-Nev.) blamed the poor night on overcoaching, too many statistics, and not letting Reagan be Reagan. Immediately afterward the polls showed a slight upswing in Mondale's strength, although the President's huge lead remained largely intact. Mondale's performance had revived spirits among Democratic field troops. Suddenly there was a feeling that a massive Reagan sweep, carrying with it Republican candidates all down the line, might not be inevitable. The President postponed setting his schedule for the last weeks of the campaign, which would have sent him into states with closely contested congressional races, like North Carolina's.

A few days before the first Reagan-Mondale debate a feisty, high-spirited Geraldine Ferraro touched down in Greensboro and Raleigh to sample the southern exposure in her pioneering campaign. In both cities she attracted enthusiastic crowds. Perhaps more significant, all the top state Democratic leaders turned out, in marked contrast to their response to a Mondale visit to western North Carolina in August (when neither Hunt nor Edmisten appeared). Governor Hunt introduced the vice presidential nominee in Raleigh and compared her chances for victory to those of another Italian-American—Jim Valvano, the North Carolina State University coach who led his basketball team to a national championship in 1983 against overwhelming odds. "The polls had him losing five weeks out too," Hunt said of Valvano.

Ferraro devoted as much of her high-voltage rhetoric to the Hunt-Helms contest as she did to the national race. "The people of North Carolina don't want to back death squads in El Salvador," she said. "The people of this state don't want leaders who smear the good name of Martin Luther King . . . who drag their feet on the Voting Rights Act. North Carolina has moved past the politics of division, and that is another very good reason you're going to elect Jim Hunt." The right-wing ideology of Senator Helms, she said, "is out of step with North Carolina, out of touch with your traditions and totally out of line."

Some in the estimated crowds of six thousand in Raleigh and three thousand in Greensboro undoubtedly turned out simply to see Ferraro and had no intention of voting for her. Small anti-abortion groups with placards protested in both cities. As Hunt noted later, however, there was excitement and electricity in the air during her visits. One mother said, pointing to her five-year-old daughter, "I wanted [her] to come and see this. . . . I think it's important." "I came to make a statement," said another woman carrying a sign with a photograph of a fetus. "I'm opposed to her stand on abortion."

Overall, state Democratic leaders seemed pleased with the response to Ferraro, but North Carolina Republicans were ready to unlimber their most potent weapon. On the night following his unimpressive first debate with Mondale, President Reagan flew from Louisville to Charlotte on Air Force One with one familiar associate—Senator Helms—and another, until then, surprise backer—H. Edward Knox, the unsuccessful Democratic candidate for governor. Knox's wife and brother had openly moved into the Reagan camp in the summer, following Knox's defeat at the hands of Rufus Edmisten, but Knox had said he would support the state Democratic ticket.

At an open-air rally at noon in south Charlotte under blue skies the President attracted a crowd of more than thirty thousand people, who cheered him enthusiastically during his twenty-two-minute speech. The rally was a "political extravaganza" which included more than ten thousand American flags distributed to the crowd, patriotic medleys, sky divers, and thousands of helium balloons. When Reagan introduced Knox and announced he would be national cochairman of Democrats for Reagan-Bush, there was a gasp from the crowd. In his speech Knox talked of Charlotte's growth and prosperity. "This city and many other cities have prospered since you took office," he said. "We don't want to turn back, do we, ladies and gentlemen?" Knox asked the crowd, which responded with a loud "No." Knox praised Reagan's leadership style and concluded, turning to the President, "You made us proud to be Americans."

In his speech the President enumerated the glowing statistics about the economy which had marked most of his campaign appearances. Saying he needed support in Congress to continue his program to renew America, Reagan made a strong pitch for Helms: "Do you know how hard he works for your state? He's one of my greatest supporters too. And we need him back in Washington. North Carolina could not have a greater export this year."

Reagan also endorsed by name other Republicans on the ticket—Jim Martin for governor and Alex McMillan, the Republican candidate for Congress from the Ninth District. In his introduction of the President, Helms recalled how he had urged Reagan to run for President as early as 1973. "The fury of his critics notwithstanding, Ronald Reagan is a great President because he is a great human being," Helms said. "Americans want the President to be strong and decisive. They don't want a promising politician in the Oval Office."

The President included other local touches in his speech. He mentioned North Carolina's 8 percent unemployment four years earlier compared with a 6.5 percent rate today. He criticized school busing for racial integration. He said Democrats "favor busing that takes innocent children out of the neighborhood school and makes them pawns in a social experiment that nobody wants. I don't call that compassionate." The crowds did not applaud those remarks, and later Charlotte's school superintendent, Jay Robinson, expressed concern about the President's statement. "To suggest going back to all-neighborhood schools—which would mean re-segregation—is shortsighted to say the least," he said. "In my opinion, it would tear the conscience out of this community."

Reagan also renewed his call for voluntary group prayer in public schools and voiced support for tax credits for parents who send their children to private schools. Conspicuously absent from the rally was Charlotte's black mayor, Harvey Gantt, who was not invited and said he did not think it appropriate anyway for a Democratic official to appear at a partisan Republican function. Gantt had succeeded Eddie Knox as mayor, with the latter's support, but he had responded critically when Knox's wife and brother endorsed Helms.

Most politicians of both parties agreed that Reagan was a powerful drawing card in North Carolina. There was considerable doubt, though, whether Knox's defection would be a political asset for the Republicans. Newspaper editorials again labeled the former Charlotte mayor "Turncoat Eddie," and one said Knox had "found a home" and could look forward to "obliging Republicans" stepping forward to "help clear up [his $300,000] campaign debt."

The final Helms-Hunt television debate on Saturday, October 13, in Charlotte reflected new wariness on the part of both candidates. Their supporters had been reporting negative responses to name-calling and mudslinging. The rise in voter indecisiveness signaled public annoyance with the longest and costliest senatorial contest in history.

Held at the Adam's Mark Hotel in conjunction with the annual convention of the North Carolina Association of Broadcasters, the debate for the first time included a live audience. Several dozen television and radio officials attended. Also there, as invited guests of Senator Helms, were Senate Majority Leader Howard Baker (R-Tenn.) and Senator Robert Dole (R-Kan.), chairman of the Senate Finance Committee.

Under the format for this debate the candidates were sitting at desks and direct questioning was limited. As a result the exchanges were less rancorous and the overall tone restrained.

The debate began on a positive note, as Helms praised the upbeat attitude in America and attributed it to Reagan's influence. Hunt underlined his gubernatorial service for eight years. "I represent a tradition that has deep roots in the North Carolina soil. A tradition of sound progressive government that has moved this state forward over the years."

In his first question the governor quoted "one of the senator's closest political allies" (the Reverend Jerry Falwell) as saying he hoped and prayed "for the day when we won't have any public schools. The church will have taken them over." "Do you agree with that statement?" Hunt asked Helms.

Helms replied, "Of course not" and criticized Hunt's definition of 'radical.'" "He uses the term 'radical' to blast anybody and anything that's not liberal," he said. Noting that Hunt had opposed President Reagan's economic policies, he went on to name organizations with which he had worked closely—chambers of commerce, veterans' organizations, and farm groups

—and then mentioned Senators Dole and Baker, who were in the audience, and President Reagan, who had been in Charlotte earlier that week. "Now, Governor," he concluded, "are all these people who are supporting me part of some right-wing political conspiracy?"

Hunt later reminded Helms of the issues on which the senator and Reagan had disagreed, including the bipartisan rescue plan for Social Security, which both Baker and Dole supported. Hunt reemphasized that he did not want North Carolina to be known for "narrow, intolerant leaders who claim that God is on their side. Rather I think we should try to be on God's side. I respect Senator Helms's views, but I could not disagree with him more strongly about the course our state and nation should take."

Much of the first half of the debate covered familiar differences between the candidates on increased spending and tax increases. Helms charged that Hunt had not really balanced the state's budget but had favored hikes in gasoline taxes and worked behind the scenes for other tax increases. Hunt vigorously defended his record, saying he had only championed a necessary gasoline tax increase "to keep our highways going" and insisting that other increases originated with the General Assembly.

A question from the media inquired why Helms had been cool toward Gerald Ford and enthusiastic about Ronald Reagan. This led Helms to recount his early support for Reagan as far back as 1973, when he visited him in California. "I went to lunch with the Reagans at their home," he said. "And you learn a lot about people when you go into their home and talk with them. You notice the Bible on the table. . . . You gain an understanding of what they really are. And I admire this man. He's a compassionate, decent man who has been kicked around by the left-wingers in this country and by the liberal press."

Another media question mentioned that the number of undecided voters had doubled in recent weeks. "Does this suggest a backlash," the questioner asked Governor Hunt, "from the barrage of negative advertising you and your opponent have been running?" Hunt replied that he shared the questioner's concern about negative advertising. "This campaign started way back on April 1, 1983, when Senator Helms started running advertising, all of it critical, trying to tear me down. . . . Now, you may recall that . . . I asked Senator Helms if he would agree with me that we would stop taking any out-of-state money. . . . In the next debate I challenged him to . . . let's cut out the negative advertising. In both these cases he said no. But we've got to do something to change this situation. The campaigns are too long. They cost too much. That money should be spent somewhere else."

Helms replied by saying: "You know what a negative ad is, don't you? It's the other fellow's ad. Now I have repeatedly suggested to Governor

Hunt that he inform me of any advertisement that we run that is not factual. He has not done that. There was one small error in one ad and we pulled it. . . . The only way we could get his record examined by the people . . . is to buy what the governor gets free because he's down here using state planes and state automobiles and state personnel to campaign, and I can't get here."

As the debate proceeded, the principals returned to such subjects as support for education, the environment, spending cuts, and the federal deficit. Hunt asked Helms what he would do to combat acid rain. Helms replied that the problem is a "question of how far you want the government to go and how fast." Hunt asked Helms about helping working women. Helms replied that the best thing for working women is a strong economy. As for loans for college students, Helms said the private sector should help. "We can't forever sit home and say, 'Let Washington do it.'"

In their closing statements both candidates spoke in a positive vein. Hunt urged that the electorate cast a vote "that you will be proud of." Helms mentioned his post as chairman of the Senate Agriculture Committee (for the second time) and declared that "the President and I need your support if the economic recovery is to continue."

After the debate partisans in both camps proclaimed "victory," but the principals refused to join them. Both had clung to familiar themes and argued their cases forcefully but not with vitriol. David Williams, a speech professor at Wake Forest University, said: "I didn't think there was a clear winner. This was a very even kind of debate." Both candidates, he added, were trying to avoid personal confrontation. Some newspaper editorialists rejoiced because the candidates had refrained from personal attacks. "It was good to see both candidates closing out their series of debates on a higher political plane," declared the *Greensboro News and Record*, "with each man giving voters positive reasons to vote for him."

The following day Governor Hunt made two public appearances, something rare for him on Sunday. At a Wake County gathering before 350 supporters he again castigated Helms's right-wing fundamentalist ties, then used evangelistic language of his own: He urged his supporters to "talk to everybody you see like you're trying to save his soul, for its future." Later that day Hunt appeared at the North Carolina State Fair in Raleigh to present an award to comedian Jerry Clower. Some ten thousand people had turned out for Clower's performance; on Hunt's appearance some in the crowd applauded politely while others booed and hundreds departed as Hunt read a proclamation. Hunt ignored scattered calls of "Vote for Jesse," but by the time he had finished speaking only a few thousand spectators remained.

30. Search and Destroy

As Congress adjourned in mid-October, Jesse Helms returned to the campaign circuit in North Carolina, having made an intriguing about-face in strategy. On a foray into the Piedmont the senator took with him two prominent, nationally known blacks: Roosevelt ("Rosey") Grier, the former Los Angeles Rams lineman and friend of the late Robert Kennedy, and Bill Keyes, a former Reagan White House adviser, now head of Black PAC, an organization attempting to win black supporters for conservative candidates.

Helms explained that he "hadn't done anything to communicate one on one" with blacks during his twelve-year senatorial career, except those he knew personally in Raleigh and Washington. "I think after the election maybe I ought to do a little better. I ought to make an effort to communicate more—not for political purposes but so we can have an understanding about what brotherhood is and about what sound economics are and that sort of thing."

Grier, the tall, beefy athlete who had wrestled Kennedy's assassin, Sirhan Sirhan, to the floor in Los Angeles and had since turned to religious revivalism, was an enthusiastic campaigner. "I believe this man Jesse Helms is a great American. . . . He's my brother," he said. Keyes noted that Black PAC was pushing candidates who "favor traditional moral values" and said he was not "bothered" by Helms's past hostility to civil rights legislation. He had known Helms for six years, he said, and "found him to be a very caring person."

At his first public appearance with Grier and Keyes, in Greensboro, Helms was also accompanied by three Republican senators—Chic Hecht of Nevada, John Chafee of Rhode Island, and Robert Kasten of Wisconsin. But for his trip the next day to small, predominantly black Livingstone College (750 students), in Salisbury, the senator had with him only the two out-of-state black visitors and his press secretary, Claude Allen, also black. Helms had been invited to speak on the college's lecture series, and when he showed up, he was greeted by some one hundred silent black students locked together arm-in-arm outside Varick Auditorium. Helms extended his right hand to one of the students, but the youth refused to shake hands. Helms moved on, saying "Just the same, I love you." Asked by reporters why he refused to shake hands, the student said: "Why should I put my hand in the dirt?"

The program before an audience of about one hundred began, as one reporter noted, like a "tent revival" with Grier testifying about his Christian faith and his belief that Helms will help steer the United States as "one nation under God." Helms's speech was short and got right to the point. "I didn't come here with the anticipation of getting any votes," he said. "I know how you're going to vote. I knew when I came in here. If you want to boycott, that's fine. But at least I came here to tell you where I stand." Helms went on to say that he hoped to start a dialogue with blacks after the election. The common denominator, he said, would be "faith in the Lord." The students who remained outside, he added, were "shooting themselves in the foot" by not attending, because blacks stood to gain the most from the political and economic system. "They better start listening to the people with whom they think they do not agree."

Helms spoke calmly during his formal talk, but grew agitated during the question-and-answer period that followed. He charged that blacks were being used by the Democratic Party, which had been "jerking you around" for years. "You have the most to benefit by an expanding private sector. You don't want to be a captive of the welfare system in Washington, D.C. You want a job." Helms insisted that a particular segment of the population should not be singled out because of past mistreatment. "People who brought slaves over here were blacks themselves," he said. "Remember that. I never owned a slave. I wouldn't own a slave, doubt my family ever owned a slave. . . . This system—the free enterprise system—is open to everybody."

At one point when Helms again mentioned the students boycotting his speech, a faculty member interrupted to note that there were students inside the auditorium. Another commented that Helms had said little in his speech about where he stood. Helms bristled and charged that one question was a "political statement." He showed annoyance over students whispering in the audience and declared: "I'll let you finish your conversation, and then I'll go on, okay?"

Later the students outside said they had boycotted the lecture because they feared Helms might use the appearance in his television advertising to give the appearance of having black support. Jim Hunt quickly took note of the new Helms initiative. "I think he's going to have to do a lot more than just haul Rosie Grier around with him [to win black votes]. I don't think [Helms] has shown that he believes in equal opportunity. I don't believe he has indicated by his own example . . . he believes in equal employment opportunities. He has, throughout his career, had his appeal to prejudice and to fear and to things that divide people, and I think the black people of this state know that very well."

Other black leaders also castigated Grier's endorsement. "A black carpetbagger is as bad as a white carpetbagger," said Kelly Alexander, Jr., of Charlotte, vice president of the state NAACP. Irving L. Joyner of Raleigh, president of the North Carolina Association of Black Lawyers, said: "Rosie Grier is obviously misinformed about the history of Jesse Helms. And before he allows himself to be trotted in, he ought to conduct an assessment of the commodity he's being asked to represent." Joyner also said he thought that by using Grier Helms was appealing to moderate whites by showing he was supported by blacks. "I see his use of Rosie Grier as a ploy to say to some moderate whites that he is not as bad as he has been painted to be on the race issue."

Jack Betts, a *Greensboro News and Record* journalist who had covered Helms over a ten-year period, saw something else in the Livingstone encounter: "The over-riding impression one gets from witnessing Helms in such a setting is that the senator is not only uncomfortable before a black audience, but that he does not know how to handle himself, does not understand the people he is facing." Betts went on to note that other southern politicians who had earlier held views on civil rights similar to those of Helms—such as Senators Strom Thurmond and Robert Morgan—had long since appointed blacks to office and picked up black support.

Press aide Claude Allen said Helms's Livingstone visit was not politically motivated—but then commented that the black vote totaled 12 percent of the total in the 1978 election and could go as high as 20 percent in November. "That is a lot of new registered voters, and they can't be neglected." For his part, the senator, who had earlier called Hunt's appeal to black voters "racist," acknowledged no inconsistency in his new emphasis. Although Helms had never lectured at a predominantly black school before, he said he accepted the Livingstone invitation because, had he not, the media would have said "he's afraid to come." Gary Pearce, the Hunt campaign director, speculated that Helms was "using a back-handed way of injecting a racial tone into the campaign" to bolster the possibility of a white backlash vote against Democrats. Or, he noted, Helms may have been trying to tone down the perception that he was intolerant of blacks. Others felt Helms's about-face reflected apprehension about the closeness of the campaign.

Meanwhile, Helms stepped up his campaign in other unfriendly areas. The perception among Jewish groups that Helms was anti-Israel had led pro-Israel PACs to make Hunt the third-largest recipient of their contributions in 1984 (some three hundred thousand dollars worth). To try to counter that perception, Helms's National Congressional Club sent out a national "Jewish mailing" of its own to seven thousand individuals around the country. In addition, Helms's chief foreign policy aide, James Lucier, met Jewish leaders on a week-long trip to Israel arranged by Marshall Breger, a Reagan White House aide. And in late August Helms himself met for two hours with a group of twenty prominent Jewish leaders in New York City at the Regency Hotel. Earlier he had shifted his position on the West Bank issue.

To try to offset Hunt's attacks on his alliances with authoritarian figures abroad and to tout his foreign policy experience, Helms unveiled an October surprise. At a Raleigh press conference he announced that twenty-two current United States ambassadors and one former ambassador, ten of them representing American interests in Latin America, had endorsed his reelection campaign. On hand at the press conference to praise Helms were J. William Middendorf, ambassador to the Organization of American States, and Lewis Tambs, ambassador to Colombia, who called the senator's experience an investment that shouldn't be wasted. Middendorf described Helms as a "good team player" and a "special friend" of the Reagan administration on Latin American policy.

In a press release the Helms camp said the endorsements were a "historic event" and described the ambassadors as being "on the front line of the President's foreign policy." As a senior member of the Senate Foreign Relations Committee, Helms had been involved in confirmation of most of them. The next day thirty-six former ambassadors responded by saying that the endorsements violated a well-established tradition of political neutrality among diplomats. Lawrence S. Eagleburger, number-three official at the State Department until the previous summer, said the ambassadors "showed terrible judgment. It's damned well embarrassing to the Department of State. It opens the door to ambassadors participating in the election every two years." "An active-duty ambassador who engages in partisan politics diminishes his office and undermines his or her own ability to serve the United States abroad," the American Foreign Service Association, representing twelve thousand career Foreign Service officers, said in a statement. None of the ambassadors was subject to the Hatch Act, the law limiting participation in politics by federal employees, since they were top White House appointees, but criticism was widespread. "Something just doesn't smell right about the ambassadors giving their support to the senators who confirm them," said Congresswoman Patricia Schroeder (D-Colo.), chairman of the House Civil Service Subcommittee. William van den Heuvel, who had worked in several Democratic campaigns and was ambassador to the United Nations during the Carter administration, said that Helms "has a history of terrorizing people in the State Department and blocking appointments. How does it look when these ambassadors, in their fawning obeisance, endorse him?. . . They'll be seen as politicians who are on a string and are identified with Jesse Helms."

The State Department said the endorsements did not represent its official view. It also indicated they were frowned upon and released a March cable from Secretary of State Shultz which said that "ambassadors have been discouraged from extensive participation in partisan political campaigns. That tradition was based largely on the historical concept that American foreign policy should be conducted in a non-partisan manner."

Several days later United States Ambassador to Mexico John A. Gavin denied he had endorsed Helms. "I have not given, nor will I give, any candidate authority to use my name for political purposes while I hold this office," Gavin told the *Washington Post*. Speaking for Helms, Claude Allen apologized for "any inconvenience" caused by the use of Gavin's name and said it was based on a birthday greeting and other correspondence from the ambassador. "We'd like to think our diplomats were conscientiously doing America's work abroad and far too busy to dabble in North Carolina politics," observed the *Greensboro News and Record*. "But, alas, we were disappointed."

In still other ways the tempo of the campaign picked up in mid-October after Congress adjourned. Both Helms and Hunt launched meet-the-voter tours in every part of North Carolina. From the beginning Hunt had told his staff: "We've got to win this race person-to-person." He had continued that emphasis even as his own strategists sought to match Helms's costly media campaign, which had been in progress for nineteen months. "I think that getting out and doing this grass-roots campaign, being with the people, is by far the most effective," Hunt said in October. "The best place in the world to campaign is at the check-out counter in a grocery store. That's the way I do. You get into conversations with people, they tell you things they're concerned about, you really get the feel of folks."

During the summer, while Congress was in session, the senator had confined his public appearances to the weekends and had not done much personal campaigning. He accompanied Bush and Reagan on their visits to North Carolina, but even on those occasions he returned immediately to Washington. The Helms campaign was less tightly organized at the grass-roots level than Hunt's, which had its "keys" in every county and hundreds of volunteers, and thus was less dependent on appearances by the candidate to build enthusiasm among local workers and supporters. As the election approached and public weariness with the television campaigns heightened, however, the Helms camp showed more interest in getting its candidate out on the hustings.

Both candidates continued to hear more complaints about negative advertising. At a rally in Raleigh Hunt told his supporters that the television airwaves had become so cluttered that "[we] can't get our campaign messages across. We can't use TV like we've done in the past. It won't get through in the current climate." As Hunt worked a campaign crowd at a Raleigh breakfast, a construction company official told him both candidates ought to "knock it [negative advertising] off." Hunt told him he'd tried without success to get an agreement with Helms to drop negative advertising. "I used to take my kids out and give them a good hard licking for what they [the candidates] are doing," the official later told a reporter.

After the television debates Helms and Hunt developed campaign themes out of thrusts that had proved successful on the airwaves. Hunt stepped up his barrage against Helms's ties with "a nationwide network of right-wing extremists" who "claim they have a special mission to save America, and anyone who disagrees with them is considered an enemy." Helms retaliated by defending his alliance with the Moral Majority's Reverend Jerry Falwell and said religion could keep America on the right track. "I hear all the humanists say, 'You must not let religion or Christianity show its head in the political process.' I say to heck with that. This country was founded on those principles. . . . I believe we began having our problems when we decided to make a god of government instead of realizing that this is a government created with and by God's guidance."

Helms's aides labeled Hunt's criticism of Helms's ties to a wide spectrum of right-wing groups, including some with racist and anti-Semitic ties, as "guilt by association" and pointed to Helms's support from Reagan and thirty Republican senators as evidence that he was in the Republican mainstream. "We could expound on and undertake a campaign against Jim Hunt's labor unions connections, the radical feminist connections, the socialist connections," declared Claude Allen. In the same session he added: "We could go back and do the same thing with the queers." Later he called a reporter and apologized for the remark, calling it an indiscretion. Will Marshall, Hunt's aide, labeled Allen's reference to "queers" as "entirely in character with the tone of the Helms campaign."

Both sides continued their invective. Hunt charged Helms with lying when he denied he had taken negative stands on Social Security; Helms claimed that Hunt had dissembled when he disagreed with Mondale about raising taxes but supported doing the same thing by "closing tax loopholes." Hunt handed out a four-page campaign letter signed by Helms concerning Social Security and called it full of "slick distortions" about his (Hunt's) stands on Social Security. Helms declared, "The only association Jim Hunt ever had with Ronald Reagan is to cuss him out and criticize his programs." Hunt's campaign reprinted and distributed a 1981 *Wall Street*

Journal story saying that Helms "apparently had a pet name—a euphemism—for blacks. He calls them 'Freds.'" Helms backers put out a forty-nine-page pamphlet of derogatory drawings of Hunt, including one picturing him in a pigsty. The caption asked: "Will Jim support tax-funded abortion for poor animals?" In another mailing the great-great-nephew of General Robert E. Lee, Retired Vice Admiral Fitzhugh Lee, railed against modern-day "carpetbaggers" such as the Reverend Jesse Jackson who "have invaded the South." A Hunt supporter replied: "Jesse Jackson is the first carpetbagger born and raised in South Carolina."

The *Washington Post* proclaimed that the "Hunt-Helms race has polarized the electorate" and said that North Carolina's three R's in the contest were "Race, Religion, and Registration." On the last "R," figures released by the State Board of Elections on October 19 showed that, as registration books closed, North Carolina had the largest number of registered voters in its history—nearly 3.3 million, or 77 percent of those eligible to vote. This represented an 18 percent increase from the number registered for the 1980 presidential election. Robert W. Spearman, board chairman, said: "North Carolina certainly is in the top of all the states in eligible people registered."

That, of course, told nothing about how many of those eligible voters would get to the polls. North Carolina's bitterly partisan struggle had aroused the two major warring coalitions—the Democrats and black civil rights organizations versus the Republicans and a network of white, fundamentalist church groups. "The two reverends have done very well here," said elections board executive director Alex Brock. He referred to the Reverend Jesse Jackson and the Reverend Jerry Falwell, both of whom had spearheaded registration drives among their followers all over North Carolina. Falwell had warned his supporters that if Helms were defeated, "the whole nation [would] be set back, in my opinion, five to 10 years in the battle to return this country to sanity."

A closer look at the figures revealed that, while the Democrats had picked up more potential voters, the Republicans had grown as a percentage of the electorate. In 1980 there were 2.91 registered Democrats for every Republican; in 1984 that ratio had dropped to 2.73. The percentage of black registrants had increased over the four-year period, but Republicans had shown a larger upsurge in the shorter period since the 1984 primaries. David Price, state Democratic Party chairman, said: "Our effort over the past four years to increase voter registration has succeeded beyond our most optimistic expectations." "I just can't believe it," said David Flaherty, state GOP chairman. "The Republicans are the highest they've ever been. I'm sure many of those who registered Democrat will vote Republican."

Thad Beyle, associate professor of political science at the University of North Carolina at Chapel Hill, had a more objective analysis: "When you sort it out, it's bound to benefit the Republicans more," he said. "The margin between Democrats and Republicans is closing, slowly, due in part to the trend of younger voters to register Republican. . . . This election depends, of course, on who does the best job of getting their voters to the polls. We are evolving into a two-party state."

Release of the new registration figures in mid-October was followed by that of the latest fund-raising statistics from the Federal Elections Commission, which revealed that the North Carolina race had become the costliest in history. As of the end of September, expenditures by both campaigns had reached $20.7 million, eclipsing the $20.5 million spent two years earlier in California. Helms had raised $12.5 million and Hunt $7.8 million. Hunt allies had raised another $1.04 million through the North Carolina Fund.

"We've just had to raise more in order to try to stay in this game," Hunt said. "And of course we're still being outspent two or three to one." When asked at a campaign rally whether he thought there should be limits on campaign spending, Helms replied: "I do not, and I don't think the First Amendment does. Not one nickel we have spent or raised has been tax funds." He added he was proud to have the support of so many thousands of people who wanted him to stay in the Senate.

As an Indian summer lingered in North Carolina, Hunt took off on a whirlwind, almost breakneck, tour of his old stomping grounds, the Coastal Plain. Touring shopping malls, factories, hospitals, tobacco warehouses, and crossroads villages, in what one reporter called a determination to "shake hands with every undecided voter between Rocky Mount and Greenville," he made as many as fifteen stops per day. As he finished one day, hot and perspiring in shirt sleeves, in the little village of Winterville where one thousand partisans had shown up at an agricultural rally, Hunt sounded his keynote theme: "The real differences when you get right down to it and sweep all the mud away is: What do you, the people of North Carolina, want your senator to do?" He framed the decision as a "classic choice" between a doctrinaire right-winger and a pragmatist who focused on jobs, education, and agriculture.

Helms took off in his twenty-seven-foot motor home called "Avocado One," crisscrossing the same eastern Carolina flatlands, reporter Chuck Alston of the *Greensboro News and Record* reported, "like a circuit rider visiting his flock . . . exhorting the gospel of free enterprise, limited government and moral values" and citing the "devilish ways" of his opponent. "The real issue in this campaign, my dear friends, is who will tell you the truth," Helms declared to crowds of supporters chanting "Jes-se! Jes-se!

Jes-se!" "There's one thing I will do, I'll tell you the truth. Governor Hunt has a real problem in that regard. . . . [He] should install a WATS line for listeners to learn the 'falsehood of the day.'"

"What began as an ideological crusade for both sides," reported David Rogers of the *Wall Street Journal*, "is ending more as one long personal mission of search and destroy."

31. A Dead Heat?

As North Carolina reached the end of its costliest and most polarized senatorial campaign, both candidates agreed it was too close to call. But in the polls a slight movement toward Helms could be detected. On the final weekend a special Gallup Poll showed Helms leading 49 to 46 percent, while a *Washington Post*–ABC News Poll put Hunt up 46 to 45 percent.

The Tar Heel electorate was thoroughly weary of the mudslinging and media barrages, which, by some estimates, had approached twenty thousand television commercials. It was probably true, as the *London Economist* noted, that most of the voters had already decided how they would vote and little of the last-minute invective and attempted arm-twisting made much difference.

In the final days, the tone of the campaign became, if anything, even harsher. The governor's forces charged that an anti-abortion bill proposed by Helms in 1981 would have outlawed certain birth control devices used by millions of American women. Helms called Hunt a "consummate liar" and his allegations an "outrageous smear." The senator's wife, Dorothy, appeared in a television commercial in which she described the Hunt spot as "disgusting and dishonest." Hunt replied that the ads were accurate and that "if he [Helms] doesn't believe they are accurate, let him go argue with Dr. Charles B. Hammond, president of the N.C. Ob Gyn Society." Hunt maintained that the bill, by defining human life at the moment of conception, could have opened the door to laws prohibiting forms of contraception that work after conception takes place. In 1981 physicians had testified against the Helms legislation, along the lines Hunt described, at a Senate subcommittee hearing presided over by Senator John East, who said the thrust of his colleague's bill was to return authority to establish abortion policy to the states. But the bill never came before the full Senate for a vote, and East said he doubted it would be resurrected.

Both candidates began to mimic each other in tactics and language. For example, in response to the long-fought battle by Congressman Charles Rose and the Hunt forces to have the Federal Elections Commission investigate relations between the National Congressional Club and its subsidiary, Jefferson Marketing (they charged that that company's cut-rate pricing practices were illegal), Helms's lawyers filed a complaint with the FEC accusing the governor of election law violations. The complaint alleged that various arms of the Hunt campaign were funneling illegal money into the contest. It accused the governor of using his office "to provide each of his political committees with cut-rate services, including transportation." It also charged that the defunct North Carolina Campaign Fund, a Hunt operation, transferred its mailing list, which cost more than $1 million to develop, to the Hunt Exploratory Committee for $1,750.

Hunt's camp described the lawsuit as a "ludicrous" attempt to deflect attention from the FEC investigation of the Helms organizations. The lawsuit to probe the multi-million-dollar National Congressional Club combine had been initiated two years earlier by Rose after his own Republican campaign opponent had been aided by Congressional Club contributions. But Rose's suit had been stalled by the FEC and the federal courts, which expressed concern about revealing confidential corporate information until the investigation was completed. Just before the election a federal district judge, Louis F. Oberdorfer, ruled that the results of the FEC investigation would not be released for another thirty days, on a date well beyond November 6. The Hunt forces were bitter about further delay of a lawsuit which had already been stalled for more than two years.

The Helms forces suffered a blow during the final week, when the political action committee of the Veterans of Foreign Wars announced it had withdrawn its endorsement of the senator. The director of the VFW PAC, Fred von Renbow, said a reexamination of Helms's voting record had shown it fell short of the requirements for an endorsement. He blamed the faulty information on a computer error. The withdrawal came on the same morning Helms had distributed and read part of a lengthy statement mentioning fifteen pieces of legislation he had voted for or sponsored on behalf of veterans. In the release Helms also declared: "I am proud to have been endorsed by the Veterans of Foreign Wars' political action committee." Helms later claimed that the head of the VFW, Billy Ray Cameron of Sanford, worked for the Hunt campaign, but a Hunt aide denied it. When told of the VFW reversal, Hunt commented: "That's exactly what he [Helms] deserved. He's voted against the veterans every time he's turned around."

The stress had begun to show on both candidates. At a Raleigh news conference Helms engaged in a verbal free-for-all with British-born journalist Julian Harrison, called him a "jerk" and a "liar," and asked supporters to eject him from the room. "Sweat popped out on Helms's face," a reporter wrote, "and he waved his arms in the air" as he reacted to Harrison's question about Helms's demand that spring that President Reagan recall his ambassador to El Salvador, Thomas R. Pickering. Helms said his letter to the President had only requested Pickering's "temporary" recall. The letter accused Pickering of interfering in the runoff election between José Napoleon Duarte and Roberto D'Aubuisson, whom Helms had defended against accusations that he had led right-wing death squads. Helms later accused Hunt's campaign of sending Harrison to the news conference—a claim that both Hunt and Harrison denied.

Earlier the *Wall Street Journal* had reported a similar episode in Charlotte. "[Helms's] courtly manners" wore thin and he "erupted in anger at a questioning reporter and swore at him in a hotel lobby." The *Journal* said Helms "quickly sought to make amends but appeared shaken, hastily lighting a cigarette when he was in the privacy of a room."

Governor Hunt had also exhibited anger during the campaign. During the third television debate, when Helms asked him what "war" he had served in, Hunt could barely contain his rage as he responded: "I don't like you challenging my patriotism." As the campaign ended, Hunt seemed worried about name-calling and mud-fighting. "North Carolina deserves better than this," he told one thousand mayors at a convention of the North Carolina League of Municipalities in Winston-Salem on the last day of October. "It has not been good for the state. North Carolina should not be known around the nation as the home of negative multi-million-dollar campaigns."

Nevertheless, Hunt continued attacking Helms and charged that negative assaults from both sides were Helms's fault. "Unfortunately, turning the other cheek doesn't work," he told reporters after his Winston-Salem speech. If elected, Hunt said, he would "not rest" until Congress and the nation found ways to ensure that future campaigns would be different from his battle with Helms. He spoke of limiting campaign spending and fashioning a code of ethics and new policies for television advertising. In a newspaper interview published on the Sunday before the election, Hunt defended his taking the tough road in responding to Helms's attacks. You can't remain on the defensive, he said, when they keep pounding at you.

"That's part of why we've had to come back strong and tough and put on an ad that shocked a lot of people, while it was true [the 'crumpled bodies' ad]. You've got to defend yourself, and sometimes you have to defend yourself with an offense. And everybody who's played ball or done anything else knows that." So the governor continued his pressure on the senator's record right up to the eve of the election.

Meanwhile, the so-called "macabre wild card"—the execution of convicted murderess fifty-two-year-old Velma Barfield four days before the election—was played on its judge-ordered schedule. The state took the life of Mrs. Barfield by lethal injection at two o'clock on the morning of Friday, November 2. Placard-carrying crowds, including opponents and supporters of capital punishment, gathered outside Raleigh's Central Prison. The event, the first execution of a woman in the United States in twenty-two years, had little visible impact on the senatorial race. The execution was widely covered by the media. Governor Hunt, who had refused to commute her sentence, again received wide publicity, as he had earlier when he announced his decision not to intervene. The governor canceled his campaigning on the morning of the execution and remained in his office.

Seven days before the election Helms had appeared glum as he confronted the VFW controversy and lost his temper with a reporter. The following day, though, his mood was upbeat as he arrived at his Wake County campaign headquarters, where over one hundred volunteers and supporters awaited him with a cake for his forty-second wedding anniversary. "I've got some bad news for you," Helms said slyly. "We just got a poll, our poll. We don't have but 54 percent of the vote." Helms's aide Carter Wrenn confirmed that the poll showed the senator leading Hunt by 54–46. It came on the heels of a *Charlotte Observer* poll which gave Helms a 47–43 lead, with 10 percent undecided.

As the cheering subsided after Helms's announcement, the senator went on to chide his two traveling aides, both in their early twenties (he called them "storm troopers"), who, he said, lacked stamina to keep pace with him on the campaign trail. But then he reminded his supporters, as he had done previously, that the margin of victory in Senator John East's 1980 campaign was less than five votes in each of the state's 2,352 precincts. Wrenn added later that while he felt "pretty good," a "lot can happen between now and Tuesday."

Elsewhere in the last days of campaigning the senator seemed optimistic. At appearances in Asheville, Greensboro, and Raleigh with Senator Jeremiah Denton (R-Ala.) he lauded free enterprise and pumped for Reaganomics, blaming the deficit on the House of Representatives, where tax measures originate, and not on the White House. In Greensboro, a textile stronghold, he criticized the Carter administration's decision to expand trade with China, where, he said, "slave labor" provided an unfair production advantage. Helms said "an official of the state of North Carolina" (meaning Hunt) had lobbied for the decision.

Hunt's last week of campaigning was as strenuous as those that had preceded it. At news conferences across the state he was accompanied by a former head of the Social Security system, Robert Ball, to hammer away on that key issue. Ball, commissioner of Social Security under Presidents Kennedy, Johnson, and Nixon, declared that Helms had been an ardent foe of the system and repeatedly voted against legislation designed to increase benefits and improve finances. "His record on Social Security is consistent opposition to the measures for improving the system over his entire career in the U.S. Senate," Ball said.

Eight days before the election the governor returned to his home county, Wilson. There before a crowd of five hundred at Bill's Barbecue and Chicken Restaurant he declared: "You know Senator Helms's priorities. They are the priorities of the Congressional Club with all that powerful organization means. . . . They are the priorities of Jerry Falwell and the Moral Majority. They are financed by the Nelson Bunker Hunts and the other oil billionaires. They are the priorities of working with the right-wing military rulers and dictators around the world."

As he talked with reporters along the campaign trail, the governor was guardedly optimistic. He said he thought the momentum was "coming our way," but noted "there is a sort of national tide we're going against," meaning President Reagan's personal popularity. He shared Helms's awareness that a few voters might change the outcome. "Robert Morgan lost by only 3 and one-half votes per precinct," Hunt said of the 1980 senatorial election. "We're not talking about changing a great number of voters. We're talking about a few here, a few there."

On the final weekend before November 6 both Helms and Hunt warned of possible subterfuge at the polls. In Lexington on Friday, Helms said he would have "at least one" representative at every precinct to guard against "any irregularities." Hunt charged that Helms's "ballot security" program, which some thought might include voter challenges, was designed to intimidate black voters. He said the Democrats also would be watching for election fraud. Helms praised a letter sent by Raleigh-based United States Attorney Sam Currin, a former Helms aide nominated for a federal judgeship, in which Currin said his staff would closely monitor election procedures in eastern North Carolina. "I think that's his duty," Helms said. "I think that's the duty of every U.S. attorney."

Four days before the election a special Gallup Poll underwritten by Tar Heel news organizations and conducted October 30 through November 2 reported that Helms and Hunt remained in a virtual dead heat (49–46). The same poll showed a significant surge by GOP gubernatorial candidate Jim Martin against Rufus Edmisten. All through the campaign Edmisten had led Martin by wide margins—51 to 39 percent in September. But the newest poll showed them tied at 46 to 46 percent, indicating that Martin's vigorous and largely positive campaign was getting results.

Increasingly the looming Reagan landslide threatened Democratic fortunes across North Carolina. In the polls the Reagan-Bush ticket led the Democrats by 62 to 35 percent. Political seers in both parties had agreed that if the Reagan vote ran above 60 percent, the coattails effect could be substantial. "It is déjà vu 1972," said Walter DeVries, a pollster from Wrightsville Beach. "As Reagan stays in the 55 percent to 60 percent range, it is tending to have an effect on the other races. The trend in the polls has been consistent movement away from Edmisten and movement away from Hunt. If that continues to happen, Helms and Martin will win."

On the final Sunday before the election the Hunt forces aired an expensive (ninety thousand dollars) thirty-minute television commercial on the state's major television stations. Narrated by Hal Linden, star of the television series "Barney Miller," it was a dramatic effort to clarify the differences between the two candidates and tip the balance toward Hunt. Filmed in documentary style, it linked Helms with Reverend Jerry Falwell and the Moral Majority, Texas oil billionaire Nelson Bunker Hunt, Salvadoran right-wing leader Roberto D'Aubuisson, and Korean evangelist the Reverend Sun Myung Moon. The second half featured statements supporting Hunt from conservative Democratic leaders, such as former governor Dan Moore, and insisting that Hunt was no "Mondale liberal." The commercial ended with a look at Hunt's positive programs and a seven-minute close-up of the governor seated in his executive mansion office attacking Helms's negative ads, expressing regret for the long and expensive campaign, and vowing, if elected, to "put a stop to that kind of campaign."

On the final two days before the election Hunt concentrated his efforts on the pivotal metropolitan centers of the Piedmont, where he held news conferences and courted voters with his wife, Carolyn, at his side. In those final solicitations, Hunt touched on both his record in industrial procurement and education and Helms's negative role as a right-wing leader with poor records on Social Security and veterans' benefits. Expounding on the theme that the senator was trying to hide campaign irregularities, Hunt said: "Jesse says, 'If it ain't broke, don't fix it.' I say to Jesse, 'If it ain't crooked, don't hide it.'" Taking on the demeanor of a country preacher, Hunt's longtime friend Phil Carlton, who accompanied him on the final forays, depicted Tuesday's vote as a choice "between good and evil."

On the final weekend Helms flew from one end of the state to the other. In airport news conferences he charged that Hunt was a man "not to be trusted" and expressed the hope that he "never has another day in public office after he's finished his term as governor." The senator also linked Hunt with "homosexuals, . . . labor union bosses," and "crooks."

In eastern Carolina Helms made a big issue of his success in defending tobacco price supports in Washington. "Let's talk about Governor Hunt's repeated charges that the Senate has not been kind to the tobacco program," he said in Greenville. "He says it's because I'm so unpopular in the Senate. That's a strange thing because the tobacco program has never once left the U.S. Senate with one scar on it. All the damage that has been done to the program has been done in the House." Helms repeatedly made promises about what was to become one of the crucial national issues growing out of the campaign. "This senator," he said, "is going to continue to be the chairman of the Senate Agriculture Committee not the Foreign Relations Committee," he told the cheering crowd in Greenville.

The senator also repeatedly waved the flag of anti-Communism and urged the voters to "deliver the strongest possible mandate to President Reagan . . . as well as to his programs and supporters, including me." "Do we want to return to the kind of economic disaster created by Jimmy Carter and Walter Mondale, as Jim Hunt would have us do?" he asked in Asheville. "Or do we want the Reagan recovery to continue?" Helms frequently mentioned the "bloc vote" (telling reporters later he was referring to blacks). "He's [Hunt's] counting on the bloc vote to win." He also accused the governor of having made an unspecified "deal" with the Reverend Jesse Jackson. But then he added he himself would attract black voters concerned about the conservative issues of banning abortion and allowing organized school prayer. Helms also denied any connection with the Reverend Sun Myung Moon, saying he had met Moon only once, in 1974, and also that he was proud of his friendship with Bunker Hunt.

The campaign ended in a blaze of charges and countercharges. Each candidate spoke, at times, about whether his competitor might crack under the strain and let the heightening tensions change the chemistry of the contest. During the last week Hunt told reporters he thought Helms was showing signs of losing his grip on himself. "He's really getting paranoid. I've noticed his desperateness, the name-calling. He really can't take the pressure. I'm amazed at the way he is acting. I hope he lasts out the remainder of the campaign." Helms spoke similarly of Hunt, saying, "He is desperate, he is harried, he is frustrated, he is frightened, and that's the size of it."

Yet, as election day dawned, neither the senator nor the governor had broken under the strain of one of the hardest-fought political struggles in North Carolina's history.

32. One of a Kind

Early Tuesday evening, November 6, even before the lines had diminished at some East Coast polling places, Dan Rather, Tom Brokaw, and Peter Jennings began telecasting news of Ronald Reagan's avalanche. On the fifty-state wall maps in the network election centers state after state lit up for Reagan, as results from exit polls were analyzed and announced. It was a thunderous affirmation for the incumbent president, encompassing all age, economic, sexual, and ethnic groups (except blacks and the jobless). The Reagan-Bush ticket won 59 percent of the popular vote and the greatest electoral romp in history—525 votes, leaving only 13 for Mondale-Ferraro.

The President's landslide could be explained simply in the words peace, prosperity, patriotism, and personality. Mr. Reagan's victory stemmed from citizen confidence in a booming economy; command leadership exercised by an attractive, relaxed chief executive; the prevailing climate of peace, uneasy though it might be; and an earnest but inept Democratic opposition campaigning on issues perceived as bankrupt by a majority of the voters. Beneath the surface the President's triumph seemed to represent the second stage of a political realignment, a turning away from the welfare state toward the "Opportunity Society."

In North Carolina and other states of the old Solid South this shifting alignment appeared even more dramatic than it did in the nation as a whole. Reagan carried the state by 62 percent, but the erosion ran deeper, washing out Democrats at the statehouse and courthouse levels along with their brethren at the top of the ticket. Pundits carefully noted that, nationally, the Democrats gained two Senate seats and lost only fourteen House seats—a relative standoff in a presidential election year. But North Carolina voters unmistakably tore away the remnants of one-party solidarity. Some Tar Heel seers called it "de-alignment" rather than "realignment," meaning that voters on both sides became less party oriented and more independently selective. Democrats continued their abandonment of the the straight party ticket at the state level, indicating that something more than Reagan's popularity was involved.

As in 1972, the Republicans won the Tar Heel governorship, a Senate seat, and several additional congressional seats, plus numerous legislative and county courthouse positions. Such massive shifts didn't occur outside the South. One Tar Heel analyst described the factors at work as Reagan, recovery, religion, race, realignment, and Rufus. One wag commented slyly: "North Carolinians didn't want to elect a governor named Rufus." Another said three factors helped Jesse Helms win—"outside money, inside money, and sanctimony."

A shrewd North Carolina judge anticipated the key issues eight months before the election. "If the national ticket is Reagan-Bush versus Mondale-Jackson," he said on March 2, "that will have plenty of impact. And if either Rufus Edmisten or John Ingram gets the Democratic nomination for governor, then look out. The Democratic Party will be ruined. Jesse will benefit from all this, especially if the economy doesn't collapse and the foreign policy situation doesn't blow up." The judge's prophecies largely came true (if you substitute Geraldine Ferraro for the Reverend Jesse Jackson.)

Congressman James G. Martin's victory margin over Attorney General Rufus Edmisten (54 to 46 percent) fell short of the President's but exceeded Jesse Helms's narrower edge over Jim Hunt (52 to 48 percent). Martin scored well for several reasons. His integrity and solid leadership qualities overwhelmed Edmisten's business-as-usual partisan politics. Toward the end of the campaign the attorney general was openly described as a boozer and womanizer. The phrase that best described him for many Tar Heels was that he simply "wasn't gubernatorial." Martin's program not only offered fashionably conservative tax cuts for business and the affluent but also championed elimination of the state sales tax on food, which would benefit the middle class and the poor. Ideologically, Martin stood near the mainstream of the state's conservative Democratic leadership. He refrained from mud-slinging and built his name-identification campaign skillfully as the electorate became disillusioned with the national Democratic ticket and his shopworn opponent in North Carolina.

At the same time the Democratic candidate for lieutenant governor, Robert B. Jordan III, held off his Republican challenger, John H. Carrington, to become head of the party's decimated forces, just as Jim Hunt had done in 1972.

When Governor Hunt's mentor, former congressman Richardson Preyer, arrived at the Raleigh Inn early Tuesday evening, he encountered Eli Evans, president of the Revson Foundation, and Hunt's chief adviser, Phil Carlton. Evans had been a speech writer and Carlton the state office manager for Preyer during his unsuccessful quest for the governorship in 1964. The three wondered if this election night would resemble the one ten years earlier. They soon discovered it would.

Governor Hunt and Carolyn reached their fourth-floor suite at the Raleigh Inn around eight o'clock. It was shortly afterward that the television networks announced Jesse Helms the winner. Senator Helms remained at his Raleigh home watching the returns with his family until it appeared his victory was assured. Then at a few minutes after eleven he and Dorothy went to the ballroom of the Raleigh Hilton, his election-night headquarters, to greet his ecstatic supporters, who were chanting, "Jes-se," "Jes-se," "Jes-se." A beaming Helms began by paying tribute to Ronald Reagan. "Let me ask you a question. Aren't we proud of our great President? . . . What a victory he has achieved today; and it all began in North Carolina in 1976." Then Helms turned to his own triumph. "Now look at what you have done to me for the third time! . . . How can I even begin to thank so many thousands of you across this state and across the nation who have worked so hard and sacrificed so much and supported us in every possible way with your prayers, your love and your faithfulness to principles?"

Helms's enthusiasm began to expand as his jubilant supporters pressed toward him cheering and hugging one another. This victory, the senator said, "has sent a signal throughout the world that North Carolina is a God-fearing, conservative state. A state where a majority of people believe in the free enterprise system and believe that it ought to be allowed to function. . . . A state where people believe in school prayer, and they want it restored. . . . You are the kind of Americans who will make sure that these principles do survive." He added that North Carolina was a state where people "certainly reject politicians who try to be all things to all people."

Helms exhibited his knack for anecdote which had characterized his rise to national prominence. "Please be mindful that it was not Jesse Helms who won this election. It was you." He recalled a saying that his father was fond of repeating: "When you see a turtle sitting on a fence post, you know he didn't get there by himself. . . . I didn't get here by myself!"

Finally Helms turned to a subject which surprised many in his audience.

He extended an olive branch to the state's black voters, who had strongly supported his opponent. Helms said he intended to work for all people, "especially black citizens, who have the most to gain from a strong and flourishing free enterprise system." Helms went on to explain that he had wanted to reach out to them during the campaign but thought that would have been seen as a political gesture. (The senator did bring Rosie Grier, a black athlete, to accompany him on campaign forays across the state and spoke at a predominantly black college.) "Whether or not you [blacks] voted for me today," he concluded, "you have my hand of sincere friendship. I will do all I can to bring our people together."

Meanwhile, at the Raleigh Inn, supporters of the entire Democratic ticket had gathered to hear the news, good or bad. A reporter for the *News and Observer* wrote of the scene in the ballroom. "A hush fell when ABC projected the Helms win (at 8:43 P.M.). Members of the crowd, who had come to celebrate, paced the floor nervously with somber faces. . . . Hunt's son, Baxter, emerged about 11 P.M. and said: 'Unless there's a marked change . . . obviously we're headed for defeat. Things look bad right now, but we'll wait to see the remaining votes.'"

On the fourth floor most of the governor's top aides—Phil Carlton, Richardson Preyer, Joe Grimsley, Arthur Cassell, Felix Harvey, Gary Pearce, Stephanie Bass, Joe Pell, Mike Davis, and John Bennett, among others—had come and gone during the early evening to watch returns along with Hunt's media adviser, David Sawyer. As the outlook darkened, the governor, along with members of his family—his wife, children, mother and father, brother and sister-in-law—began to realize that the night would not be a long one after all. As his aides departed, Hunt wrote his concession statement prior to going downstairs shortly after midnight to concede.

As the governor and Mrs. Hunt appeared amid loud cheers and applause, some wept openly. "Our long and difficult battle is over," Hunt said, his own eyes glistening. "We have fought for what we believe. We have carried the torch forward and that flame will never die. The people of North Carolina have made their choice. While we may disagree, we must respect it, and I wish Senator Helms the best. Yes, we have suffered a disappointing defeat, and yes, it hurts; but we are not beaten in spirit. . . . I may be beaten, but I am not bowed. I may be disappointed, but I will not be bitter."

In North Carolina it is the custom for defeated candidates to visit the winner's headquarters to congratulate the victor personally. But the passions aroused by the senatorial campaign dissuaded Hunt from attempting such a journey. Nor did either winner or loser remain for a press conference. The next morning the governor visited his office, where messages of condolence were pouring in. Later in the day he met with Governor-elect Jim

Martin, at the latter's request, to start the process of transition. On the following day Jim and Carolyn Hunt left for an undisclosed destination (later revealed as Jamaica) for a week's vacation. The governor told his press secretary, Brent Hackney, "You'll see me when you see me."

Senator Helms and his wife left Raleigh almost immediately, headed for a vacation at their Lake Gaston home. There he was besieged by callers offering congratulations. But the small-town fire chief's son who had risen over twelve years to become one of the Senate's most prestigious figures had serious matters of state to ponder.

Elections, with their frozen-in-glass images of voter preferences, have a way of clarifying the national mood. The November balloting did that in North Carolina; but the principals still had their theories about what happened and why.

Out of 2,239,051 votes cast in the senatorial race Senator Helms prevailed by only 86,280, a tangible victory (52 to 48 percent), but narrow enough to indicate the intensity of the competition. The senator carried fifty-two of North Carolina's one hundred counties, winning substantially in the small towns and villages of the central and western Piedmont, where many of his enthusiastic blue-collar textile worker and religious fundamentalist supporters dwelled. He also scored well in the western mountains, a traditional Republican stronghold. Hunt led in the northeastern rural areas and also carried, by narrow margins, the largest urban counties of the Piedmont corridor from Raleigh to Charlotte. Results from exit polls of 2,500 voters, published by a national newspaper wire service, showed that Helms won a majority among Tar Heel whites, males, and the older, more affluent voters. Those who called themselves born-again Christians split 60 to 40 for Helms, while those who said they were conservatives voted 3 to 1 for the senator. Hunt carried the women's vote by 57 to 43 percent, captured a small majority of voters 49 and under, and won almost two-thirds of the votes among the poor. Professor Merle Black of Chapel Hill pointed out that Helms carried only counties in which Reagan won at least 60 percent of the vote; but those counties were numerous. Still, it was a close election.

In his victory statement Senator Helms reechoed themes he had sounded over his years in the Senate: that North Carolina was a "God-fearing, conservative state" and that its voters had responded to his call for restoring and supporting the principles he espoused, especially free enterprise and a moral society. Later Helms credited his victory to the registration of thousands of new voters by fundamentalist churches. "The governor was obviously counting on a somewhat heavier turnout of our black citizens," he said. "He knew he would get 99 percent of these and we knew it. So our people just turned out better than his did."

Helms's camp acknowledged that the Reagan popularity had been a major factor. "President Reagan was sent back to Washington with a mandate," said Claude Allen. "That mandate was to continue the economic boom that this country has experienced under his administration, and Senator Helms was part of that mandate." Carter Wrenn spoke of the Mondale tax increase issue as an important ingredient. "I think that taxes, the economy and continuing recovery ended up being the biggest part of the whole election," he said. "Reagan and Helms, anti-taxes . . . Mondale and Hunt, pro-taxes." Some thought that clever television ads in the closing days hit home. They cited the thirty-second spot of a well-dressed young woman in a new-car showroom saying she couldn't buy a new automobile because increased taxes would eat up her monthly payments. Helms's chief aide, Tom Ellis, thought that Helms and other state candidates had coattails of their own—that they had created their own individual images and carried other Republicans along with them. One state political scientist spoke of a "triple-coattails effect"—meaning that Reagan, Helms, and Martin had swept different voting groups into the Republican column. The staff of the North Carolina Reagan-Bush campaign sent flowers to Governor-elect Martin's campaign headquarters on Friday after the election with a card reading: "Congratulations! and thanks for bringing us in on your coattails!"

In the other camp Governor Hunt characterized the Reagan avalanche as the most powerful factor in his defeat. "I lived a couple of years in Nepal, so I know what an avalanche is. It just sweeps everything in its path." In a letter to newspaper editors who had supported him, the governor said, "In my view, Senator Helms got a substantial—perhaps decisive—lift from President Reagan's tremendous popularity." Other Hunt supporters shared his view of the awesome Reagan popularity. "It was like a hurricane coming off the coast," said J. Phil Carlton. Yet there were other influences at work, notably in the areas of race and religion.

From the start the Reverend Jesse Jackson had been a key figure in the senatorial struggle. In the early eighties, the governor had appointed him to the board of the state's new School of Science and Mathematics. After Jackson visited Hunt in the governor's office in 1982, Helms forces used a photograph of that visit in their fund-raising literature. Jackson's presidential candidacy generated enormous excitement among Tar Heel blacks in general, even though some black leaders were not enthusiastic. Jackson's dynamic role in the registration drive helped lift the number of black voters on the books from 451,000 in early 1983 to 619,000 in the fall of 1984. In Wake County alone the number of blacks registered jumped from 21,987 in 1980 to 31,672 in 1984—a 44 percent increase. By comparison the number of white registrants in that county increased by 23.8 percent (from 131,941 to 163,345).

In the November election Hunt's forces hoped that black voting would rise as high as 70 percent of those registered. After the election they were disappointed to learn that the figure totaled only 63.48 percent, according to a study by the Voter Education Project of Atlanta. A study of thirty-five largely black precincts indicated that Hunt got 98.8 percent of that vote and Helms only 0.3 percent. Hunt's campaign codirector, Joseph Grimsley, thought the lower-than-expected turnout was a question of "organization." He acknowledged that blacks had worked hard, but stated that their failure to do better was a "shortcoming of the whole system."

Part of the problem could have been that fewer blacks were on local ballots than in the spring primaries, and the national Democratic ticket also failed to inspire support. Blacks have always turned out in lower percentages than whites, according to Professor Black. Blacks, he noted, are generally poorer and don't perceive politics as making much difference in their lives, and they have more difficulty getting to the polls.

The backlash against black voter registration, however, was only part of the skillfully unfolding Helms strategy. The idea had been to chip away at Hunt's associations, his record as governor, and his character. With massive applications of television and radio advertising over a twenty-month period, the attack made devastating inroads in the store of goodwill Hunt had built up during his years as governor. The thirty-second spots that questioned the consistency of Hunt's positions (asking, "Where do you stand, Jim?") became a continuous feature of the Helms offensive.

The governor found himself constantly on the defensive. When Walter Mondale won the Democratic presidential nomination and promised to raise taxes, the Helms electronic blitz kept Hunt squirming to get off the tax-increase hook without repudiating his party loyalty. Helms, the superb phrasemaker, summed it up succinctly in the second television debate when he said: "[Hunt's] a Mondale liberal and ashamed of it, and I'm a Reagan conservative and proud of it."

As Reagan's popularity rose, Helms took advantage of it. His reelection campaign sent a recorded telephone message into homes featuring the voice of President Reagan endorsing Helms. The campaign mailed prepared form letters to out-of-state supporters asking each one to write a designated Tar Heel urging him or her to vote for Helms. Over his wife Dorothy's name, the campaign dispatched thousands of letters in an effort to get 63,000 birthday cards filled with $63,000 to help celebrate the senator's 63rd birthday. Included in the birthday mailing was a color photograph of

Helms kissing his fifth grandchild, Katie, on June 22 when she was a day old.

When Hunt's forces sought to get off the defensive and dominate the agenda, they had trouble finding a theme. They had already attacked Helms's support of "unfair" corporate tax reductions and his neglect of Social Security and veterans' benefits. The major thrust in the final weeks was a full-scale assault on Helms as the "high priest of a nationwide network of right-wing extremists." In the growing conservative climate the attack never drew blood. Indeed, Hunt's linkage of Helms with right-wing dictators abroad and fundamentalist Moral Majority preachers at home caused him serious problems.

For one thing, the majority of North Carolinians were not much informed about controversies in faraway El Salvador and Nicaragua. (One politician said he heard a voter say, "Who's this fella Dubby-son?") The larger problem lay in the governor's attack on the Reverend Jerry Falwell and fundamentalist preachers in general. Attacking preachers of any kind is dangerous in North Carolina. Beginning two years earlier, Falwell and his associate Lamarr Mooneyham had laid the groundwork for a massive voter registration drive among their church members across North Carolina. The center of their strength lay in small textile and blue-collar towns of the Piedmont—precisely where Helms scored heavily on November 6. Previously Hunt had always done well in those areas. But this year, while he won the larger urban counties, such as Mecklenburg, Forsyth, Guilford, and Wake, by narrow margins, he lost in the smaller communities and the Piedmont countryside.

After the election Falwell said his Moral Majority organization had registered 150,000 new voters in North Carolina. (Mooneyham, head of the group's national field office in Lynchburg, Virginia, put the number nearer 200,000.) "We worked on a daily basis with 2,400 pastors and churches [in North Carolina]," Falwell said. "I've been feeling this landslide for five months." Mooneyham said the organization had concentrated on the Interstate-85 corridor, a 200-mile zone between Charlotte and Durham. He said the churches drove their members to the polls. "The churches . . . did the same thing they do on Sunday on Tuesday—the machinery was already in place."

State Elections Director Alex Brock agreed. He noted that the black registration drive had lifted the statewide black registration substantially over the fifteen months before the election. "The minority voted in record numbers," he said. "But they didn't even come close to numbering what the Republicans did, plus the Democrats who voted Republican." Howard Lee, a black consultant to the state Democratic Party and former mayor of Chapel Hill, said that efforts by white fundamentalists and Reagan's influence on the rest of the GOP ticket were simply too much to overcome. "We [blacks] did what we said we would do," he said. "When you look at loyalty to the party, up to this point, blacks have stayed loyal."

In some ways Hunt's problems mirrored Mondale's at the national level. He failed to find a coherent campaign theme—a simple and specific motif. He struggled to shift gears in response to the senator's pounding on the Mondale tax increase and the main "character" issue: the governor's use of state transportation for political purposes. The state Democratic organization was plagued by factionalism—the Eddie Knox defection and Rufus Edmisten's inability to mend party wounds. The governor's decision to lash out at the senator—and to tip over into mud-fighting—disillusioned some of his more idealistic backers, who had hoped he would distance himself from Helms and remain above the battle. One of those supporters, who regretted Hunt's aggressive attacks as well as his opposition to the nuclear freeze and his support of capital punishment, put it this way: "Enthusiasm for the governor among his strongest supporters seemed to decline at the very moment Helms's people gained encouragement."

Partisans in both camps agreed that the Helms campaign produced more effective television advertising than Hunt's. Often, on both sides, as one commentator said, it was "the politics of distortion, half truths and character assassination" where "ends are used to justify means" and "truth often takes a back seat." Hunt strove to follow the high road, but the pressures of the campaign, and his determination to fight back, occasionally led his camp into exaggerated charges—such as the attempt to link Helms with the Reverend Sun Myung Moon and the television ad that featured crumpled bodies in El Salvador.

In the minds of contending strategists such hard-hitting advertising served its purpose. The largest chunk of the $25 million spent over twenty months went for television commercials. An estimated seventy-eight hundred television spots were broadcast during the last five weeks. Hunt's media adviser, David Sawyer, said the Hunt camp made eight different Social Security ads. "People said they didn't like the negative ads, but our polls showed they changed people's minds. On Social Security you could watch a 10 to 15 percent shift depending on who was on the air." Both sides used a nightly television ad tracking poll and responded to each other accordingly. It was a highly sophisticated search-and-destroy technique, and money was no obstacle.

Helms's church leaders, who played a major role in the senator's victory, were not openly disturbed about the negative campaigning. But many of Hunt's supporters felt differently. "I strongly disagree with Senator Jesse

Helms's post-election assertion that his victory demonstrated that North Carolina was a 'God-fearing state,'" wrote a Methodist minister to an Eastern Carolina newspaper. "On the contrary, it proves once again that a majority of North Carolinians do not believe in 'the brotherhood of man under the Fatherhood of God.' The new religious right brazenly supports the senator, those 'religionists' who preach continuously about family values and morality and yet have little or no proclamation concerning social justice, human dignity and racial inclusiveness. They, much like the Pharisees of old, 'have neglected the weightier matters of the law, justice and mercy and faith.'" Another Democrat, who had studied North Carolina politics for three decades, decried the view that Senator Helms always put principles first. "Helms does change positions where expedient—on farm price supports and Israel," he said.

As the Democrats surveyed the vastness of the party's devastation, they had differing reactions about the future. Senator Sam Ervin, the party's elder statesman, spoke up from his mountain retreat, saying: "I think the Democratic Party in North Carolina is going to have to run as a team . . . to quit single-shotting for themselves." His view of what the party had become had much in common with what Virginia's Charles Robb said of it: "There's a feeling that our party has become not a party of the whole but simply a collection of special interests that are narrower than the national interest." Mississippi Democratic Chairman Steven Patterson said it in a somewhat different way in a letter to other party chairmen: "The Democratic Party has become the party of the needy, their platform one of redividing the pie. But the younger voter wants to be part of a world of growth. The Robin Hood ethic of the Democratic Party this year makes sense only in the confines of a Sherwood Forest that never expands. . . . That world is not the America of personal computers, expanding career opportunities, swifter communication and exploding high-tech industries in which the baby boomers dwell."

When Jim Hunt and his wife returned from their Jamaican vacation, the governor announced he had no interest in succeeding Charles T. Manatt as chairman of the Democratic National Committee. The job, he said, was too "time consuming." Nor was he interested in the presidency of the University of North Carolina system, which was opening in 1986 on the retirement of President William Friday. The governor, however, declined to rule out another Senate race in 1986 against Republican Senator John East. When asked about it, he replied: "I don't know, and I have given no thought to that. I've just been through a tough campaign. It was a long one, a hard one—we gave it all we had—and I'm not about to start thinking about politics again."

But it was evident that at forty-seven and still imbued with the ambition that had marked his career from the earliest days at Rock Ridge High School, Hunt would be heard from again. His defeat, by only 86,280 out of 2,239,051 votes, was comparatively small. In view of the formidable obstacles—the Reagan avalanche, the booming economy, the Democratic slump, Helms's political skill—he had done well to get within four percentage points of his opponent. "I don't think that things I stand for have been rejected," Hunt said, referring specifically to education and jobs. "I think people as we go along will feel good about the leadership we provided and what we've done together. . . . I still believe in the state. I believe in the goodness of North Carolina." There was also a spark of good news in another area: Hunt's multi-million-dollar campaign—with some nine million dollars spent—had ended in the black.

As the reanointed Senator Helms surveyed the political landscape from his new position of power, belated acknowledgement of his prowess appeared. "The outcome of the North Carolina Senate race should dispel once and for all one of the most persistent of Washington myths," wrote Bill Peterson in the *Washington Post*, a Helms adversary, "that Jesse Alexander Helms is a political dinosaur out of touch with the mainstream of his party and state. Helms is an innovator, one of the most skilled politicians of our time. He has a genuine affinity with his state, and an innate grasp of how to motivate its voters. He has raised the politics of confrontation and negative campaigning to a high art."

Almost as if to confound his liberal critics again, Helms set about helping resolve an important national issue growing out of the November election. Immediately after the election the senator again reiterated to an old friend, the editor of the *Goldsboro News-Argus*, that he intended to remain chairman of the Senate Agriculture Committee, as he had repeatedly promised during the campaign. He would not, he said, move to the chairmanship of the Senate Foreign Relations Committee. Before the election, speculation had been rampant that Helms would take that post if the incumbent chairman, Senator Charles Percy of Illinois, were defeated and the Senate remained in Republican hands. Percy was indeed defeated and the Democrats failed to win Senate control.

Since Helms had the necessary seniority, it was his decision to make, and few doubted his desire to move. Another factor threatened to complicate the situation: the Republican who would take over Agriculture if Helms made the change was Senator Richard Lugar of Indiana, a professed opponent of tobacco and bad news for Tar Heel farmers. That problem evaporated when Senator Robert Dole of Kansas won the Senate majority leader post, also sought by Lugar, making it possible for the latter to succeed Percy at Foreign Relations. This pleased the Helms camp, since it blocked Senator Charles Mathias of Maryland, a GOP liberal who would have been next in line. Through it all, though, Helms stuck by his word, despite urgings from his New Right allies to abandon the Agriculture Committee post. Helms said of this: "If there is one job in the Senate I would like to have it is Foreign Relations Committee chairman, and there it was; all I had to do was bend a principle. [But] if I can't keep my word, I don't belong around here."

All these games of musical chairmanships left Helms on the high road, both at home and in Washington. Even the Reagan administration reportedly had not welcomed the prospect of Helms's stronger hand in foreign relations. Helms's first major move following the election had underlined his professed determination to remain a man of his word, one for whom principles came before personal preference.

Helms gave no indication that he would deviate from the gadfly role he had played under both Democratic and Republican administrations, especially concerning State Department appointments. Even before he was freshly endowed with Senate seniority, the senator had shown his enhanced power in foreign matters by persuading twenty-two ambassadors to endorse his campaign against Hunt. Early in Secretary of State George Shultz's tenure Helms had mounted a stubborn fight over the appointment of Richard Burt, an arms control advocate and former *New York Times* reporter, as assistant secretary of state for European affairs. Burt won Senate confirmation, but not before Helms had won appointment for one of his former aides, Robert T. McCormack, as assistant secretary of state for economic affairs. This was only one of dozens of encounters between New Right forces and Republican moderates. The prospects were for more of the same in the second Reagan term. In late November a State Department official told a North Carolina newspaper editor that the department faced the future with "dread" on issues where Helms might be involved. With the leadership of the Senate transferred from one moderate Republican to another—from Howard Baker to Robert Dole—there promised to be no lack of opportunities for renewed clashes among Republicans when Congress reconvened in January.

Of several disturbing questions that arose out of the Helms-Hunt campaign one of the most important was the burgeoning role of money in politics. The two contenders spent almost $25 million, the largest sum in senatorial election history. The total would probably run far in excess of that if unrecorded expenditures at the local level were included. Senator Helms, whose National Congressional Club oversaw the dispensing of the giant share of his spending, which reached some $15.6 million, saw no problems here. In fact, the senator insisted that because of "media bias" against him he needed such funds to get his message across to the voters.

Helms's position echoed some of Supreme Court Justice Sandra Day O'Connor's reservations concerning PAC contributions and First Amendment rights. In a case which sought enforcement of a law imposing a strict one-thousand-dollar limit on expenditures by independent political action committees, she commented in November: "It's a pretty hollow right to be able to join a [committee] if it's limited to only $1,000. . . . A right to speak through a group means being able to pool your assets to amplify your voice." Lawyers for two conservative PACs contended that the law under discussion, passed in 1971 but never enforced, was unconstitutional. By the end of 1984 the Supreme Court had not ruled on the case, which brought the right of free speech into conflict with political reform efforts. The Federal Elections Commission and the National Democratic Party favored the bill and some kind of campaign spending restraint; the FEC's general counsel told the court that any curb the law placed on free speech was outweighed by the need to protect the electoral process. The American Civil Liberties Union, in an unusual alliance, joined the conservative PAC representative in opposing the legislation.

Governor Hunt, whose campaign raised a smaller amount ($9.8 million), also voiced concern about excessive spending. In the candidates' first television debate in July he challenged Helms to join him in cutting off all out-of-state contributions. But the senator refused. Helms's twenty-month television ad campaign was credited with helping reduce Hunt's 20 percent lead in the opinion polls to practically zero by the closing weeks and playing a large part in the senator's victory.

In 1983 prominent New York and Washington philanthropists of both parties had joined forces to form a nonpartisan "Citizens Against PACs." Their goal was to pressure Congress to eliminate corporate, labor union, and special interest PACs that make "ax-to-grind" contributions to candidates. Philip Stern, one of the movement's leaders, said: "We want to make it uncomfortable for Congress to continue accepting PAC money." But the drive made little progress, since incumbents ordinarily receive 77 percent more in PAC donations than challengers. Several bills were brought before Congress to provide public financing for political candidates, but they received little support.

There is no doubt that money, in amounts that astonished even the most seasoned observers of North Carolina politics, played a central role in the Helms-Hunt campaign. Those who profited from it and those who, in the end, were hurt by it remained hung up over what, if anything, should be done. North Carolina voters grew thoroughly weary of the television ad blitz, but there were abundant signs that it had a powerful influence on the outcome of the election.

In a post-election interview with the *Salisbury Evening Post* William C. Friday, the University of North Carolina system's president for thirty years, spoke to that issue and others. "I think our state went through a very difficult experience," he said. "It bothers me that this whole thing slid into character assassination and almost obscene use of money and dragging the campaign on for months and months and months." Friday urged Governor-elect Martin to appoint a bipartisan commission to study the election and repair the damage. Elaborating on the need for a bipartisan commission, Friday concluded: "I move around a lot in circles out of North Carolina . . . and I know that it didn't help North Carolina a bit. This shouldn't happen again. We are wiser people than that, a more intelligent people."

Since his victory over Nick Galifianakis in 1972, Senator Jesse Helms had proved over and over again that he was no anti-McGovern aberration soon to disappear, as most Democrats had anticipated. As a champion of Ronald Reagan at a crucial moment early in his march toward the presidency, Helms stood at the forefront of the GOP triumphs of the early 1980s. Closer home, he helped his friend John East win North Carolina's junior Senate seat in 1980. In 1984, running against the state's most popular Democratic governor in the twentieth century, he scored a comfortable victory. His coattails, as his senior aide Tom Ellis contended, probably had something to do with Republican successes all up and down the line in North Carolina. Like Governor George Wallace of Alabama, the senator had become a sort of folk hero of the populist stripe, attracting wide attention and support beyond his home state.

Senator Helms established a new pattern in Tar Heel politics. In this century North Carolina had never sent mavericks or extremists to the Senate (with the brief exception of Robert R. "Our Bob" Reynolds in the 1930s). The Tar Heel electorate consistently favored moderate conservatives of the southern Democratic school. Helms, however, broke the mold. His emphasis on flamboyant fundamentalist religion and belligerent ultraconservative economics mixed powerful elements of Old South populism with Reagan's New Right. But the Helms agenda ranged beyond the President's in its inflexible ideology. "Having Jesse Helms representing conservatives in the United States Senate," one Tar Heel editor wrote, "is roughly equivalent to having an avowed Socialist representing the liberals."

The senator's vision was to reduce government to its bare essentials in economic controls but to enhance its regulation of personal morals. Such an explosive combination had seldom made much headway in American politics. Southern demagogues of the Theodore Bilbo–Cole Blease–Huey Long school had combined some of these ingredients in bombastic appeals to the down-home constituencies of small-town, rural America. But Helms had managed to make his New Right politics agreeable both to the affluent business community and the blue-collar and rural masses. He had become a new force in southern politics, a 1980s version of Eric Hoffer's True Believer.

A long-time Helms watcher observed that if you lifted the dome of the United States Capitol, several Gary Harts would tumble out, but only one Jesse Helms. As far as North Carolina was concerned, Helms was one of a kind—the state's own unique political personality who came across as an individual not afraid to speak his mind or champion unpopular causes, or use any hard-line tactics necessary to win. In an age when most politicians spoke with many tongues, that inflexibility of mind and purpose had become Jesse Helms's greatest strength—and perhaps his greatest vulnerability.